Warrior Women

An Archaeologist's Search for History's Hidden Heroines

Jeannine Davis-Kimball, Ph.D.
with Mona Behan

WARNER BOOKS

An AOL Time Warner Company

PHOTO CREDITS
Kernal A. Akishev/*Issyk Kurgan*—102, 103 (right), 104, 105, 171; ©Gala Argent/Dr. Tamara Lobanova—103 (left); Sergei I. Rudenko, *Frozen Tombs of Siberia*—107; Herve Lewandowski/Louvre MNC 624, Reunion de Musés Nationalaux/Art Resources, NY—115; *Entre Asie et Europe: L'Or des Sarmates*—116; Azov Regional Museum, Azov, Russia—117; *After Teinshan Petroglyphs: A Testimony of Fertility Worship*—158; *After Marija Gimbutas.* The Language of the Goddesses—164; Courtesy of the Institute of Archaeology, Kishinev, Moldova—166; Boris A. Litvinskii. Excavations at Takhti-I Sanguin—171; Giancarlo Ligabue and Sandro Salvatori, eds., Bactria: An Ancient Oasis Civilization from the Sands of Afghanistan—174; Viktor Sarianidi, The Golden Hoard of Bactria: From the Tillya-tepe Excavations in Northern Afghanistan—181, 183, 184; Courtesy of the Trustees of the National Museum and Galleries of Northern Ireland—201; S. A. Pletnva, ed., Stepi Evrazili v Epokha Erednevekovia—232 (top); E. & J. Frankel, LTD, as representative for D. Erdenebilig—222; all other photos from author's collection.

Copyright © 2002 by Jeannine Davis-Kimball, Ph.D.
All rights reserved.
Warner Books, Inc.
1271 Avenue of the Americas, New York, NY 10020
Visit our Web site at www.twbookmark.com.

 An AOL Time Warner Company

Printed in the United States of America
Originally published in hardcover by Warner Books, Inc.
First Trade Printing: February 2003
10 9 8 7 6 5 4 3 2 1

The Library of Congress has catalogued the hardcover edition as follows:
Davis-Kimball, Jeannine.
    Warrior women: an archaeologist's search for history's hidden heroines / Jeannine Davis-Kimball with Mona Behan.
    p. cm.
    Includes bibliographical references and index.
    ISBN 0-446-52546-4
    1. Women, Prehistoric—Russia (Federation)—Pokorovka Region. 2. Women, Prehistoric—Eurasia. 3. Women—History—To 500. 4. Women heroes—Russia (Federation)—Pokorovka Region—History. 5. Women heroes—Eurasia—History. 6. Human remains (Archaeology)—Russia (Federation)—Pokorovka Region 7. Human remains (Archaeology)—Eurasia. 8. Pokorovka Region (Russia)—Antiquities. 9. Eurasia—Antiquities. I. Behan, Mona. II. Title.
GN635.R8 D38 2001
    305.4'09'01--dc21
ISBN 0-446-67983-6(pbk.)   2001026878

Cover design by Brigid Pearson
Book design by Mada Design, Inc./NYC

TO TISA, MARY, STEVE, JOHN, CHRIS, LESLIE
AND TO MATT

ACKNOWLEDGMENTS

My curiosity about people who lived in foreign lands began when I was in the lower grades, compelling me to pursue the thoroughfares and paths of far-off lands, and providing the underlying background for my work in Eurasia. So many people deserve acknowledgment that the task is daunting, beginning with my sixth grade teacher, Frank Knight, who charged me with our meager library of adventure books, to a sundry of college professors in Spain and California who encouraged my passion to understand other cultures, to decipher the significances of their art, and who motivated the quest of archaeology. My first adventures in the former Soviet Union were possible because of the support of Irina Shemashko; and the understanding of Kazakstan's many nationalities and incredible archaeology would not have been possible without my first guides and teachers, Nurilya Shakanova, Almanjol Kalishev, and Beken Nurapiesov. Leonid Yablonsky deserves special thanks for our years of collaboration in the Ural steppes, and Elena Yablonsky for constant support of our projects. A multitude of other scholars in Moscow and St. Petersburg, Russia; in Almaty, Kazakstan; in Kishanev, Moldova, and in Ulan Bator, Mongolia, have each contributed to my understanding of their people, today and in the past. Special thanks go to Meiram and his brother, Sairam Kadar, who opened the doors of the Kazaks' yurts in Bayan Ulgii province, and to Aigul Mckei, my invaluable translator. Llagvasueren and Benbadorj were my special guides and teachers as we searched the ancient monuments in western Mongolia. To all the others who so generously allowed me to come into their life, to photograph them, to eat and sleep in their yurt, and to ask endless questions—as well as "students," young and old who have accompanied me on these expeditions, I sincerely thank you.

I owe much gratitude to my editors, Caryn Karmatz Rudy, Molly Chehak, and Anne Montague, at Warner Books for their guidance in making the nearly always obscure subject matter clearer. If there are errors, of course, these are my responsibility.

And finally, my husband, Warren Matthew, who proffered such good advice when I was confronted with a dead language, insisting I take Russian instead, who has provided myriad logistics and support (including carrying loads of books from air terminal to terminal), has my most grateful appreciation.

CONTENTS

PREFACE   xi

CHAPTER ONE   THE PATH TO POKROVKA   1

CHAPTER TWO   AN ARCHAEOLOGIST IN THE FIELD   14

CHAPTER THREE   THE POWER OF THE HEARTH   30

CHAPTER FOUR   THE POWER OF THE SWORD   50

CHAPTER FIVE   THE POWER OF THE SPIRIT   67

CHAPTER SIX   RICH LEGENDS:
                   FROM GOLD MAN TO GRIFFIN   96

CHAPTER SEVEN   THE ADVENT OF THE AMAZONS   112

CHAPTER EIGHT   CHINA'S MYSTERIOUS MUMMIES   132

CHAPTER NINE   ANCIENT FERTILITY RITUALS
                   IN THE TIEN SHAN   153

CHAPTER TEN   MOTHER GODDESSES AND ENAREES   169

CHAPTER ELEVEN   IRISH WARRIOR QUEENS
                   AND THE DAMSELS OF DEATH   186

CHAPTER TWELVE   FROM CELTS TO MONGOLS:
                   WOMEN OF BUSINESS AND KINGMAKERS   211

CHAPTER THIRTEEN   THE LEGACY OF WARRIOR WOMEN   234

GLOSSARY   241

BIBLIOGRAPHY   249

INDEX   254

PREFACE

My work lay underground, but I couldn't keep my eyes off the sky that July day in 1994. The temperature hovered well above 100 degrees Fahrenheit and the sky was scrubbed to a whitish blue by the unrelenting sun, but I knew how quickly the weather could change in this part of the world and I kept glancing anxiously to the east. Sure enough, around 10 A.M., just as it had almost every morning for the past four weeks, a charcoal-colored smudge appeared on the horizon, foretelling the fast-moving clouds that would sweep through every afternoon and dump so much rain on the hard, sandy soil that we'd have to ford an instant lake as we scrambled back to camp.

An archaeologist from Berkeley, California, I was coleader of a joint American-Russian team excavating kurgans, or burial mounds, on the extensive collective farm named Pokrovka, located on the Russia–Kazakstan border. Leonid Yablonsky, a gifted and sometimes volatile archaeologist, led the fifteen-person contingent from the Russian Academy of Science, and I was in charge of the eight American scientists and volunteers. We were nearing the end of a grueling two-month dig of burial mounds that had belonged to the Sauromatians and Sarmatians, nomadic tribes of herders and fierce warriors who had ruled vast portions of the steppes more than two millennia ago.

The day's rain promised far more than soggy boots—if we didn't move quickly enough to remove the day's finds from the kurgan, valuable artifacts and skeletal remains would get damaged or lost. "Let's get cracking, people," I called out, and turned my attention back to the meticulous work of the dig. As we unearthed, cleaned, tagged, photographed, and recorded each new discovery, we had no time for speculation and wonder; the fragile skeletons would disintegrate under the hot sun in a few hours, if the rain didn't flood the burial site first. Yet despite my single-minded concentration on the logistics of our work, I was conscious of a growing sense of excitement. For as one of the crew exposed the contents of the latest grave, I realized that we had chanced on something I had never seen before: the skeleton of a woman—a girl, really, thirteen to fourteen years old when she had died—interred with a sizable collection of bronze arrowheads in a quiver, along with what once had been a finely wrought iron dagger. I pulled the brim of my hat down for more shade and turned to one of the volunteers who, by my side, was peering into the dark catacomb. "Mary, see all that armament in the burial?" I pointed into the pit. "This could be a very interesting find."

It wasn't until months later, once I had carefully scrutinized the fruits of our dig, that I realized exactly how interesting it had been. That summer day yielded nothing less than the most profound discovery of my career, a cache of bones and artifacts that would help change established notions of a woman's place in ancient nomadic societies and lend credence to tales around the world of warrior women and priestesses of great power.

Perhaps I am so fascinated by these women of high status because my own path to professional and personal achievement was such a long, convoluted road. Unlike the lucky few who know what they want to be at an early age, I came to my career as an archaeologist rather late in life. The sole clue to my future occupation might have been my childhood penchant for digging in the dirt and making elaborate mud pies, carefully laying them out to bake in the sun. Born in Driggs, Idaho, in 1929, I discovered my calling only after three marriages, six children, and a varied résumé that included stints as a nurse in Idaho, an administrator in a convalescent hospital in southern California, an English-language teacher in Bolivia and Spain, and a failed cattle rancher in South America. Although I had completed a degree in Hispanic studies at the University of Madrid, I didn't finish my American undergraduate work until my children were grown, earning a bachelor's degree in art history from California State University at Northridge at age forty-nine. I was the first woman in my family to graduate from college.

I had taken a few undergraduate anthropology courses, but it wasn't until I began working on my master's degree and cataloging Near Eastern art for the Los Angeles County Museum that I started to suspect my true passion was ancient civilizations. I became very curious about the collection's two hundred bronze plaques and animal statuettes from Eurasia, a legacy of the steppe nomads. Although these artifacts were between two and three thousand years old, the casting was impeccable, the colors either mellowed to a soft verdigris or the lustrous reddish hues of a fine old port. The detailed depictions of flying deer with massive antlers twined over their backs or a tiger savagely attacking a horse enthralled yet perplexed me. I felt they held some special significance to their owners that I couldn't quite reach. I puzzled over the meaning of the ubiquitous recurring coils and scrolls that marked the hip and shoulder joints of these beasts. At the same time, I found that my interest in the Mesopotamian city-states and empires that dominated my course of study, with their rigid hierarchies controlled by a handful of kings and priests, had waned. I became much more curious about the free-roaming lifestyle of their far-off Eastern neighbors, the Eurasian nomads who had created those enigmatic plaques and statuettes.

The more I learned about the history of the steppes and pored over obscure Soviet maps of the region, the more fascinated I became.[1] The very scope of the land dazzled me—definitions vary, but in the broadest sense, these immense grasslands sweep from the forested eastern slopes of Hungary to the lush fields of Manchuria, reaching into the southern fringes of Siberia and down through the high Tibetan plateau. Sliced into two distinct portions by the Altai Mountains, the steppes stretch for rough-

---

1. *Steppes* is derived from the Russian word for plains or grasslands.

ly six thousand miles, spanning nearly a third of the world's land mass. The Volga, Don, Dniester, and Dnieper rivers snake through these rolling pasturelands, which, depending on the time of year, can be a straw-colored mass of prickly wild grains or an emerald carpet of waist-high grasses dotted with pink hollyhocks and purple lupine.

With temperatures that ricochet from 130 degrees Fahrenheit in the summer to 30 below in the winter, the Eurasian steppes have long possessed a reputation for being one of the least hospitable regions on earth, yet a succession of influential cultures have called it home. Here is where the Silk Road threaded from China to Rome, its paths so thick with caravans laden with precious cargo that even today, satellite photos reveal the compacted depressions of the ancient routes. Here is where Attila the Hun thundered out of the eastern mountains with legions of mounted warriors, plundering and massacring the settled populations on the steppes' borderlands and hastening the fall of the Roman Empire. Here is where Genghis Khan built his own massive empire, the greatest contiguous dominion the world has ever witnessed, and where his grandson Kublai Khan presided over the refined and learned Chinese court that so intrigued Marco Polo. The fifth-century-B.C. Greek historian Herodotus was fascinated by the steppes; he interrupted his account of the Greco-Persian wars to include the exploits of the region's fearsome nomadic tribes, including the Sauromatians, whose genesis he traced to the Amazons. Like most historians—even modern ones—he concentrated on the raids and rampages of the steppe peoples, but common sense told me there was more to these societies than war, rape, and pillage, and I was drawn by some unexplained magnet to explore their world.

My master's degree in hand, I embarked on a Ph.D. program in Near Eastern studies at the University of California at Berkeley, a decision that finally brought my career ambitions into focus. In 1985, I went on my first archaeological dig, excavating at Tell Dor in Israel, which is situated just north of the famous ancient port of Caesarea on the Mediterranean coast.

I hadn't really considered going on a dig—my interest still lay primarily in art history—but my Ph.D. adviser, who was directing the university's excavation, needed supervisors for the flock of volunteer archaeologists that converged on this site.

So I found myself at Tell Dor, a massive mound stretching along the Mediterranean, a mound with a very long history. It is mentioned by name in the Bible, but even before that the seafaring Phoenicians of the second millennium B.C. had coaxed royal-purple dye from tiny sea animals living along its coral reefs. Today, we can still see their dye vats carved into the surface of the natural coral jetty extending into the sea just below my excavation square. Tell Dor's cliffs yielded some fine examples of Bronze Age pottery, and over thousands of years all the ancient Near Eastern peoples, as well as the Greeks and Romans, had built settlements here.

After excavating from before dawn until 2 P.M., my duties included everything from taking notes during the afternoon pottery readings to rubbing my professor's legs when he got cramps (tasks, I might point out, that my male colleagues were never asked to perform). As far as the actual archaeology was concerned, I was allotted a beautiful five-by-five-meter square of dirt that lay on an incline sloping down to the sea. Unfortunately, the scenery was its sole reward. The Romans who had lived in this area had been ecologically magnificent: whatever garbage the former inhabitants had tossed into my five-meter square long ago had been completely biodegradable. I wasn't privileged enough to recover even a single worn, bronze coin as we hauled bucket after bucket of gray, ashy soil to the top of the mound. It was painstaking, fatiguing, and remarkably nonproductive work, and the major anthropological highlight of my six weeks there was observing the scuffle that broke out every working morning in the shadowy side-kitchen as the wealthy volunteers stabbed at a jar of peanut butter spotlighted by a single bare bulb.

Still, I was hooked. I loved the freedom of working outdoors, and digging for artifacts that might reveal some tiny clue to the mystery of an ancient world fired my imagination and lent purpose to every task. I hoped that archaeology would shed light on the original sources and meanings of the variety of motifs that most intrigued me as an art historian: the scrolls and coils of the nomadic bronzes, the seashells that bloomed unexpectedly in Christian and Islamic architecture, the strange zoomorphic forms that were celebrated by so many diverse cultures. Also, as I learned more about the methodology of some past excavations, I became increasingly skeptical about relying on others' interpretations of the excavations, wary of the occasional sloppily compiled data and knee-jerk explanations (such as the widely accepted assumption that if a person was buried with a dagger, that person had to be a male). And I was frustrated by the lack of interest exhibited by many historians and archaeologists regarding the status of women in the societies they studied. I realized that the answers to the questions I found most pressing lay not in museums and research libraries, but out in the field. Time would prove me right—the most thrilling and profound discoveries of my career lay in wait in the Eurasian steppes.

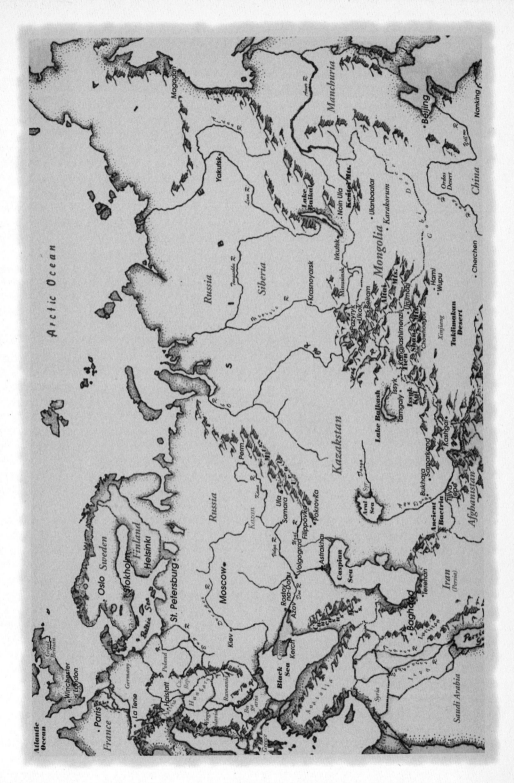

Map of Eurasia with the important archaeological sites of the first millennium B.C.

Warrior Women

An Archaeologist's Search
for History's Hidden Heroines

CHAPTER ONE

THE PATH TO POKROVKA

"I read [history] a little as a duty,
but it tells me nothing that does not either vex or weary me.
The quarrels of popes and kings, with wars or pestilences, in every page;
the men all so good for nothing, and hardly any women at all . . ."
—*Catherine Morland, in Jane Austen's* Northanger Abbey *(1817)*

In 1985, I had my first, long-awaited glimpse of the land of the nomads. My husband, Warren Matthew (Matt), an engineer by profession and an intrepid traveler, and I made the long journey to Samarkand and Bukhara, two cities in present-day Uzbekistan that once had ranked among the most important ancient cities and later oases caravan stops dotting the Silk Road. Matt was an aficionado of Sovietology, and we knew that Intourist, the government agency that assigned official escorts to all foreign visitors, was infamous for its overbearing style and excessive zeal, particularly when it came to ensuring that Soviet citizens didn't become polluted through contact with outsiders. Indeed, our Intourist guide, Natasha, was a charming young woman, but she dutifully hovered by our side like an anxious watchdog, making sure that we followed her beeline from the officially sanctioned hotel to the officially sanctioned bus that would whisk us to the officially sanctioned sights of the day. We were confined to separate tourist sections in restaurants and airport waiting rooms. Guards at Intourist hotels blocked—sometimes quite forcefully—

ordinary Soviet citizens from entering these hallowed premises (although Matt and I noticed that they made certain exceptions in the evening for shapely young ladies in tight dresses and stiletto heels).

We chafed against all the restrictions, and were further dismayed upon reaching our Central Asian destinations. We had expected romantic locales suggestive of the heady times when entrepreneurs from the East and West met and traded exotic goods and even more exotic tales of their travels. Instead, we found the Intourist amenities were now dominated by the shoddy and singularly unattractive 1960s-era Soviet architecture, the former caravansaries reduced to piles of rubble.[1] Although they weren't quite as magnificent as they had been in the fourteenth century, the mosques and madrasahs (Islamic colleges), as well as the palaces that had been the pride of Uzbek emirs, whetted my appetite for exploring the region further. Most of these buildings are the legacy of Tamerlane, the Turkish conqueror who balanced his lust for war with a passion for Islamic art and architecture.[2] The structures he commissioned in Samarkand, the capital of his vast empire, are masterpieces, featuring exquisitely crafted tiles fired in azure, white, and turquoise glazes, with bands of abstractly lettered, black or gold-lustered inscriptions praising Allah. The iwans (arched reception halls of the mosques) still stand tall and elegant on dusty streets near the outdoor bazaars; here groups of old men huddle in the courtyard, spinning tales or playing chess while women sell vegetables, dried fruits, nuts, and other delicacies in shaded stalls. In one such stall, a boy of about eight took my hand and led me around the marketplace, patiently identifying the exotic wares in the gentle tone adults usually reserve for small children. The scents of ripe fruit and spices suffused the air, helping me to imagine the babble of long-gone traders, the snorts of camels, the braying of donkeys rising over the shrill voices of youngsters zigzagging in a game of tag.

---

1. Caravansaries were roadside inns with large central courtyards that provided food and shelter for travelers and their livestock along the Asian trade routes.
2. Tamerlane (also spelled Tamburlaine) died in 1405, and when his embalmed corpse was exhumed five hundred years later, Soviet archaeologists found a tall figure lame on the right side, thus corroborating his Central Asian name, Timur Lenk, or Timur the Lame.

The next year signaled the dawning of glasnost, the era of openness ushered in by the new Soviet General Secretary, Mikhail Gorbachev. Excited by the prospect of traveling free from Intourist's distrustful eye, Matt and I returned, only to find that change came slowly and cautiously to the people of the Soviet Union. Up until now, a free exchange of ideas with foreigners might have been enough to earn a citizen a trip to the gulag, a miserable labor camp of unimaginable hardship, in Siberia. We were met by cold and hostile stares if we asked directions, and it was almost impossible to engage in even a short friendly conversation with a Russian citizen. But not all were terrified. One elderly gentleman, striking in his poise and well-dressed elegance, deliberately drew us into the street near the Kremlin in full view of the police when we asked him for directions to the Lenin library.

"Yes, you go to the next street," he replied in an unnaturally loud voice, turning to glare in the direction of the gray-uniformed military officers patrolling near the Kremlin walls. "Turn left and go two more streets. It's near the Metro stop." As we thanked him, he seemed reluctant to leave, but finally turned and crossed the street, his contempt for the Soviet authorities still evident in his deliberate stride.

Frustrated by our inability to penetrate the tourist facade, we returned home and I vowed never to return to the USSR unless I first established connections with Soviet scholars who could grant me access to the information and sites needed for meaningful research. Work on my Ph.D. dissertation and a period spent fighting breast cancer sidelined my quest for two years, but paradoxically, I finally achieved the Soviet contacts I sought in that sunny bastion of Western decadence, Los Angeles. In 1989, "Nomads of Eurasia," a Kazak art and ethnography exhibition, arrived in southern California, and I made the acquaintance of several of the curators. One was Irina Shemashko from the Institute of Ethnography in Moscow, who, fortuitously for me, also turned out to be the institute's Communist Party Secretary, a position of significant power. She paved the way for a trip later that year to the Soviet Union, arranging for the

The Nomadic Way

Nomadic is a term that laypeople and scholars alike tend to associate with any group of people who move from place to place. Historically and archaeologically, it has been applied to everyone from the Paleolithic hunters and gatherers who moved about constantly in search of game and edible wild plants to the more recent Gypsies, the Romany, of Central Europe.

Most of the present-day nomads of the Eurasian steppes, however, practice what is known as pastoral nomadism (or transhumance), meaning that they travel in small kinship groups consisting of three to five families who assemble in portable villages, called *auls* in the Kazak language. They engage in little or no agriculture, depending on their herds of horses, sheep, goats, yaks, or camels (or combinations thereof) to fulfill most of their needs.

Pastoral nomads travel along loosely established routes to their spring, summer, and fall pastures; in winter, the aul dwellers return to permanent homes built from clay-dabbed logs or mud bricks in sheltered river valleys, or in southern-exposure locations, frequently below huge rock escarpments that radiate solar heat and thus warm the atmosphere. Their migrations can range from a few dozen miles up and down mountains (known as a vertical migration) to more than a thousand miles across the steppes (referred to as a horizontal migration, usually along a north–south route). The duration of their stay in any encampment varies greatly, depending on seasonal conditions that determine the availability of grass and water.

Once a group arrives at its destination, each family sets up its dome-shaped shelter, called a *yurt* in most languages (except in Mongolia, where it is known as a *ger*), which has been used by steppe nomads since the

An elderly Kazak woman in her yurt. She and her family were among the sixty thousand Kazaks who immigrated to Kazakstan after the demise of the Soviet Union but later returned to their pastures in western Mongolia.

early first millennium B.C. One yurt and all the family's household belongings can be transported on the back of three camels. The walls of these portable dwellings consist of a series of expandable wooden lattices, bound together to form a circle and supported by long ribs of curved wood that fasten into an open circle at the top, allowing the smoke to escape from the hearth. (When it rains or is extremely cold, a covering of felt is pulled over the opening.) Handwoven woolen bands are laced between the ribs to hold them firmly in place when gale-force winds hit, and are embellished with colorful designs that hold special amuletic significance, intended to ward off misfortunes that might befall the family. The roof and the exterior walls are covered with blankets of thick woolen felt; the interior walls are hung with decorative multicolored felt carpets and reed mats woven together with brightly dyed yarn in abstract designs. More felt rugs serve as floor and seating at the back of the yurt, and neatly stacked boxy leather suitcases function as the family's chest of drawers.

Few nomads possess chairs or tables; instead, most sit cross-legged on the carpeted area directly opposite the wooden door to rest, visit, or eat. As you enter the yurt, men's lariats, saddles, and other riding tack are found to the left of the door, while women's accoutrements, including cookware, cheese-making equipment, and sewing supplies (I have even spotted an occasional portable sewing machine), are stored to the right. Sleeping arrangements vary with age: babies are swathed tightly and laid in cradles, children snuggle under blankets on multiple layers of thick felt carpets, and the adults sleep on single cots, surrounded by drapes suspended from the ceiling that afford a modicum of privacy in these snug and eminently practical dwellings.

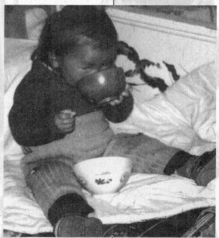

Mongol child at breakfast.

necessary travel documents, scholarly contacts, and for our guide, Nurilya Shakhanova, a Kazak curator at the Ethnographic Museum in Leningrad.[3] Matt and I flew to Almaty,[4] nestled among the Tien Shan Mountains in southern Kazakstan, to live in a small graduate-student hostel and study with scholars from the Kazak Academy of Sciences for a month. They were generous with their knowledge and collections, and I learned much about the hundred different nationalities of Kazakstan (most of whom had been transferred there during Stalin's reign of terror), the steppes' rich history, and the intriguing array of artifacts displayed in the excellent historical and archaeological museums.

To cap off our visit, we returned to Moscow by train, our first trip across the steppes, leaving the Almaty station during a driving early winter rain, which soon diminished as we followed the fertile alluvial plain along the foothills of southern Kazakstan. We skimmed the tip of the forbidding Kyzyl Kum desert, plowing through mile upon mile of flat, almost featureless scant grasslands, and ending with a flourish of rolling hills before pulling into Moscow's Kazansky railway station. The three-day journey covered only a small portion of the steppes, but it was enough to give us a taste of their varied terrain. It also gave us a taste of the still-present Soviet paranoia. As we neared the city of Turkestan, a friendly fellow passenger, a professional wind engineer, told me that the train might pass by an imposing mausoleum Tamerlane had built for Ahmed Yesevi, a twelfth-century mystic, and he urged me to take some photographs. As I stood in the corridor of the vagon to watch through the train window for this monument, I noticed the conductor glaring suspiciously at me. Just as we were pulling into the station, I laid the camera on my compartment seat, covering it with a scarf, and settled in to watch the fascinating Central Asian faces of the milling crowd on the platform.

Suddenly, two KGB agents appeared at our door, apparently alerted

---

3. The city, founded by Peter the Great in 1703, was rechristened with its pre-Soviet name of St. Petersburg in 1991, the dawn of perestroika.
4. Known as Alma-Ata during the Soviet period.

by the conductor even before the train had arrived in the city. Looking like a couple of young heavies in a grade-B mobster movie, dressed in black suits, with pomaded dark hair slicked back, they took seats on either side of our compartment. One brandished a sheaf of papers in my face before slamming them on the table. "You should not be on this train," he said in very proper but accented English. "It is forbidden to foreigners."

"Why?" I replied. I tried to think what might have caused this sudden unwanted attention, then remembered the suspicious conductor and glanced at the scarf that rested against the KGBer's thigh. "We're on our way to Moscow from Alma-Ata, and the Kazak Institute bought the tickets for us."

He thrust the top sheet at me, sternly saying, "Sign this. Here, on the line." I turned to Nurilya, our Kazak companion, who had joined us in the compartment. Now very pale, she only stared with wide black eyes, first at me and then at the two men.

"Nurilya, what does this say? What do they want?" She stared speechlessly back at me—my first up-close demonstration of KBG-inflicted terror. I peered at the page filled with Cyrillic script, wondering what to do, when the train whistle shrilled its warning that we were about to depart. The tension created by the KGB men was palpable. Matt muttered in a low voice, "Don't sign anything! We don't know what it is."

"Sign! Here!" the agent demanded again, jabbing at the paper with a slender pointed finger. "Here!" I picked up the pen and scrawled my name, hoping that we would make it to Moscow and Irina's protection. The men in black grabbed their papers and jumped to the station platform from the now-moving train.

At the next stop, two even tougher-looking men boarded and stood guard in the corridor, while a middle-aged dishwater blonde claimed the other half of the visibly shaken Nurilya's compartment. Suspicious of this new traveling companion, I struck up a conversation with the woman, who maintained that she was going to her son's wedding in Uralsk. Given her grungy housedress, her broken nails, and lack of luggage, it was pretty evident that she had received a phone call commanding her to immediately board our train, and I realized we had a third agent in our midst.

The trio finally disembarked at Uralsk, and only later did I realize that our route had taken us by the Baikonur missile-launch site, and the smoke-belching factory that my wind engineer said produced ceramics was, in fact, the source of the tiles that covered the Soviet spaceships. Because this route passed through a large sensitive military area, it was naturally off-limits to all foreigners.

Later Nurilya told us that although the ticket agent had put us on the wrong train, the Kazak Institute was unjustly reprimanded for contributing to the security breach. I still wonder what the consequences were for Nurilya's "lapse" of vigilance.

Despite our rather unnerving encounter with the KGB, I returned home to Berkeley eager to relay the Kazak Institute's offer to establish a working relationship with an American organization. I made several efforts to interest UC Berkeley in this invitation, but to no avail. In fact, I couldn't find a single member of the International Area Studies staff who had even heard of Kazakstan. Finally, with the help of a Nolo Press book on non-profit organizations and advice from Dr. Alton Donnelly, a family friend and a professor of Russian history, I established the Kazakh/American Research Project, Inc.[5] Now our work could begin in earnest.

Looking back, I can't really blame the UC Berkeley staff for their lack of enthusiasm. Little was known about the non-Russian Soviet republics at that time, and even after the dissolution of the Soviet Union in 1991, information about the area's historical and cultural significance remains skimpy. The ancient nomads themselves left behind no written records, and while Greeks such as Hellanicus and Herodotus wrote of steppe dwellers in the fifth century B.C., they freely interspersed their more sober portraits of military campaigns, industrious farmers, and nomadic herders with tales of one-eyed men called Arimaspians, griffins that guarded nuggets

5.   In 1997, the name was changed to the American-Eurasian Research Institute, Inc., and the Center for the Study of Eurasian Nomads and Zinat Press were established as subsidiaries.

of gold that tumbled from mountainous crags, and tribes of fierce, man-hating female warriors. In the fifth and twelfth centuries, when Attila the Hun and Genghis Khan were building their respective empires, it often fell to the peoples they conquered, from the terrified Slavs to the Western Europeans, to report on their conquerors' beliefs and customs—circumstances that never result in a complete, much less flattering, portrait of a culture. These accounts added much to the mystique of the remote realm, but did little to enlighten foreigners about the true nature of Eurasian nomads.

In modern times, despite all the advances in archaeology and many excavations in the area, very few treatises on ancient steppe societies have been published outside Russia. Only the Scythians, a nation of warlike nomads and traders who had lived north of the Black Sea, had attracted attention in the West, thanks to the hoards of gold treasures found in their kurgans. (See "Discovering Russia's Early Nomads," page 10.) It wasn't until Leonid Yablonsky invited me to excavate with him in 1991 that I was able to really delve into the historical and archaeological problems surrounding the tribes who fascinated me: the Saka, who occupied the eastern steppes and the Tien Shan and Altai mountains from the eighth through third centuries B.C.; the Sauromatians, who lived in Russia's southern Urals and along the Volga and the Don rivers in the sixth and fifth centuries B.C.,[6] and the Sarmatians, another nomadic confederation of mysterious origins who began displacing the Sauromatians around the fourth century B.C.

Leonid Yablonsky's friendship became incredibly important to me throughout the dig. Initially, his taciturn and somber manner was somewhat off-putting, but I soon learned that he possessed a quiet charm. When given a chance to discuss his beloved excavations south of the Aral Sea, he won me over with animated accounts of the dry desert heat and

---

6. Russian archaeologists date the Sauromatians in the lower Volga and Don river regions from the seventh century B.C. while the tribes in the southern Ural steppes are dated from the sixth century B.C. As always, new archaeological discoveries could alter the traditional dating schemes.

Discovering Russia's Early Nomads

A surge of interest in the Early Iron Age nomadic legacy began in the seventeenth century when, during the Russian expansion eastward through Siberia, explorers turned fortune-hunters discovered that huge earthen mounds, easily spotted because they are visible for miles against the horizon, contained tremendous golden treasures. Hundreds of irreplaceable artifacts were melted down, lost in this gold rush, until 1716, when Peter the Great's newly established Kunstkammer (Russia's first museum) received about sixty gold artifacts donated by two Siberian entrepreneurs. Astounded by the intricacy of these hoards, the czar issued an edict: The crown would pay more for intact works of "Scytho-Siberian" art than the value of the metal. Today golden deer and crouching tigers—once exotic imports fashioned by Greek craftsmen commissioned by royal Scythian chieftains or priestesses who were buried in great mounds across the Eurasian steppes—dazzle visitors to the Hermitage's Gold Room in St. Petersburg.

Far to the west in Ukraine, Russians excavated a huge kurgan in the mid-eighteenth century, but they did not recognize it as being Scythian until seventy years later in the northern Black Sea region, when they opened the Kul Oba kurgan, revealing the remains of a chieftain, his wife, and a retainer. Spurred on by the singularly exciting discovery of burial mounds containing hundreds of horses, intricate Animal Style plaques, and huge bronze cauldrons, intensive Scythian exploration—followed by excavations—was in full swing in Ukraine and the northern Caucasus Mountains by the second half of the nineteenth century.

Russian historians in the early nineteenth century, believing that the Scythians' eastern neighbors had been Sauromatian and Sarmatian tribes, began consulting the works of Herodotus and other ancient authors in an attempt to locate these nomadic homelands. But it wasn't until 1905 that the first Sauro-Sarmatian kurgans in the lower Volga and Don river regions were excavated. Curiously, the Russians never identified the Sauromatians that Herodotus associated with the Amazons until 1929, probably because it required that kurgan architecture and artifacts from many burials be compared before a clear cultural picture could be visualized.

The Second World War—the "Great War," as it is called in Russia—brought archaeological excavation to a halt until the late 1940s; large-scale, handsomely financed Soviet excavations resumed north of the Black Sea, where the massive Scythian kurgans dominated the landscape, and in the Don and Volga region, only recently recognized as also being Sauro-Sarmatian territory.

Far to the east in the Siberian Altai Mountains, in the 1950s and early '60s the Russian archaeologist Sergei Rudenko's excavations included five great kurgans that were identified as Pazyryk (see Chapter 5), and the lavish art that he found was labeled "Scytho-Siberian." Although he meticulously recorded the presence of women in the Pazyryk burials, Rudenko dismissed them as wives sacrificed to accompany their royal husbands to the next world, not women of power in their own right.

Around the same time Rudenko was delving into Siberia, another Russian archaeologist, K. F. Smirnov, encountered more Sauro-Sarmatian nomadic burial sites near Orenburg in the southern Ural steppes and wrote an excellent summary of his findings, which helped explain the distinctions between the different groups of steppe nomads. He credited the women in these burials with a more prominent role, going so far as to publish an article in 1982 identifying the population living in the lower Don River region in the fourth century B.C. as "Amazons." Smirnov's colleague Marina Moshkova excavated west of the Ural River and along the middle Volga in the 1960s through the 1980s, publishing many articles and editing volumes on the origins of the Early Sarmatians. Although the Russian and then the Soviet scholars had for decades excavated the ancient nomadic kurgans, it wasn't until 1975 that the Soviets mounted the first traveling exhibition of the Scythians' dazzling Animal Style gold ornaments and elaborate equestrian trappings that the legacy of the steppe nomads began to excite Western interests.

remote locales. I was intrigued by his passion for excavation, and noted a rare, wide smile emerging through his salt-and-pepper beard and his dark brown eyes shining with amusement.

The following year, with the breakup of the USSR imminent, Yablonsky could no longer excavate in Turkmenistan. He showed me his survey of the Pokrovka cemeteries, which, although in the Kazak steppes, were just within the Russian border. "If you'd like," he said, "we can excavate these kurgans together." I eagerly signed on. As we worked I developed great respect for his skills and his knowledge of kurgan archaeology. He was also an excellent physical anthropologist, who was able to sex and age skeletons *in situ*. He had learned this skill as a young student when he assisted the then-leading Russian physical anthropologist, who was too elderly to jump in and out of excavated pits, and therefore most appreciative of young Yablonsky's agility. Some of this esteemed scholar's lessons were decidedly less than scientific. "Do you know how to distinguish a make skull from a female?" Yablonsky shook his head, and the professor replied, "When you hold it, if it has bumps that's a male, and if it's so smooth you want to pet it, that's a female." No matter how he learned them, Yablonsky's skills in physical anthropology were invaluable in our excavations.

Even before my excavations with Yablonsky at Pokrovka, Russian archaeologists had excavated and noted in their reports that there were female warriors and priestesses in these societies, and a couple of them had written articles defining the Sauromatians as a "female dominated" tribe, but because of the Cold War and the paucity of communication between the East and West, nothing had appeared in English on this topic. In reality, Soviet archaeologists were little concerned with this issue, preferring to concentrate on the more spectacular burial mounds of male chieftains. As a consequence, even in archaeological circles, the prevailing Western concept of ancient steppe nomads was that they were a pack of merciless warlords with jet-black hair and dark, slanted eyes, who marauded on tiny ponies throughout Europe, the Middle East, and eastern Asia, besieging cities and wiping out the men before carrying off the women for new breeding stock.

The true story, of course, is much less gory and infinitely more complex. As I interpreted our archaeological finds from Pokrovka, it became evident that the Sauromatians and Sarmatians were a variegated culture

A Sarmatian woman as reconstructed from her skull.
(Three views. Reconstruction by Leonid T. Yablonsky.)

of Caucasoids in which women enjoyed a measure of power and prominence far beyond what previous researchers had ever imagined. And, in hunting for clues about these lost women, I realized that the steppe maidens and matrons who fought bravely on horseback or made prognostications with the aid of bronze mirrors had counterparts the world over. Many were enmeshed in warlike, seemingly male-dominated societies, a number of which crossed paths with the Sauro-Sarmatians in some fashion. Each discovery seemed to force me to look deeper and further to ferret out other hidden women of history, and my search eventually encompassed the Golden Age of Greece, the Vikings' reign of terror, the Celtic warrior queens, and the women wrestlers in the courts of the Mongol Empire. But it all started in the plains of Kazakstan, at the sacred mounds where Iron Age nomads once came to bury their dead.

CHAPTER TWO

AN ARCHAEOLOGIST IN THE FIELD

The life of an archaeologist is a fascinating one, but it is certainly not what action-adventure movies would lead you to believe. The *Indiana Jones* myth—the idea that archaeology consists of swashbuckling forays into exotic lands that yield swift and spectacular results—is one that needs dispelling. In fact, those forays are highly criticized by real archaeologists, because the swashbuckling destroys the archaeological record, a record that is very fragile and crucial to preserve.

In real life, a strong back, a knack with a shovel, and the ability to recognize when the shovel should be laid aside and the trowel and small brushes be brought to the fore are much more useful than prowess with a bullwhip or being able to outrun careening boulders. Our bounty is much more likely to consist of clay pots, the bones of ancient animals, and arrowheads than hoards of precious gems. An iron constitution that allows one to adjust to strange but nutritious (and always monotonous) food also helps; after a couple of weeks on the steppes our volunteers fantasize about "gourmet fare" like hamburgers, ice cream, and pizza.

With the demise of the Soviet Union, the train trip from Moscow to Sol Iletsk, once a pleasant thirty-six-hour journey, has become increasingly hazardous as increasing numbers of ruffians are now free to travel within Russian borders. Boisterous singing concerts inspired by the vodka bottles passed hand to hand became aggressive shoving contests, and sleep was difficult for our Russian and American crew. As the train pulled into the station, the loud voices carried through now-glassless windows, and both Leonid Yablonsky and I breathed sighs of relief when our crews were finally assembled. The teeth-jarring twenty-five-mile ride from the train to our Pokrovka camp over the broken-asphalt highway, with us sardined on unpadded wooden benches in the back of our Russian military truck, was a less hazardous trip but infinitely more uncomfortable.

Our volunteers also must realize that they're venturing into territory without ready access to state-of-the-art medical facilities. When one young woman became seriously ill, Yablonsky had to drive four hours to the nearest airport at Orenburg and then summon up all his charm and influence to land her a ticket to Moscow. Due to the lack of clinics and stores, we always have to pack all the medical supplies we might possibly need during a dig. On one extensive drugstore run before a trip, the pharmacist pensively looked over my stash of varied antibiotics, bandages of all types and sizes, analgesics, antibacterial ointments, motion-sickness pills, and antidiarrheal medicines. He shook his head. "I hope you get well *very* soon," he said in a sympathetic voice.

Most of the time my little speech about spartan living conditions, unfamiliar foods and customs, hard labor, and seemingly modest finds succeeds in weeding out the eager but unsuitable souls. However, once in a while a mismatch slips in. I was forced to send one pleasant and eager woman home after the pervasive dust from the dig kicked her asthma into overdrive. To be sure, more than a few volunteers found that pitching dirt for hours under a glaring sun could be exhausting. This last group included Dr. Michael, who accumulated many overtime emergency room hours so that he could enjoy more frequent and longer vacations to engage in his favorite pastime—archaeological excavations. Michael's concept of excavating was relaxing on his shovel handle and dreamily looking off into the horizon. When I once reminded him of the tool's real purpose he just smiled broadly and said, "Ah, this is just fine." (This is in contrast to Matt, my dear septuagenarian husband, who revels in pitching dirt more than anyone on the team.) I forgave the doctor his laid-back archaeological work ethic, though he earned his keep when our new and inexperienced driver limped into camp one morning at dawn covered with dirt and crusty dried blood. He had fallen asleep while driving and when the front wheel of his massive Russian truck jerked into a deep roadside gully, he somehow pitched free of the rolling vehicle. I summoned Michael from a deep sleep and he responded in true surgeon's fashion. Without benefit of a crisp white examining table, X-rays, and other medical niceties, he initiated a full exam. After a speedy but thorough series of tests, he determined, much to everyone's relief, that the driver had no broken bones and that his bruises, scrapes, and lacerations were not immediately life threatening. He did, however, have him sent him back to Moscow, as the risk of infection was much too great for him to remain in camp.

We had an interesting succession of drivers during our various excavations, a fact that might not seem important unless one understands the status of this job in Russian society. When the Soviets opened up Siberia to development in the 1940s, nearly every commodity, from lumber to flour, could be transported only by truck over immense distances on poorly maintained, frequently icy roads. Trucks break down and they freeze up in subzero weather; if vehicles are immobilized on isolated Siberian highways, drivers will succumb very quickly in the cold. As only a few elite were ever permitted to own automobiles, the demand for garages staffed by trained mechanics, equipped with a multitude of diagnostic computers, also never existed in this immense country. Gas stations dispensed gasoline (at least part of the time) and provided absolutely nothing else. The elite drivers were trained mechanics who had passed those tests before they were allowed a driver's license, and they repaired minor and major breakdowns with rudimentary equipment. The skill and danger involved make these astonishingly well-paid jobs. In 1992, I was told that drivers made about the same salary as Gorbachev did.

Drivers were tightly regulated by their union, so we had little say in who our driver would be—he usually came with the vehicle we rented. Occasionally we'd get a prima donna or a less than forthright character, such as one who claimed he couldn't work for several days running because both his parents had just been decapitated in a motorcycle accident; we found out later that he simply had been too hungover to drive. Sometimes, though, we lucked into an obliging and responsible fellow, such as Piotr, who faithfully hauled drinking and cooking water to camp in ten-gallon galvanized cans and shopped for bread at the nearby village, and a young Chechen named Sasha, who never missed a day's driving in two seasons.

The second prerequisite for our American volunteers was the ability to communicate on friendly and professional terms with our Russian staff and volunteers. Several of our Russian crew returned summer after summer to work with us, and although they had other professions and came to us during their vacation time, they were talented and efficient amateur archaeologists who often taught the finer aspects to our novices. Red-haired Mitya, for example, a capable and personable architect by profession, was responsible for assembling our huge, former-Russian-army kitchen tent as well as the canvas lean-to roof attached to a rare steppe-tree that sheltered our outdoor dining accommodations. Before excavating, Mitya also helped choose our kurgans for each season, and then surveyed and mapped them for size, height, and location in relation to the other kurgans.

Cleaning the skeletons and artifacts is a crucial task that requires a delicate touch, for none of these can be moved until they have been completely revealed and their location accurately recorded. Much of this cleaning fell to Olga, a geologist, and Tanya, a medical doctor, although Jan and Julie, two of our American volunteers, were quite dexterous and developed these skills in rapid order.

Digging nomadic burial mounds requires removing huge quantities of dirt from the pits. Often the principal burial—the one in the center that the kurgan had been constructed for—was in a catacomb, a tunnel-like construction that extended from one end of the pit. Catacomb burials were particularly difficult to excavate, as the hard-packed "roof" must be preserved intact, although the interior height could be less than a yard. Big Tolya, one of our amateur archaeologists, was a specialist in identifying the fragile line between virgin soil and the ancient pit and in determining exactly where the catacomb lay. A slightly built high school teacher, Big Tolya had brought his son, Little Tolya, on excavations since the child was five years old. Now fifteen, Little Tolya towered over his father, had a prodigious appetite, and let it be known that he adored American peanut butter, proclaiming it tasted like beer nuts, a commodity recently introduced into Russian cuisine. The somewhat eccentric crew was rounded out by Slava, a diminutive, wiry Russian who excavated alongside Big Tolya. He kept his profession a secret, eliciting much speculation on our part when he arrived each morning at the breakfast table dressed in go-to-town finery. After eating, he frantically rushed to his tent to change into excavating garb while our truck driver honked impatiently. What kind of job could necessitate such an odd routine? Finally, after many seasons with us, Slava confided to my husband Matt that he designed top-secret electronics for Soviet military aircraft. We never would have guessed!

At the beginning of each excavation season, I arrive in Moscow lugging mounds of excavating equipment from the States—shovels and trowels, tiny paintbrushes and small bulb syringes (to remove dust from fragile bones), even a wheelbarrow or two. Leonid Yablonsky meets me, and after I clear customs—in typical Soviet fashion, sometimes they hardly notice me, other times the ordeal is unnerving—we load the military truck, only to soon unload, lugging the equipment and luggage to Yablonsky's sixth-floor, turn-of-the-century apartment. The entry of his apartment is already overflowing with cartons piled higher than my head, for he has been shopping for the food that we will need in camp: Russian apple butter, pasta, sacks of sugar, Polish pâté, *gretchka* (bulgur wheat—though it is disdained by most "foreigners," this nutty grain was my favorite), canned Argentina beef, and boxes and boxes of loose tea imported from India.

Yablonsky and I then take the Metro to his favorite shops to buy a few cans of the instant coffee that would ensure the much-needed afternoon pick-me-up and, if we're lucky, a five-pound salami and a round of smoked Gouda from Holland; magically these tasty tidbits won't spoil without refrigeration, and we carefully apportion them throughout the summer.

That was our routine each season we excavated together—but no one could have predicted how special 1994 would prove to be.

The overland route from Moscow to Pokrovka and the homeland of the Sarmatians in the first millennium B.C.

Early on the morning appointed for our departure to the site, our Russian crew arrived. Under Mitya's supervision, they hauled everything from Yablonsky's apartment and meticulously packed the truck so the load wouldn't shift, reserving a modicum of legroom at the front where four men could ride on a padded wooden bench to Pokrovka, on the southern edge of Siberia. This was truly an awful trip—three days in a windowless compartment, bouncing on a backless wooden seat. As we pulled out of Moscow, Yablonsky directed from the truck's passenger seat, while Matt and I brought up the rear in our small red Neva, a wonderfully tiny four-wheel-drive vehicle. While at gas stations or in towns along the way, we never spoke a word so that the "mafiosi" wouldn't hear our foreign accents and rob us (or worse). After three days of cooking over a campfire and sporadically washing with a cloth dampened from our drinking water, we arrived at Pokrovka. Just as a massive red sun tilted over the horizon, we excitedly began setting up a makeshift shelter at our old campsite on the left bank of the Khobda River. Tomorrow the work would begin!

After the kurgans are selected and surveyed, the excavations begin with the removal of the mound to expose the ancient virgin soil—called cat's-eye because of its yellow mottling on a buff-white background that contrasts with the dark, humus-soil stains on the earth signaling the location of the burials or other pits. At Pokrovka, the sandy topsoil is completely devoid of stones or rocks, so that over the 2,500 years since these mounds were constructed and during the last 50 years they have been plowed on this collective farm, they have eroded to a shadow.[1] From one of the collective farms Yablonsky hires a scraper, a huge tractorlike machine with a blade attached to the front. As it removes a four-inch depth of soil during

---

1. In other areas where we've excavated, such as in southern Kazakstan, large stones were layered with soil to construct the mounds. These kurgans can't be plowed and there is less erosion, so the mounds are more easily identified. This was also a drawback, as they were easily identified by grave robbers.

each swath back and forth around the central balk, Yablonsky and I follow on foot, watching for any indication of ancient soil disturbance or other anomalies, such as a burial from the medieval period.[2] Frequently we find evidence of a ditch that encircles the kurgan, revealed by black humus soil that had filled the depression, and sometimes the mourners erected a wall of yellow sand around the important central pit. These peculiarities of kurgan architecture are symbolic vestiges of the nomads' religious beliefs. For example, the yellow wall may have signified that the person buried there was of elevated status (because of the extra labor required).

Chronologies of the Early Nomads

Saka	eighth to third centuries B.C.
Scythian	seventh to third centuries B.C.
Sauromatians	late seventh/early sixth to fourth centuries B.C.
Early Sarmatians	fourth to second centuries B.C.
Middle Sarmatians	second century B.C. to A.D. second century
Late Sarmatians	A.D. second century to fourth century

Soon we identify dark brownish elongated stains on the cat's-eye—only when we have removed the pit soil will the mysteries beneath reveal themselves. After all the kurgans are opened, the workers, who have been setting up our tents, arranging equipment, and unpacking and storing our supply of staples in the mess tent, gather their picks and shovels to begin the next process: removing the soil from the burial pits. Upon near-

---

2. A balk is the soil bank left standing as the dirt is removed on either side by the scraper or by hand, and it allows archaeologists to read the stratigraphy. For example, in a center balk, we can tell by the way the soil layers slope if the kurgan has been robbed: Level- or upward-sloping layers indicate an undisturbed mound, while downward-sloping layers indicate collapsing soil, revealing that a robber had probably dug into the central chamber. If the mound is larger than about twenty yards, three balks are left equidistant across the area.

To Die a Nomad: Ancient Burial Rites and the Construction of Kurgans

Although the Sauromatians and Sarmatians might traverse great areas in their travels, these tribes buried their dead only in their summer pasturelands, and their cemeteries certainly were regarded as holy places where, year after year, the tribes performed commemorative rituals. If nomads died in winter or during migration, their bodies were ceremoniously washed. Many of the muscles and organs may have been removed, and the cavities filled with sedge and fragrant herbs, then precisely stitched up with horsehair thread; the corpses may have been coated in wax or honey to help preserve them, as was the practice of many peoples of the first millennium B.C., including the Scythians. The bodies were then wrapped in felt blankets reinforced with cane rods, tied with woolen ropes, and during the winter placed in trees to protect them from wild animals until they could be transported to the burial grounds. Many of these traditions were recorded by Herodotus and later verified by archaeologists when they excavated the frozen Pazyryk tombs in southern Siberia.

Once the nomads arrived at their summer pastures, they would either bury the bodies in existing kurgans or construct new ones. These burial mounds, some of which date to the Bronze Age, can be imposing structures: The resting sites of the great chieftains—which the Russians call czar kurgans—just inside the Kazakstan border near Pokrovka rise roughly 100 feet over the plains and stretch 350 feet in diameter. Our Pokrovka kurgans were much less grand. Housing the remains of the nomadic middle class, they average about 65 feet in diameter and probably stood about 6 to 9 feet tall until erosion and agricultural development took their toll.

In regions where rocks are plentiful, the mounds were built from stones layered with soil. At Pokrovka, they were constructed entirely from soil and sod, since

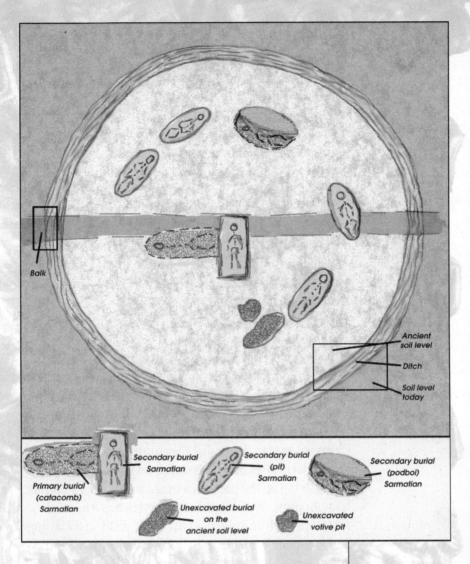

Balk

Ancient
soil level

Ditch

Soil level
today

Primary burial
(catacomb)
Sarmatian

Secondary burial
Sarmatian

Secondary burial
(pit)
Sarmatian

Secondary burial
(podboi)
Sarmatian

Unexcavated burial
on the
ancient soil level

Unexcavated
votive pit

there are no rocks in this portion of the steppes. The nomads would clear a circle and dig an elongated oval or rectangular pit in the center to a depth of six to eight feet. The hardpan (the clay-ridden dirt known to Russian archaeologists as cat's-eye because of its yellow and white color) makes digging difficult even with modern equipment, and I can only marvel at the effort required in ancient times, using picks fashioned from deer antlers mounted on wooden handles. Sometimes they'd slice a six- to eight-inch ledge into the sides of the pit,

Schematic of the various components that make up a kurgan and the types of burial pits and their placements within the kurgan.

which helped the gravediggers to get in and out, and provided a place to anchor the small tree branches covered with cane, grasses, and possibly textiles that formed a canopy over the deceased. In addition, some kurgans also contained catacombs (five- to six-foot-long tunnels without outlets) extending from the end of the central pit, or else *podbois* (horizontal niches dug along the side of the pit), both of which were used for burials. Occasionally, a kurgan boasted more elaborate construction, such as a sunken wooden cabinlike structure to house the deceased and the funerary offerings.

Once the chambers had been dug, the bodies were laid to rest, entombed in a wooden sarcophagus plastered with clay or simply wrapped in a felt blanket. The earlier Sauromatians at Pokrovka always oriented their dead toward the rising sun—that is, the top of the head pointed toward the east—but, not having compasses, the orientation could vary slightly north or south of east. In contrast, the Sarmatians preferred to bury their corpses with the heads pointing toward the south, but again there could be a deviation east or west of south. The orientation of the skeleton was one of the criteria that we used to determine the culture and time period, as both cultures placed the deceased in a supine position, lying on the back with the face upward. Items that might prove useful in the afterlife, such as a joint of mutton, an iron knife used to cut the meat, and clay jugs of koumiss (fermented, slightly alcoholic mare's milk), broth, or water, were placed in the burial chamber. A variety of other mortuary offerings would also be laid in the chamber, reflecting the status of the deceased. These might range from a quiver of bronze arrowheads to a stone-carved ceremonial altar, fossilized seashells to rare glass beads. When everything was in place and the corpse protected from cascading dirt, the mourners filled in the pits; in the larger and perhaps more prestigious burials, they also built a wall of packed yellow clay about two feet high circling the pit. Dirt and sod were then piled on top, creating a mound. During all this time—undoubtedly several days or even weeks—they feasted on ritual foods.

Given how labor-intensive these undertakings were, it isn't surprising that the majority of kurgans were reused many times through the centuries; many of the ones we excavated at Pokrovka contained from two to thirty burials. Occasionally mourners would add a corpse by entering through a dromos (tunnel) and pushing aside skeletons to make room for the newly deceased. More often, fresh pits were dug laterally around the center through the top of the mound to avoid disturbing the earlier burials, suggesting that the gravediggers knew the location of the previous burials and thus were members of the same clan. The respectful placement, especially the positioning of later burials directly over a long-deceased female figure, also hints of ancestor worship, which would have been in keeping with religions of the time.

Judging from the piles of horse bones and ring of horse skulls found at the edges of some large kurgans, the nomads sometimes celebrated during or after the construction of the mounds with a banquet at which they consumed horsemeat, a ritual food. We also discovered seeds from a hallucinogenic plant at one burial—a rare find indeed, since organic material doesn't tend to preserve well—suggesting that they also might have burned these plants and inhaled the intoxicating vapors as part of their rites as they laid their loved ones to rest.

---

ing the bottom of a pit, they turn the next phase over to a skeleton cleaner, who removes tiny amounts of dirt using tools such as spoons, knives, and flour scoops, and only then patiently brushes away dust to ready this burial for the final steps. The first of these is to photograph every aspect, which I do in detail before Mitya and his crew begin the next, to precisely measure and draw the tomb and skeleton. (The initial drawings are made in pencil and later are inked onto white vellum.) By late afternoon Yablonsky and I identify and remove each artifact while Mitya records their exact locations on his drawing. We examine the long bones for evidence of diseases such as tuberculosis and arthritis, which leave traces there; the pelvis and skull will reveal the sex and age of the deceased. This routine is actually never monotonous. It is sometimes puzzling and frequently exciting, and it continues over the summer as almost each day we clean and document another burial.

Perhaps the most common mistake laypeople make about an archaeological crew is that, after a long day on the dig, we all sit around and engage in excited conversations about our finds, interpreting the artifacts and speculating about the light they shed on long-vanished civilizations. The truth is a little less dramatic: We are so busy working against the clock once the kurgans are exposed that there's little time for discussion and wonderment. After dinner, we write up our notes, check drawings for accuracy, wash and piece together potsherds, and then promptly fall asleep on our cots. Not at all Indiana Jones-ish. Our best camaraderie begins at the end of a hard week's work when the vodka bottle emerges after supper and we all gather around the open fire. The Russians sing mournful ballads while Yablonsky strums his guitar, and the Americans are occasionally coaxed to warble an old pop tune.

On this particular dig, as we complete burial after burial and kurgan after kurgan (and all must be excavated before we leave), we are all becoming weary of the primitive living conditions and heavy work (I fantasize about a long, hot shower). We feel changes in the weather pattern; soon cold autumn rains will make tent camping intolerable. Our last major task of the season (and one of my favorites) is to photograph all the objects in context, meaning that the artifacts from each burial are assembled for their final portrait together before being separated forever: pottery, too fragile to transport to Moscow, will be left in the Orenburg Museum and the other artifacts packed for their trip to the Moscow Institute. We pick a day when most of the fieldwork is complete and the weather is good—sunny, no wind, no black clouds glowering on the horizon, and no gray overcast, drizzly skies. In the center of the campsite Olga carefully removes the artifacts, first from the trunk where they have accumulated over the long summer, then from tiny boxes, mating those from each burial before handing them to me. I arrange them on the blue satin sleeping bag that serves as a backdrop, add a measure marked in black and white centimeters, and insert the numbers and letters that identify this burial. Yablonsky and I take turns photographing each assemblage before I pass it back to Olga, who restores each artifact to its original wrappings. Everyone gathers to watch, and now, with a season's worth of reflection under our belts, Yablonsky and I try to identify the unusual, commenting on an aspect of a particular bronze plaque or offering a theory as to what purpose a stone carving might have served.

Preservation in the Pokrovka Burials

Organic materials, such as cloth, wood, leather, and flesh, generally are preserved under two conditions: extreme cold, which creates permafrost, and extreme dryness, such as the conditions found in hot, sandy deserts.

At Pokrovka, we occasionally came across fragmented wood branches that roofed a burial, or planks painstakingly hewn for a sarcophagus, as well as traces of reeds and felt mats that had wrapped the body for burial but now looked like a collection of gray ashes. Fragments of woven cloth were preserved if a bronze mirror had been placed under the body— the copper in the alloy protected the cloth from bacteria as the corpse deteriorated. But Pokrovka has neither permafrost nor the year-round aridity of a desert, so nonorganic materials constitute the major bounty of the tombs. These materials yield invaluable insights into the lost cultures of the Sauro-Sarmatians.

Unless the skeletal material has been crushed, the Pokrovka alkaline soil preserves the bones quite well, so even the small and delicate skulls of children have survived the 2,500-year journey to our age, while the adult skeletons reveal their stature and much about their diet and health. Almost without exception, we encountered animal bones in the burials, usually those of sheep, along with some camel and horse bones. Some Russian scholars consider these to have been sacrificial offerings, but I believe that the sheep joints were meant for a different cultural purpose—as meat for the long journey to the otherworld—and the horses and camels were generally meant to be ritually ridden.

Bronze and silver hold up well in the Pokrovka soil, and gold preserves eternally. By stylistic comparison, we know that craftspeople from faraway cities fashioned a variety of prestigious grave offerings from these metals. The Sauro-Sarmatian women indulged in a single style of earrings—coiled bronze wire covered with gold foil—and both men and women sported ornamental and amuletic plaques, some attached to leather belts that identified the owner's status, clan, and tribe. Functional and decorative horse trappings were a must, as were the ubiquitous trilobed arrowheads (one burial contained over two hundred); I can well imagine how nomads schemed about terrorizing their enemies in the next world—repeating the events of this life, galloping at top speed across the steppes, twisting backward in their saddles, launching volleys of these deadly arrows.

While the soil at Pokrovka renders iron into a rusty phantom, we still managed to uncover iron arrowheads now molded into clumps, small remnants of armor plaques, and daggers and swords over a yard long, in both men's and women's burials, which were interesting examples of the traditional Sauro-Sarmatian weaponry style. Other preserved items indicating social status include seashells, already fossilized when collected by the priestesses from some unknown ancient seabed remote from the Pokrovka burials, semiprecious stones, and even imported coral and amber carved into beads, as well as amulets made from boars' tusks that must have imbued their owners with extra prowess.

Fired clay pots were in virtually every burial because food and drink were necessary for the journey to the other world, yet spindle whorls, the small flywheels used for weighting a spindle and regulating its speed, made of stone or fashioned from potsherds—and the occasional "pseudo–spindle whorls" cut from soft chalk—were found only in women's burials (see page 60). Sacrificial altars of carved stone and fired clay were the hallmark of priestesses, and among their uses, they may have served as mortars to grind the chunks of colored ores into powder; these magical colors then became body or textile paint. Each funerary offering not only bespoke the deceased's station in life, it was also a practical or ritual item intended to serve him or her well in the next world.

Grave Encounters

Sometimes we can piece together the scenario that occurred when a tomb was plundered, a fact that became vividly clear to me in the summer of 1994. We were opening a small mound in Pokrovka Cemetery One when we encountered the burial of a man who had died between the fourth and second centuries B.C. We stopped the mechanized scraper, and Yuri, an archaeology student who is our assistant, excavated both fully articulated legs and the skull. The other bones were missing, so we once again started the scraper, careful to avoid the immediate area of the burial. Soon, though, we discovered more bones on the opposite side of the kurgan. As I finished excavating the perfectly arranged bones of an arm, I realized what probably had happened. Shortly after this fellow had died, a grave robber had dug into the mound. When the thief came upon the corpse, he grabbed an arm and jerked it in an attempt to move the body, probably to extricate some valuable artifacts, such as the dead man's belt encrusted with precious metals. But the body was partially decomposed, and when the arm abruptly separated from the shoulder the grave robber, in shock, hurled the severed limb across the mound. Who knows how much more we would understand about ancient civilizations if so many burials had not suffered the destructive interference of grave robbers?

CHAPTER THREE

THE POWER OF THE HEARTH

I had risen before dawn and carefully picked my way through the yurt so I wouldn't disturb the other tenants. I seemed to be the first person awake in the entire aul this unusually clear morning, and I settled comfortably on my folding stool just outside the cluster of huts to jot down some observations in a field notebook. That's when I saw him: a yak bull about twenty yards away, trotting straight toward me. With his curved, pointed horns, pyramid-shaped hump, and long tangle of shaggy brown and white fur, he could have been the love child of an ox and a bison on a bad hair day. I knew from years on an Idaho cattle ranch how dangerous foul-tempered bulls can be. This one looked docile enough, but appearances can be deceiving, and I certainly couldn't claim any expertise in yak body language. As he lumbered closer, I quickly weighed my options. Option 1: Run back into the yurt, waking all the inhabitants and probably giving everyone a good laugh at the expense of the nervous *sheteldyk* (outsider). Option 2: Sit very still and hope that he would ignore me.

Even though a male yak can stand six feet high at the shoulder and tip the scales at more than 1,200 pounds, and this one seemed close to those dimensions, I didn't want to wake everyone up, so I settled on the latter course of action. My decision was rewarded by the sight of the massive beast trotting benignly by, his attention riveted on a herd of yak cows across the shallow ravine. Who said archaeology was dangerous?

This encounter occurred in 1996, when my ethnographic expedition was observing a Kazak aul at their *jailou,* or summer pasture, nestled below Tavan Bogd in western Mongolia.[1] It wasn't the only disconcerting experience we would have during our many stays with the nomads. I'll never forget Matt's expression when, as an *aksakal*—"white-haired one," or honored elder—he was handed the cooked head of a sheep and told to apportion the eyes, tongue, ears, and brain to the people he considered most deserving of these tidbits. But the intimate glimpses of nomadic life afforded by short visits and longer research projects were exhilarating and immensely instructive. At first, the inhabitants of the aul would be rather reserved and self-conscious, but after they got used to the foreigners in their midst, they would relax and go about their daily life, which afforded us invaluable insights into their unique culture.

Although they inhabit the same region once ruled by ancient steppe nomads, the Kazaks cannot be viewed as the true ethnic descendants of any of the nomadic tribes who once lived in Eurasia. Instead, they are a mixture of the many groups who lived in these lands throughout the millennia, including a variety of Caucasoid, Turkic, and Mongol tribes.[2] Still, an examination of contemporary steppe cultures is integral to unlocking the mysteries of the Sauro-Sarmatians, the Scythians, and the Saka, another Iron Age nomadic confederacy. The lifestyle of these long-vanished tribes deprived archaeologists of many of our tools: the written histories, architectural ruins, and troves of revealing artifacts that settled popula-

---

1. Tavan Bogd, which means "Five Gods" in Mongol, is a group of five mountain peaks on the Russia–Mongol border; they are the highest in Mongolia.
2. Both the Mongol and Turkic peoples originated in northwestern Mongolia and speak Altaic languages.

Sarmatians from Pokrovka to the British Isles

Around 400 B.C., the Sauromatians began to be displaced by people known to ancient authors as Simatians or Sarmatians. No one is certain of the origins of these people; although they were also Caucasoids and spoke an Indo-Iranian language, their skeletons revealed a variety of ethnic types, with some being tall and large boned— very much like Vikings (see Chapter 12)—while others were shorter and delicate in stature. My theory, based on a number of notable comparisons between funerary offerings, is that some of these people might have been younger generations of Saka who were forced from their territories near the Tien Shan Mountains or the southern Aral Sea by the need for additional summer pasturelands. Around the third century A.D., they began migrating westward and eventually these expert horsemen equipped with sophisticated weapons and armor constituted a real threat to the Roman legions guarding the Danube frontier. The enterprising legionnaires, however, defused the situation by recruiting some of the Sarmatians to join their army. In A.D. 175, more than five thousand of the steppe tribesmen (most likely along with their families) were dispatched to the northern English border to guard Hadrian's Wall, which helped repel incursions into Roman Britain by the Picts and the Celtic Scots. Twenty years later, the Sarmatian regiment was redeployed to Gaul (the ancient designation for France and Belgium) to quell a rebellion. Later they were returned to Britain, and as they grew old, the battle-weary Sarmatians retired to a veterans' home in Lancashire. (It seems as if they had taken to the British climate, proving that almost anything is better than the weather of the steppes.) The Sarmatian presence in Gaul and Roman Britain never ceases to fascinate me—I always wonder how many unsuspecting modern-day Frenchmen and Britons, as well as Americans of those extractions, possess the genes of the ancient steppe warriors.

tions typically leave in abundance. The houses of the dead are the only dwellings our footloose subjects left behind, forcing us to rely on the often meager clues to be culled from the bones, burial offerings, and physical features of the kurgans. Due to this handicap, ethnography is a critical weapon in the arsenal of the burial archaeologist, and in this I am fortunate in my choice of cultures. The strong oral tradition of the steppe nomads has preserved many highlights of their history, and there are few places on earth that have witnessed the continuity of customs and the means of livelihood as the Eurasian steppes; when one eliminates outside factors such as the effects of Sovietization, it's remarkable how little the lifestyle of the Kazaks, Mongols, and other peoples still practicing pastoral nomadism has changed over the course of 2,500 years. As Alma Kunenbaeva, an ethnographer from Kazakstan teaching at UC Berkeley, told me, "Our society still keeps the old tradition, such as the rites of passage. These are important for the survival of the tribe."

As a scientist, I know it is somewhat risky to extrapolate the ways of the past from present customs, yet questions keep arising in my digs that I think could be solved if I know how nomads today solve the problems of everyday life, from how they cook their food without any apparent fuel to how they care for babies in these harsh climates and mobile conditions. My solution is to go to their summer pasture, sleep in their yurts, eat their food, watch what they do with their children and animals, and ask questions.

I thought it would be difficult to obtain the support I would need for such a trip. Yet all it took was an e-mail correspondence with a Kazak official in the Mongolian Ministry of Foreign Affairs, and I was off. For six weeks in the summer of 1996 in the western Altai Mountains, I became a nomad. Traveling over the bumpy mountain trails by Jeep from one camp to another, I observed the basic tasks of the aul. I watched the women milk yaks, sheep, and goats, then boil the milk until it was slightly caramelized over a dung fire kindled in the tin stove in the center of the yurt. They then cut and dried the cheese, called *kurt,* on the sloping

(above)
Kazak children in western China watch while milk is boiled in a cauldron over an open fire. To the right is a bag where the liquid from the milk (whey) is drained. Later the cheese, a winter food staple, will be dried in the open sun either on a rack or on the roof of the yurt.

(right)
A Kazak woman in western Mongolia milks a yak. The milk will be made into cheese that will be stored for winter use.

roof of their yurt. *Kurt,* a winter staple vital to their subsistence, is so hard it must be soaked to be edible.

At another aul, the men showed me how they rigged a tripod of poles to which are attached a pair of wooden arms. These arms counterbalance a huge stone; by pumping the arms, the stone is moved up and down, creating the momentum to twirl stiff rawhide into supple leather strips for finely braided lariats and bridle reins.

I did sometimes find clues that helped to unravel questions I came up with during our excavations. During the 1993 excavations at Pokrovka, we had discovered twenty-two skeletonized horse heads around the kurgan's perimeter, and in the burial a sizable bronze container perforated with a number of inch-wide holes. I had no idea what its purpose might have been until four years later, when I sat watching a Kazak family prepare a sheep for dinner in our honor. After the fragrant meat had boiled in a large round-bottomed kettle set directly over the flames, my hostess, using a metal pan with a perforated bottom, scooped chunks of meat and bones from broth and dumped them into a basin. Suddenly, I understood what the bronze sieve had been used for 2,500 years ago: the mourners had cooked horse meat, scooping it from its broth as they partook of a ritual feast that I imagined honored their deceased kinsman.

A young Kazak mother nurses her child who is swathed in a cradle. By being in the cradle many hours each day, the child is protected from falling or getting burned on the stove

In a high Altai camp called Dayan, I watched closely as a young mother cared for her six-month-old daughter according to what surely was an ancient tradition. Each afternoon she swaddled her undiapered baby tightly in a cradle, which has a small round hole in the bottom that allows waste to drain into a container below. During the night she arose from her bed and leaned over the still-swaddled child while she nursed, pulling her winter coat around her shoulders to keep away the dark chill seeping through the felt walls. Only at mid-morning after the animals were milked did she take the child from her cradle. Later, when I encountered a Kazak doctor visiting his parents in another aul, I asked if this lack of stimuli didn't hinder the children's development. He replied, "The mothers have many things to do and it's difficult to watch the children every minute. Unlike us, the Mongols don't tie their babies in their cribs and they have many more childhood injuries, especially bad burns from the stoves. It is better this way." Weighing lack of stimulation against burns in these remote mountain valleys, I also voted for swaddling and, after closely observing the toddlers romping around the yurts, decided they had adequately made up for lost time.

Although the ancient nomads were a patriarchal people, one of the things that struck me as I watched husband, wife, and children working together was how egalitarian the auls are. Even when the tribespeople had had some contact with the domineering Russian or strict Islamic male-oriented cultures, men and women usually work side by side, and often at the same tasks. Everyone helps to assemble and strike the yurts, and while the women are charged with most day-to-day food preparation, the men also pitch in by cooking savory horsemeat in the sawed-off, fifty-gallon oil drums that serve as modern substitutes for the bronze cauldrons of yore. Women take care of the babies, but I often saw men tending to toddlers while their wives concentrated on other tasks.[3] Both sexes collaborate to make the wool felt that is used for clothing, rugs, blankets, and the exterior walls of the yurts, and they share the many

---

3. Kazak ethnographer Alma Kunenbaeva told me that steppe nomads don't consider a child to be a tribal member until it has survived a year, a period that includes the nine months spent in the womb. Until this time, the mother is expected to care for the baby with complete detachment, and she cannot cry if it dies. When it reaches the one-year mark, the child is given a name and joyfully welcomed into the aul.

Ritual feasting, a practice among the Early Nomads, is still common among the Kazaks of western Mongolia. Here they cook cauldrons of horsemeat for a celebration honoring the Kazak hero Kurumbai Batir.

duties associated with their herds of horses, sheep, goats, yaks, and other animals. Young boys help their mothers prepare food, carry water from a stream or lake to the yurt, milk the livestock, and perform other domestic duties, while girls learn how to ride and round up the herds. The women especially must be prepared to take on all the tasks involved in running the aul, as many of the men can be absent for long periods of time gathering far-flung herds or trading and buying supplies at distant outposts.

Some ethnographers seize on the nomadic Kazaks' inheritance laws as proof that this is a male-dominated society, but even that apparently inequitable situation requires a further look. It's true that the youngest son inherits the father's estate upon his death, but the daughters—and other sons—each receive a fair portion of the family's assets when they

A Kazak bride and groom at their wedding dinner. The bride wears the traditional *saulke* (pointed hat) now veiled for the wedding.

At a Kazak festival a young woman, dressed in traditional costume that includes a veiled pointed hat (*saulke*), sings traditional songs at the beginning of one of the ceremonies. This costume is nearly identical to those worn by the Saka nomads who lived during the first millennium B.C. Some of these burials were frozen, revealing many beautiful textiles.

marry. The women are not treated badly here: In addition to outfitting the new yurt, part of their dowry is invested in jewelry fashioned from silver coins and gemstones, as well as in their *saulke,* the tall, pointed hat festooned with precious-metal and jeweled plaques. One such headpiece reported in the last century was so lavishly adorned with silver and gold ornaments that it was said to be worth forty thousand horses—a valuable commodity indeed in nomadic currency. When the family has secured all the animals its pastures can handle, any surplus wealth is usually invested in additional adornments for the women, thus endowing them with a kind of portable savings account.

Egalitarianism is also reflected in the many festivals and celebrations that bring the auls together and break up the monotony of life on the steppes. Boys and girls ages six to nine compete as equals in the grueling horse races held during these fetes, riding their sturdy ponies up to thirty-five kilometers (about twenty-two miles) to the starting line and then riding hell-for-leather back over the steppes to the finish line near the aul. Nor is sex a barrier in the singing contest known as the *aites*. In these remarkable competitions that help preserve their history, one contestant sings out questions related to the current festival, while the challenger unhesitatingly must warble back the answers. And so it goes, until all the singers but one run out of questions or answers—or exhaust their vocal cords.

I watched one *aites* in western Mongolia where Kazaks were com-

Both girls and boys between the ages of six and nine prepare for a traditional horse race. They will ride between fifteen and twenty-two miles to get to the starting line and then race to the finish line near the aul.

memorating Kurumbai Batir, an eighteenth-century hero (*batir* means "hero") who had saved his Kazak tribe from the Djungars, a fierce Mongol tribe who had coerced their way west. About twenty yurts had been assembled next to a mountainside creek for this nationalistic gathering, and the customary horse races and wrestling matches already had taken place when the Kazaks started to assemble excitedly in a circle. In the center, a fifty-year-old man sat cross-legged on a brightly colored felt rug, protected from the soft but penetrating rain by his heavy black coat and hat, his back ramrod straight. He threw down

Kazak woman singing in an *aites*, a traditional competition performed by nomads. She is answering a question posed by her male counterpart concerning Kurumbai Batir, an eighteenth-century Kazak hero.

the musical gauntlet by crooning something like "What did Kurumbai Batir do on the fifth of July in 1760?" in a smooth baritone.

His challenger, a woman a few years his junior, replied in her strong, vibrato-laden soprano, "He vanquished the forces of the Djungars near the Ili River."

"Where did Kurumbai Batir lead his Kazak warriors?"

The answer was fired back immediately: "He took them to the green pastures high in the Altai where the Djungars would not follow."

These two were a good match, well versed in Kazak history and skilled at adding the theatrical flourishes and flashing eye contact that help determine the winner. My privileged position in the center of the group turned out to be a mite precarious, as several women spectators pushed ever closer, leaning on me and crushing my feet in their eagerness to see and catch every nuance of the songs. Despite a few waves of claustrophobia, I was charmed by this unique and dramatic manner of keeping history alive and happily sat through the long hours of the contest, which was suspended late in the afternoon and resumed the next morning. Finally, after three days in which alternating pairs of challengers tested each other's mettle, the *aites* was over. I asked Aigul, my Kazak translator, who had won, but to my surprise, she only shrugged her shoulders. "I don't know; I don't like the *aites*," she replied with uncustomary gruffness. I never did find out who had been declared the victor—a frustrating and anticlimactic ending to an otherwise fascinating cultural display.

On a more political level, women also clearly have a voice in running the auls. These intimate communities, which are usually composed of extended families, tend to operate mostly by consensus, rather than through edicts from an all-powerful leader. The nomads' method gives every adult some say as to the manner in which they are governed. Some women enjoy a little extra clout because they have been awarded a special status, such as being dubbed an *ana* (mother of the tribe), *hewana* (which roughly translates as Mother Eve), or *kelen* (one who comes from outside).[4] The tribal leaders tend to be men, but Bayer, my guide, once told me that a middle-aged woman was chieftain of a six-yurt Kazak aul near the Chinese border. "How come Aisha is running things?" I asked Bayer, a Communist-educated Kazak and distant relative of the clan. He shot me a disdainful look that let me know the *sheteldyk* had asked a stupid

---

4. A *kelen,* according to Kunenbaeva, is a woman who comes from outside the tribe; she accumulates status as she grows older and becomes adept at performing special duties, such as preparing bodies for burial, organizing weddings, and acting as the mistress of ceremonies at certain rituals. *Ana* or *hewana* status can be awarded for a number of reasons, including giving birth to seven sons or being a widow with responsibility for running a household. A *kelen* is a woman who has exceptional abilities and performs within the Kazak subtribe. She may replicate many functions that the ancient high-ranking priestesses performed. In contrast, the *ana* or *hewana* receives this honorary title for her responsibilities and accomplishments within her family circle, meaning her position is ranked below that of a *kelen.*

Aisha, the chieftain of a Kazak aul in western Mongolia, making rope from wool.

question. "Because she's the most adept" was his simple and telling reply.

His matter-of-fact tone underscored the fact that roles and status are dictated mostly by pragmatism, not sexual politics. The auls are small, self-reliant, elemental communities; since women play a large part in keeping everyone housed, clothed, and fed, their domestic duties are vital, life-or-death contributions, a fact that elevates the status of these women of the hearth. During my visits, I noticed that everyone had to contribute to the survival of the group. This leaves the steppe nomads without the dubious luxury of relegating females to purely ornamental functions or imposing some of the behavioral restrictions seen in many so-called sophisticated cultures (such as harems; the old Chinese practice of binding women's feet into "golden lilies"; or the pressure on even childless young wives not to work outside the home in '50s America). Even though steppe nomads embraced Islam around the tenth century, piety has often taken a backseat to practicality. This is a byproduct of their nomads' lack of access to the mosques and madrasahs that exert such a powerful influence over settled Muslim populations. Kazak women are proud that they have never worn chador, the cumbersome, traditional black robe that covers Muslim women from head to toe, nor are they forbidden to appear in public without a male relative at their side; such religious observances would impede their work and thus jeopardize the welfare of the tribe.

Although polygamy is allowed, it never gained much popularity; a flock of wives and the resulting offspring would simply be too many mouths to feed for all but the wealthiest nomads. (Besides, I doubt the outspoken Kazak women would tolerate the situation unless they had something to gain from it.) Whenever I did observe a polygamous marriage, there always seemed to be extenuating circumstances. For example, one of Aigul's grandfathers, a Kazak who lived in the Altai Mountains, had taken a Mongol woman for a second wife to quell an uprising against his tribe.

I don't mean to suggest that nomadic steppe societies are completely egalitarian. Each Kazak child must commit ten or more generations of the family tree to memory, and the ancestry is traced through the father's line, not the mother's. When a woman gives birth, she does so on the male side of the yurt, symbolizing that the children belong to the aul (that is, the father's side of the family). Divorce is a bit of a mixed bag: In auls that adhere strictly to Muslim religious law, only men can initiate it for a variety of prescribed reasons (including a wife's failure to produce children within two years of marriage). In contrast, auls that observe traditional tribal law might feature a kind of no-fault, quickie divorce if both parties agree: The bride and groom simply say "*Talakh*" (which essentially means "divorce") three times very loudly and, voilá!, the matrimonial ties are severed. If only the woman is seeking divorce, however, she must forfeit her dowry, abandon her children to her ex-husband's family, and petition her parents to take her back. For obvious reasons, this occurs only in the most radical situations, such as in cases of spousal abuse.

Overall, though, as I watched the easy camaraderie between the men and women as they performed their daily chores or chatted on the felt carpets in the yurt at night, I was pleasantly surprised by how blurred the lines were between the sex roles, and how women's domestic contributions earned them considerable influence and respect. But while it is all well and good to make a case for the egalitarian nature of modern nomadic Kazak society, can we infer that this principle also applied to their predecessors on the steppes? This is where the ethnographer, with her eye on the present, must yield to the historian and the archaeologist, with their demands for empirical findings from the past. And, indeed, there seems to be much evidence from these quarters to suggest that the ancient women of the hearth also enjoyed a great deal of power and wealth within even the most warlike of tribes.

For one thing, we have many Greek, Persian, and Roman accounts of widows of slain nomad chieftains ruling in their husbands' stead until new elections could be held.[5] It could take months, even years, for the tribes to assemble for the *quriltai* (great gatherings) during which elections took place, and the interim female leaders were far from figureheads. Herodotus wrote about Tomyris (see Chapter 4), who led her tribe of Massagetae Saka to victory against the Persian king Cyrus the Great in 530 B.C., and in the fifth century B.C. the Greek physician and historian Ctesias chronicled the exploits of Zarina, ruler of another band of Saka, who was so beloved by her people that it was said they erected a huge kurgan crowned by a golden statue after her death (although no kurgan has been excavated that can be determined to be hers).

Other ancient steppe tribes also embraced women of power. Scythian warriors used to swear oaths of allegiance on the king's hearth, that traditional female domain, and Sauromatian and Saka leaders routinely included women in their circle of advisers. In 1905, the American geographer Ellsworth Huntington noted in the *Geographical Journal* that Sarmatian women held such high positions that their tribes earned the epithet "women-ruled" from other steppe inhabitants, who disapproved of this unseemly female influence (quoted in Minns 1913, 84). In fact, women appear to have been so powerful that the Russian anthropologist Anatoly Khazanov (1994) muses, "There are serious grounds for thinking

---

5. The firstborn son of a khan didn't necessarily succeed him as ruler. Another male relative, or sometimes even his widow or an outsider, might win the tribal election, depending on who was judged to be fittest and had garnered the most influence. See Chapter 12 for more on women who served in the role of khan.

the matrilineality was . . . preserved for a long time amongst ancient nomads in the Eurasian steppes," including the Sarmatians.[6]

The archaeological evidence from some of the Pokrovka kurgans certainly lends support to the theory of matrilineality among the Sauromatians and the Early Sarmatians. The cemeteries at Pokrovka were ideally suited to suggesting a model of early nomadic everyday life, especially as far as the women in those cultures were concerned. Unlike some of the more spectacular czar kurgans, the mounds at Pokrovka were more modest affairs, housing the remains of the tribes' mainstream population—their middle class, in modern terminology. Although the central, and most important, grave in these multiple-burial structures had been robbed by ruffians ancient and new, the many peripheral graves were often left intact, affording us a wealth of artifacts to decipher.

Like many other Indo-European cultures, the Sauro-Sarmatians conceived of an afterlife similar to their earthly existence, so the dead were entombed with the accoutrements that reflected their social stations and would be of use to them in the next world. In the four years of our Pokrovka excavations, we discovered vast arrays of clay pottery, jewelry, amulets, weapons, tools, food remains, and other everyday necessities from the sixth century B.C. through the third century A.D., each one a clue to its owner's status and role. I would finger a cylindrical glass bead adorned with an indigo and cream design that looked like staring eyes, and wonder if a particular threat had caused its wearer to procure this amulet, a source of protection against the evil eye. I'd examine gold plaques hammered into the shape of snow leopards and muse over whether their owner had originally lived in the Tien Shan Mountains, the home of these magnificent animals. Every piece seemed to harbor a story and provide a glimpse into a long-ago life in a hard land.

Yet as romantic as I found these tangible fragments of history, I had to

---

6. A matrilineal society traces a family's lineage through the maternal side—that is, from mother to grandmother to great-grandmother and so on.

push aside fanciful notions when it came to the vital work of categorizing our growing inventory of artifacts. Initially, I classified each find without regard to the sex of their former owners, searching only for the status it would reveal. Three predominant statuses emerged: hearth person, priest or priestess, and warrior. The wealth of the deceased could be assessed by the quantity and richness of their burial offerings, the size of their kurgan, and other factors. Then, I assigned a status based on the nature of their artifacts to each of the 182 adult skeletons that could be aged and sexed, and noted the number of men and women who fell into each category.[7]

A full 94 percent of the men were entombed with the bronze and iron arrowheads, swords, and daggers that indicated warrior status, not sur-

A male interred with a child of about six years of age. The child had a whetstone used for sharpening knives in its right eye socket. Other children were excavated in male burials, but women were not buried with babies. To date we have no good explanation for this, nor for the whetstone in the eye.

---

7. Not surprisingly, about a third of the skeletons we uncovered belonged to prepubescent children, who couldn't be sexed through an anthropological examination, although DNA testing could determine their gender.

prising in cultures that valued military preparedness. Three percent were entombed with nothing but a clay pot or two to tide them over in the great beyond; these were most likely servants, or men who somehow had lost their animals (and therefore, their source of wealth), also to be expected because of the harsh climatic conditions. For instance, a *jut,* or ice storm, can cover the grass and wipe out a herd in a few days. Another 3 percent were buried with few artifacts but with a child at their side—definitely unexpected, as none of the women had been buried with a child, leaving Yablonsky and me completely baffled.

Other surprises awaited when I examined the female side of the equation. Not only were women generally buried with a wider variety of rich artifacts, they also occupied more statuses than the men. Roughly 15 percent of the women were buried with weapons and armor, placing them into the warrior category, and another 7 percent possessed the carved-stone altars, bronze mirrors, fossilized seashells, and other trappings that marked them as priestesses. (See Chapters 4 and 5 for more on women warriors and priestesses.) Some women—about 3 percent—were buried with both warrior and priestess artifacts, which seemed to suggest an extremely high status position. Another 3 percent had been interred with pseudo–spindle whorls, a puzzling item indeed as they were carved from chalk and therefore were too fragile to have functioned as an actual tool. I believe these might have possessed a magical significance, perhaps along the line of the old fairy tale about spinning straw into gold.

By far the largest group—some 75 percent—belonged to the hearth woman category,[8] which is characterized by functional clay spindle whorls (which many of the other women also had), bronze spiral earrings covered with gold foil, and a panoply of colored beads of stone and glass. Although all nomadic girls began riding as toddlers and continued

---

8. The percentage of hearth women grew as time passed; the Sauromatian and earliest Sarmatian graves included many warriors and warrior-priestesses, while the later Sarmatian burials contained artifacts reflecting only hearth women, some of whom had been extremely wealthy.

through puberty, when they had children and assumed the duties, responsibilities, and obligations of the household, they no longer spent long hours in the saddle, except as a means of transport.

Those from wealthier families shared the wealth in death as well as life. Some had been laid to rest in what must have been gorgeous skirts and caftan jackets. We know this because, although all traces of the fabric were lost, hundreds of tiny jet seedbeads, each handcrafted using polishers and tiny drills, had been sewn onto the sleeve and skirt hems and we found them in their appropriate positions around the skeleton. But these weren't made by our Sarmatian nomads, because bead-working was a specialty craft; years before, I had seen thousands of black and white disk-shaped beads excavated from a four-thousand-year-old workshop in Syria, and found that the craftspeople, using tiny bronze tools, had ground a stone tube before slicing off the disk beads. Luxury items such as these beads were among the barter-and-trade items the nomads exchanged with sedentary peoples. The beads the hearth women possessed in abundance were fashioned from glass, carnelian, turquoise, and other materials not found in the Sauro-Sarmatian homeland, further evidence that they were the result of trade with (or raids upon) Chinese, European, Iranian, or Central Asian peoples who had the raw materials and technology to fashion such valuable and rare prestige items. Hearth women's graves also contained bronze mirrors that were deliberately broken, signifying that the occupants had no further use for them in the otherworld.

Aside from the richness of the mortuary offerings, their very placement in the graves is a testament to nomadic women's elevated standing in general. Sorting out the order of burials in the kurgans can be a painstaking and even frustrating affair—what grave robbers didn't disturb, erosion obscured over the centuries, as walls collapsed and support timbers crumbled, filling the chambers with dirt. Still, we were generally able to determine the sex of the initial burial figure occupying the high-status central pit, and 72 percent of the time, it was a woman. Often males and other females had been laid out beside or on top of her in subsequent burials; occasionally, a burial pit might contain as many as ten skeletons or a kurgan as many as thirty-two. The position of honor wasn't reserved for warriors or priestesses—the central burial figures often were hearth women, lending further credence to speculations that the Sauro-Sarmatians might have been matriarchal societies.

So we are left with a concurrence between the old and the new, with the archaeologist, the historian, and the ethnographer nodding in agreement. Our evidence strongly suggests that the egalitarian nature of the modern steppe societies is rooted in ancient customs, prefigured in the variety and wealth of women's funerary artifacts, in their central positions in the kurgans, and in accounts of their high tribal status. As keepers of the hearth, with all that implies both on a practical and a symbolic basis, women seem to have been accorded a measure of power and wealth that many scholars still have trouble reconciling with their vision of the fierce, male-dominated warrior societies that fill the history books. Nor was women's influence confined to domestic matters; the hand that rocked the cradle also could wield a sword and decide a tribe's fate on a throw of the sheep bones.

CHAPTER FOUR

THE POWER OF THE SWORD

The prominence of the hearth women in early steppe tribes demonstrates that there was much more to these nomadic groups than the three R's: riding, raiding, and ravaging. There is no denying that the culture of war had an impact on the populations of the Eurasian steppes throughout the ages, as a succession of accomplished and ambitious conquerors periodically wreaked havoc on settled populations and migrated across the borders into China, the Middle East, and Europe.

The first full-scale attack seems to have occurred around 705 B.C., when a Russian steppe tribe known to the Greeks as the Cimmerians challenged and were defeated by the Assyrian king Sargon II but, on another front, conquered Phrygia, the kingdom of the legendary King Midas in what is modern-day Turkey. By this time, the nomads had perfected the art of fighting efficiently on horseback with bows and arrows, and raids and skirmishes were commonplace, particularly in Urartu (modern Armenia) and Anatolia. These marauding tribes occasionally banded together to create mighty confederacies and were so fearsome that they even earned a mention in the Old Testament: "Behold, a people shall come from the north, and a great nation, and many kings shall be raised up from the coasts of the earth. They shall hold the bow and the lance: they are cruel, and will not show mercy: their voice shall roar like the sea, and they shall ride upon horses, every one put in array, like a man to battle, against thee, O daughter of Babylon" (Jeremiah 50:41–42).

Around 650 B.C., one nomadic tribe in particular became renowned for its ferocity: the Scythians. They lived northeast of the Black Sea in what is now part of the Ukraine. After conquering the Cimmerians, they moved on to the Assyrian Empire in 612 B.C. and conducted frequent raids from western Persia to the borders of Egypt.[1] In the fifth century B.C., Herodotus reported on their exploits and customs in his *Histories:* At the death of a great chieftain, the "barbarians," as the Greeks called them, would cut off a part of their own ears and mutilate their own bodies, letting their blood drip onto their horses as they mourned their leader. To further commemorate their loss, the Father of History noted, the Scythians would sacrifice fifty young warriors by impaling each upright onto a strangled horse flanking the chieftain's burial mound.

Herodotus also recounted tales of another nomadic steppe tribe called the Massagetae Saka, who lived farther south and were led by Queen Tomyris into battle against Cyrus the Great in 530 B.C. after he tried to annex her territory into the Achaemenid Persian empire. The Saka won, but Tomyris's son committed suicide at the first opportunity after being taken prisoner. Distraught over his death, the furious queen searched the battlefield for Cyrus's body, lopped off his head, and soaked it in a skin filled with human blood, scornfully declaring, "[B]ut even as I threatened, so will I do, and give thee thy fill of blood" (I:204–14).

The powerful steppe tribe that perhaps fascinated the Greek historian

---

1. The Scythians earned their own mention in the Bible; the Old Testament refers to them as Gog of Magog, and the Lord proclaims, "I will bring thee forth, and all thine army, horses and horsemen, all of them clothed with all sorts of armor, even a great company with bucklers and shields, all of them handling swords" (Ezekiel 38:4).

Herodotus's Legacy

The man often credited as the Father of History was born around 484 B.C. in Caria, a Greek colony in Anatolia (modern-day Turkey). Curious and open-minded, Herodotus paired a passion for travel with a flair for writing, eventually touring many parts of both the Greek and Persian empires and recording the history, legends, and customs of the peoples he encountered. His collective masterpiece, generally referred to as the *Histories*, is a nine-book account of the Greco-Persian wars of 499 through 479 B.C. In this lengthy opus, Herodotus often strayed from military subject matters, touching upon everything from the growth of the Achaemenid Persian Empire to the Amazons and women warriors, to the bizarre burial practices of the Scythians.

Although a few other writers had previously produced histories of certain lands, their surviving works tended to be disjointed and incomplete. Herodotus was the first to use a storyteller's talent to meld accounts of many territories and times into an entertaining, unified whole. His relish of a good story actually worked against him in some ways; his tales of fantastic creatures and outrageous foreign customs, coupled with a failure to credit his sources, helped brand Herodotus as a dupe or a liar. For many centuries, the *Histories* was considered more myth than historical fact, and only in recent times have archaeologists' findings begun to corroborate many of his seemingly outlandish contentions—including those regarding women warriors and horrific nomadic burial rites (see Chapter 3 for more on Herodotus's observations).

the most was the Sauromatians, who lived between the Don River and the Caspian Sea and, like the Scythians and the Saka, were fair-skinned, long-limbed Caucasoids who spoke an Indo-Iranian language. Relying on Greek legend and tales he heard during his travels north of the Black Sea, Herodotus turned the myth of their genesis into one ripping yarn:

About a century before his time, a tribe of warrior women rode the steppes of southern Russia. The Greeks called these women Amazons, while the Scythians dubbed them Oiropata, or "killers of men." The Greeks defeated the Amazons in battle at Thermodon (now Terme, Turkey) on the southern coast of the Black Sea and set sail with three boats full of captives. The wily women managed to mutiny, seize control of the vessels, and toss their captors overboard. Alas, as skilled as they were at warfare, the Amazons were poor sailors; they found themselves shipwrecked on the north Black Sea coast, land of the nomadic Scythian warriors, and soon were locked in battle with them. It was only at the end of the day when the Scythians examined the corpses of their enemies that they realized they were women. Marveling at the bravery and military prowess of their adversaries (and thinking about the formidable children such females might bear them), they resolved to make love, not war, and the elders sent a group of their most promising young warriors to woo the Amazons. Eventually, the two groups intermarried, but the Amazons refused to be assimilated into the Scythian population, saying, "Nay, we could not dwell with your women; for we and they have not the same customs. We shoot with the bow and throw the javelin and ride, but the crafts of the women we have never learned; and your women do none of the things whereof we speak, but abide in their waggons working at women's craft, and never go abroad a-hunting or for aught else" (IV:110–16).

At the Amazons' urging, their Scythian husbands returned home, demanded their inheritances, and rejoined the women for a six-day trek northeast deep into the steppes, where their eventual progeny became known as the Sauromatians, or Sauromatae to the Greeks. Herodotus concluded, "Ever since then the women of the Sauromatae have followed their ancient usage; they ride a-hunting with their men or without them; they go to war, and wear the same dress as the men." He also noted that "in regard to marriage, it is the custom that no virgin weds till she has slain a man of the enemy; and some of them grow old and die unmarried, because they cannot fulfill the law" (IV:116,117). (See Chapter 7 for more on the Amazons.)

For centuries, Herodotus's account, along with many other tales of fiercely independent women warriors, was considered the stuff of legend, not history. Civilized Westerners such as the Greeks and the Romans were inclined to view women as delicate, submissive creatures, and they envisioned the Amazons only as a tribe of militant females capable of engaging men in combat on horseback. Then, in the 1950s, Russian archaeologists began excavating sixth-century-B.C. kurgans and discovered women's graves containing weaponry, armor, and riding gear. In their interpretations of the burials, the Russians offered few comments about these women, although they thoroughly chronicled the artifacts and social differentiation of the men. For example, Anna Melyukova, the grande dame of nomadic archaeology, waxed long and eloquent about Scythian noblemen and male warriors, and summed up the women's lot with this sentence: "Some noble women were accompanied by women and sometimes by men who are thought to have been bodyguards" (quoted in Davis-Kimball, Bashilov, and Yablonsky 1995, 43–44). I wondered whether these men were really bodyguards or whether they had been servants or maybe slaves. In 1980, the German archaeologist Renate Rolle (1989) took a more thorough look at women's status among the ancient nomads, reporting on the discovery of forty Oiropata-like graves in Scythia, and noting that roughly 20 percent of the Sauromatian warrior graves excavated in the lower Volga region belonged to women, with bows and arrows being the most prevalent weapons.

In 1994, while editing *Nomads of the Eurasian Steppes in the Early Iron Age,* I encountered the reference to a Saka woman's burial abundantly provided with bronze harness rings that had been used to harness the seven horses in her grave; in addition, a rare pole-top ornament in the shape of a long-horned ibex once stood guard as she lay in state. These offerings, which I would have expected to find only in a man's burial, complemented her fine jewelry, and it was then that I understood that women of high status were hidden by the shadows of traditional interpretations. It was time to launch a treasure hunt.

One way to search out these women is to haunt the museums where their artifacts are kept, so in 1997 I roved through display cases and the storage rooms of more than a dozen museums along the Don and Volga rivers. I verified Rolle's observations and found that although sometimes the Sauromatian women had been laid to rest with a bronze arsenal similar to those found in the Pokrovka burials, their burials had also included spears, which we'd never encountered at Pokrovka. Their repertoire of grave gifts, however, lacked the polish and luster of the Pokrovka peoples'.

The morning of the discovery had begun like any other day, but by ten o'clock the sun was punishingly hot and, atypically for the steppes, the air was heavy with humidity; this added oppressiveness seemed to presage a prodigious event. I had finished excavating a child's burial placed precariously close to an adjacent catacomb burial and the thin floor had broken away, exposing a skull lying below. The catacomb was barely lit, and peering into its opening, I could see that cleaning this skeleton would be quite a challenge for my colleague Olga. The catacomb height was lower than usual; its roof rose only about two and a half feet above the floor of the pit, giving Olga precious little space to maneuver in. This, in turn, made it difficult to avoid disturbing bones or artifacts as she worked. Squatting in a precarious bundle, she was slowly and methodically brushing away the dirt along the second set of arm bones when I noticed a strange green object resting on the skeleton's chest. Soon the unforgiving sun forced me to join two or three others in an empty pit, attempting to escape the heat by leaning into the sidewall.

If there are frustrations involved in archaeology, they certainly surfaced at that point. The heat was so overpowering that I had icy chills running beneath my skin, and even though I knew Olga had to work slowly in order to preserve the find, I was impatient for her to finish cleaning the skeleton. Contrary to the fact that I'm usually quite resigned to the slow pace of my work—I know that finding answers about these ancient people can only be achieved by rigidly adhering to the often maddeningly precise mechanics of archaeology. Sometimes, it was just the satisfaction of completing a day in this primitive and harsh environment that taught me to fully appreciate the survival abilities of the Sauro-Sarmatians. Today, though, I could barely handle the wait!

I clambered out of the pit thinking that at least Olga was fortunate to be in the shade from the catacomb's roof, so I took up a position at the mouth of the catacomb. As my eyes grew accustomed to the dim light of the interior, I saw a small skeleton, a green-patinaed cluster on the chest, the brown-rust of an iron dagger by the right leg bone, and clusters of green adjacent to the left leg bones that signaled bronze arrowheads. Judging by the orientation of the head to the east, the deceased was an Early Sarmatian (see sidebar page 32). However, the exceptionally large collection of bronze arrowheads—forty in all, we later learned—that were gathered in a wood-and-leather quiver indicated this person had lived at the very beginning of this period, perhaps around 300 B.C.

One of the volunteers, Mary, had joined me and I whispered, "Looks like this might be a female skeleton

A young warrior-priestess *in situ.* Her dagger lies by her right leg and bronze arrowheads in a quiver near her feet. A large ceramic pot and animal bones indicate the type of foods that were included in the burial for her journey to the otherworld.

Artifacts from the young warrior-priestess's burial include about forty bronze arrowheads, an iron dagger, and seashells. An amulet suspended around her neck on a leather thong (seen in the bottom row of arrowheads) is a bronze arrowhead in a leather pouch.

with a bunch of arrowheads and a dagger." Earlier we had excavated a couple of female skeletons with arrowheads, but this collection of armaments was truly astonishing. Mary beamed and muttered under her breath, "Really something if it is. Certainly hope so; that'll show 'em."

It wouldn't pay to speculate further now—we knew we'd have to wait until our photographing and drawings were completed before removing the diagnostic bones: the skull and pelvis. But neither Mary nor I could suppress our mounting excitement.

Yablonsky took the skull that our assistant Yuri proffered from the bottom of the pit and cradled it in his left arm, turning it gently, feeling its smoothness. "It's a young female," he announced. Then, examining the pelvis, Yablonsky added, "And probably between thirteen and fourteen years old."

"You're sure?" I queried.

He glowered in assent; I should have known it wasn't necessary to question further.[2]

The knowledge that we had found a female warrior buoyed us as we continued our analyses, but only after we had assembled all her artifacts did we began to comprehend that indeed this young woman had been an individual of some consequence among her tribespeople. Her arrowheads, coupled with the dagger (iron being as precious as gold then), showed that her training as a warrior within her tribe had been taken seriously. The green cluster that I had noted on her chest was an amulet suspended from a sinew thong around her neck: a single bronze arrowhead encased in a leather pouch. Another amulet also indicating potent warrior prowess, a six-inch-long boar's tusk and the largest I have ever seen, lay at her feet. In real life it must have been suspended around her small waist from a leather cord. Equally amazing were a pair of oyster shells that had already fossilized when buried, and a pink, translucent stone with a similar shape, now containing a white dried paste. These were the artifacts that later led me to deduce she was a young priestess as well as a warrior. Priestesses' burials

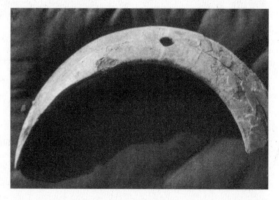

The young warrior-priestess must have valued this exceptionally large boar's tusk lying near her feet. Worn as an amulet, probably suspended from her waist on a leather cord, it certainly indicated her prowess as a warrior.

---

2   Later we had a second physical anthropologist verify sex and age on all of the Pokrovka skeletons.

Two seashells (center and lower right) and a stone containing a white residue (left), were excavated from the young warrior-priestess's grave. The white substance in the unworked stone may have been prepared as paint for body or textile decorations used during special ceremonies.

had long been recognized by Russian archaeologists by their combined artifacts, although not every artifact associated with a priestess was in every priestess burial. The two types of artifacts most consistently placed with priestesses were a bronze mirror and fossilized oyster shells that would make fine containers. As I studied more and more burials, it seemed that charcoal and colored ores—chalk, brick-red and mustard-yellow ochre, and blood-red cinnabar—were associated with body painting, that tattooing had been practiced by these ancient folks, and that some of their designs held special powers. (See Chapter 8 for more on mummified women with body painting; see Chapter 6 for designs and motifs thought to have special powers.)

We don't know exactly how this young warrior-priestess died, but the skeleton of an older Pokrovka woman suggested that her death probably was caused by a battle-inflicted wound. We found a bronze arrowhead in her body cavity, its tip bent as if it had hit a bone before lodging in her abdomen. My Irish friend and colleague Eileen Murphy (1998), who studied skeletons from a large cemetery in southern Siberia, found evidence that several women sustained damage to their left arm bones, concluding that they held up that limb to ward off blows while attacking with their right.

Most of the other warrior women we discovered at Pokrovka were interred with artifacts similar to our teenager's, although most lacked the clutch of seashells that marked her dual role as a priestess. In addition to arrows, some had a whetstone to sharpen weapons, and one from an adjacent Sarmatian cemetery had a long iron sword that measured well over three feet. Because of its length, it could only have been used for fighting on horseback. A few women were buried with legs bent in riding position, maybe to further emphasize their cavalry role, but most likely to facilitate a grand entrance to the otherworld mounted on their steeds. The warriors hadn't lost touch with their feminine side: Their graves always contained items associated with hearth women, such as earrings, beads, and spindle whorls.

The majority of these warriors had been in their teens when they died,

Bronze arrowheads as well as a spindle whorl (bottom left) and loom weight (bottom, second from left) indicate the multiple tasks this woman performed. High status is indicated by many valuable glass and stone beads (center row). We are unsure why a fragment of a bronze mirror was placed in her burial (bottom row, center) or what function the two fired clay pieces had (bottom row, right).

A bronze mirror (top), a long dagger (*akinakes*), and a spearhead (bottom) were the typical types of armament buried with Sauromatian warrior women from the lower Don River region. Two bracelets and arrowheads are in the center row. The mirror and armament indicate she was a warrior-priestess.

which leads me to believe that they started their training early and that many suspended their military duties when they bore children. From what I've observed at modern nomads' summer pastures, riding would have been the first skill they mastered. I've watched Mongols and Kazaks in the Tien Shan and Altai mountains teach their children to ride. When the toddler is about a year old, the father sets the child, boy or girl, into the saddle, and while supporting the child, he leads the horse around and around, or they ride for extended periods of time with the child sitting in front. By the time they are three or so, all the children have become proficient riders.

Once in western China, I was collecting information from a Kazak family in an aul when I spotted a half-dozen girls hanging out together, much like any clique of preteenagers, only these were on horseback. They galloped from one aul to another, racing down the gullies and up the hillsides, laughing and giggling, never dismounting for hours, as at home on

Two young Mongols who have just graduated from high school celebrate with other students by riding in the high Altai Mountain pastures in western Mongolia.

their mounts as they were in their yurts. Another time, in western Mongolia, I came across a group of Mongol teenagers celebrating high school graduation on horse-back. Several of the pairs rode double, with the girls sitting in front and controlling the steeds, the boys hanging on behind.

When it came to military instruction among the ancient nomads, boys and girls most likely were trained together by skilled mentors. Girls who demonstrated exceptional ability would have been designated as warriors and slated to receive more extensive instruction, while others would be selected for hearth-woman or priest-ess roles and concentrate on the skills needed for those vocations. The style of warfare practiced by the ancient steppe nomads was particularly well suited to women. The Sauro-Sarmatians in general rarely engaged in hand-to-hand fighting, which would have put the women at a general disadvantage when taking on male adversaries; instead, the nomads preferred to fight almost exclusively on horseback with bows and arrows, which helped compensate for a woman's typically smaller size and lesser strength. They'd ride up to the front lines of the enemy, enticing them into battle, then quickly turn and run in the other direction while firing a barrage of arrows back at the pursuing troops. When the Sauro-Sarmatian and Early Sarmatians did resort to close combat using a sword, they remained

The Fall of the Nomads

After the Sarmatians migrated westward in the fourth century A.D., they became known in the historical sources as the Alans (their descendants, the Ossets, still occupy areas in the Caucasus Mountains). They were followed by a pastoralist and loosely confederated army as fierce and warlike as any known in the past. These were the Huns, who, while undergoing ethnic and linguistic changes, were vaguely the descendants of the Hsiung-nu. The Huns swept into power by defeating the Alans in the north of the Black Sea, and continued their mobile devastation by rousting the Romans in the Balkans in A.D. 376. Allying with the Goths, a northern European tribe, and led by Attila, in the fifth century they became the best known nomadic confederacy to terrorize the West. The second was led by Genghis Khan, who in the twelfth century formed the largest empire the world had known, stretching from Manchuria in the east to Hungary in the west (see Chapter 12). In the fourteenth century, however, misfortune struck the known world in the form of bubonic plague that ravaged not only Europe but also the Golden Horde, descendants of the Genghis Khanite and an exceedingly prosperous Turkic–Mongol confederacy, who wandered over the vast steppe east and west of the Volga River.

It was not long before the Chinese and Rus' (early Russians) rebelled against their Mongol masters, fragmenting the once-mighty empire. Another blow to the nomads' dominance was the invention of gunpowder; accomplished archers, they found it difficult to amass guns and ammunition and they never really embraced this new technology. The settled peoples of Eurasia, however, quickly realized the potential of the new weapon, and used it to render the bows and arrows of nomadic marauders obsolete.

In the early eighteenth century, the territorial ambitions of czarist Russia posed another threat. By 1725, a line of Cossack fortresses snaked along Kazakstan's western periphery, while another row cut through Kazak pastures west of the Caspian Sea. Agricultural settlements soon followed, pushing ever more pastureland under the plow. By 1865, most Kazak nomads were under Russian domination.

The centralized and increasingly powerful governments of both China and Russia asserted a growing presence on the steppes, finally carving it up between them in the nineteenth century. Russia declared sovereignty from the Ukraine through Siberia and down to the Afghanistan border, while China claimed what is now known as Xinjiang, Inner Mongolia, and Manchuria as its prize. The influence of these governments proved disastrous to the nomadic way of life, as wave after wave of farm-minded settlers displaced the nomads by encroaching on their pastureland.

This was especially true in Russia, which in the 1920s saw the migration of millions of settlers into Central Asia and then, a decade later, the invasion of the Bolsheviks. Hungry for funds to nurture their impoverished revolution, the Bolshevik army invaded the nomadic auls and at gunpoint seized the women's jewelry and gold- and silver-encrusted ornaments from their *saulkes*, which constituted the family savings account. A decade later, Stalin's soldiers confiscated the nomads' herds and forced the tribes onto collective farms, mandating that they grow grain and potatoes. There was a major flaw in this plan: The nomads had no notion of how to raise crops on a sustainable scale. Those who could fled to western China and Mongolia, but millions starved during the 1940s until the survivors reluctantly adjusted to their new situation. Then, in the late 1950s, came the final blow: Soviet premier Nikita Khrushchev opened the "Virgin Lands" to agriculture in northern Kazakstan and southern Siberia. Millions of acres of waist-high prairie grass that had never been cultivated, and constituted a major part of the Kazak nomads' range, became dry-farm wheat land—some areas harvesting grain in a reasonable quantity, others yielding far less than subsistence-level production.

Today erosion from cultivation and the wind has reduced the rich pastures to less than mediocre farmland, and a tattered vestige of the nomadic way of life survives only in the Xinjiang and western Mongolian mountains. The free-roaming communities that produced powerful empires and legions of women warriors are no more, their legacy reduced to little more than a quiverful of tarnished bronze arrowheads in a warrior's grave.

---

on horseback, wielding swords well over three feet long that increased the reach and power of the combatant.

Although we're not sure exactly what roles women played in the ancient military hierarchy, the fact that few contemporaneous authors reported female warriors participating in raids or full-scale invasions leads me to believe that women were mainly used in defensive situations or as auxiliary troops. Renate Rolle (1980) notes that even the Scythian women, whom the Amazons dismissed as stay-at-home softies, were sometimes "entrusted with the safety of the herds and protection of the pasturelands when the menfolk were at war, wounded or dead." I have no doubt that the Sauro-Sarmatian women also defended their herds from predators, including neighbor or foreign tribesmen who roamed the steppes looking for animals they could steal to increase their wealth, or to carry off a young woman—as, according to ancient traditions, wives had to be brought into the men's clan to add variety to the breeding stock. Women might have participated in hunts for predatory animals such as the massive wolf or the wild boars whose tusks were valued, or, for sport, the saiga, a breed of antelope.

It's not difficult to picture Sauro-Sarmatian women acting like their counterparts, the Hsiung-nu, a bellicose nomadic steppe tribe that bedeviled sedentary Chinese populations during the Han Dynasty. Basing his account on Han annals, the English historian Homer Dubs described a Chinese attack in the second century B.C. on a fortress that a band of

Hsiung-nu had built to help them control the caravan trade in southern Kazakstan. Scores of the Hsiung-nu chieftain's concubines rushed to the defense of their enclave, shooting arrows at the attackers from the top of a tower. The concubines were reported to be ferocious and brave—in fact, the Chinese recounted that they were the last to leave their posts, fighting on even after the chieftain was shot in the nose with an arrow and the fortress was set on fire.

Today, there are few traces of the women warriors in steppe nomadic culture. Modern Kazak and Mongol nomads still train both girls and boys to be accomplished riders, and Mongol girls are taught to handle a bow and arrow alongside the boys; the fact that the women of the steppes are no longer instructed in other types of combat isn't surprising, really—neither are the men, as the nomads' fighting days have long since faded. (See "The Fall of the Nomads," page 63.)

Still, the military exploits of warlike steppe tribes such as the Sauro-Sarmatians and the Hsiung-nu had far-reaching and notable conse-quences, as settled peoples and other nomadic tribes fled when confronted with the nomads' fury. Consequently, their territories expanded, chang-ing forever the gene pools of Europe, the Middle East, and China. When the Sarmatians were pushed westward by the Huns, in the fifth century for example, many settled in the mountainous valleys of northern Spain as Alans; these Spanish descendants have blond hair and blue eyes, a tes-tament to their Sarmatian roots. And in the streets of Eastern Europe, it's not surprising to find inhabitants with the almond-shaped eyes and dark complexion of the Mongols. Nor is a little genetic variety the nomads' only legacy. As the next chapter reveals, steppe religious beliefs, the province of the priestess and the shaman, also proved to have a lasting effect on world civilizations.

CHAPTER FIVE

THE POWER OF THE SPIRIT

Matt and I had just settled in for the night at a small hotel in Hutubei, a city in the rocky desert region of western China that was off-limits to foreigners. It was the fall of 1991, and we had received permission from the Xinjiang Institute of Archaeology to view a series of Bronze Age petroglyphs in the Tien Shan Mountains the next day. A sultry evening had followed on the heels of an oppressively hot day, and I had opened all the tall windows in our room before we retired, hoping to catch any hint of a breeze. In a classic case of be-careful-what-you-wish-for, the curtains stirred slightly just as we slipped into bed. Within seconds, a cascade of sand came blowing in so fast and hard that every surface in the room was dusted with coarse, black grains before we could slam the windows closed. No rain fell, but the gale raged for more than an hour as Matt and I lay awake in our sand-choked bed. The next day we surveyed the hotel courtyard, amazed at the damage wrought by the Black Storm, as the Chinese call these walls of wind just shy of tornado force. Bushes and trees had been uprooted, tiles and moldings had been torn off buildings, and even the sculpted fountains we had admired the day before had been transformed into heaps of twisted metal. Black Storms can occur throughout the year, but in the summer the only warning you'll have that one is looming is a period of intense heat before the sky darkens and the wind sweeps in with its load of punishing sand.

Given natural phenomena like this to contend with (not to mention the extreme seasonal temperature fluctuations and torrential rains I've already described), I can certainly understand why primitive peoples would have seen the storms of the steppes as the acts of vengeful gods. It's difficult not to take such brutal weather personally! And indeed, the Sauro-Sarmatians, as well as other regional tribes, worshipped a panoply of nature gods, attributing a divine presence to the sun and moon, thunder and lightning, mountains and lakes, the rain and, of course, the wind. They prayed for spring showers that would bring verdant fields for grazing, performed ritual libations to ensure the fertility of their herds, and sought omens of favorable weather conditions before launching a raid.

The worship of nature gods was only one component in the complex system of religious beliefs reported by ancient observers and revealed by the burial artifacts of the Sauro-Sarmatians, Saka, and Scythians. The nomads' free-ranging ways brought them into contact with a number of theologies, and they seem to have been influenced by—and, in turn, to have influenced—the Greeks, Romans, Persians, Indians, Thracians,[1] and others. The result in the steppes was a polytheistic brew of ancestor worship and animism, perhaps with a little Zoroastrianism thrown in for good measure, all of which seemed to have been presided over by the third major group of women entombed in the Pokrovka kurgans, the priestesses.[2]

---

1. Although there is a modern Thrace, or Thráki, in Greece, I'm referring here to the ancient region in the eastern Balkan Peninsula.

2. Animism is the belief that all natural phenomena and inanimate objects possess a living soul. Zoroastrianism, based on the teachings of a Persian religious leader who is thought to have lived in the sixth century B.C., includes a belief in an afterlife, sacred fires, and dualism—the notion that the universal spirits of Good and Evil are locked in a perpetual struggle until the day when Good will ultimately triumph.

The Gods of the Scythians

Historical accounts and an examination of the cultic objects they left behind suggest the Saka and the Sauro-Sarmatians may have worshipped along lines similar to those of the better-documented Scythians. As is often the case, Herodotus (IV, 59) is our primary reporter here; he linked them to their Greek counterparts, something the nomads themselves wouldn't have done.

Scythian God/Goddess	Greek Counterpart	Domain
Tabiti	Hestia	Goddess of the hearth and family
Papaios	Zeus	Sky god
Api	Gaia	Earth goddess
Argimpasa	Aphrodite Urania	Patroness of fertility and marriage
Oitosyros	Apollo	God of crops and herds, defender against wild animals and disease

King Idanthyrsos (c.450 B.C.) pronounced Tabiti the Queen of the Scythians and associated her with ancestral spirits. Apparently, Tabiti was one of the most ancient figures in their religious lore, and was linked with the fire cult. Oaths made on her hearth were sacred; broken vows would cause the great chieftain to fall ill and were punishable by death. In her book on Scythian gods and goddesses, the historian Yulia Ustinova says Tabiti was an incarnation of primordial fire and a symbol of supreme authority, and her exalted position, along with the general dominance of female deities in the Scythian pantheon, has been interpreted by other scholars as evidence of the prominent role women may have played in an earlier matriarchal society.

The religious leaders of the ancient nomads were almost always women, perhaps because that sex was credited with greater intuitive powers that would facilitate communion with the gods. As we'll see in Chapter 10, the few males who were buried with religious artifacts seem to have been transvestites or eunuchs, whose feminine trappings reflected either their attempt to assume the women's power or their predisposition to the effeminate. As with the hearth women and female warriors, most of our knowledge of the world of the priestesses must be deduced from their burial artifacts. Archaeologists have been particularly fortunate with this group, unearthing a number of unrobbed priestess graves and frozen tombs that preserved organic materials usually lost to time, such as textiles, wood, food residues, flesh, and even the seeds of psychoactive hemp plants (which still grow in wild abundance in many areas of the steppes, as a few of my young volunteers have discovered to their delight). These artifacts yield many insights into the nomads' complicated belief system and amply demonstrate the power and wealth of their religious leaders.

Seven percent of the Sauromatian and Sarmatian women we excavated at Pokrovka belonged to the priestess sisterhood. Their graves were distinguished by a variety of accoutrements unique to their station: stone and clay sacrificial altars, fossilized seashells, carved bone spoons, and amulets embellished with a specific Animal Style, usually a snow leopard motif. Some of the graves contained small chunks of ochre, cinnabar, and chalk ores, and although we could assume they were cosmetics to beautify, I doubted this. I instead speculated that the pigments were ground for ceremonial purposes because other Eurasian women of this time, whose remains had been mummified and who were identified as priestesses, revealed faces, arms, and hands decorated not only with geometric designs, but with Animal Style zoomorphs. Unlike those of the hearth women, the mirrors buried with priestesses were left intact, signifying that these tools would be needed in the next world, probably for divination and perhaps for healing. Some of the women were buried with few ritual artifacts—a bronze mirror and a single seashell, perhaps—while others boasted a vast array of valuables. This disparity suggests the existence of a religious hierarchy that ranged from the modest priestesses of the hearth who served the interests of individual households, auls, or clans to the powerful and wealthy spiritual leaders who sat at a chieftain's side and

One of the earliest-dated priestesses excavated at Pokrovka was interred with a mirror and a seashell, both seen at the right. The position of her legs, termed "riding position," may indicate that symbolically she rode horseback to the otherworld.

The highest-ranking priestess excavated at Pokrovka. Three small gold felines were attached either to her headdress or at the neck of her bodice. A temple pendant, made in the style of others from Kazakstan, lies near her right cheek, possibly revealing contact with the Saka. A sacrificial stone altar, an elaborate engraved mirror, and several seashells indicate her high status.

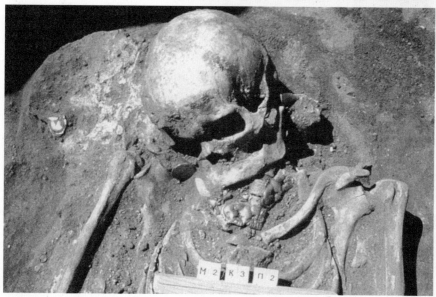

used their skills to provide guidance and ensure good fortune for an entire tribe or confederacy.

Like the women warriors, the priestesses would have begun their training in childhood, with candidates chosen for their intuitive powers or a family history of spirituality—still the criteria for steppe religious leaders today. Accomplished practitioners instructed the acolytes, and their education took years. Unlike women warriors, priestesses did not seem to have forsaken their duties when they reached childbearing age; many of the priestesses exhumed at Pokrovka and other sites were middle-aged or older when they died. Once initiated, their duties were many. They practiced the healing arts and served as oracles channeling the voices of the gods. They stoked the sacred fires of the hearth and interpreted divine will using sheep shoulder blades and anklebones, searching for propitious signs regarding when to wage war, strike trade agreements, or change pastures.[3] They appeased the gods through prayer and sacrifice, libating their altars with koumiss and other white liquids, offering choice pieces of meat and cheese, and perhaps using cultic spoons to ritually feed the gods or representations of the gods.[4]

Occasionally, camels or horses were sacrificed at priestess burials, but we uncovered no evidence of human sacrifice at Pokrovka. The practice seems to have been rare among the Sauro-Sarmatians in general; there is evidence that a priestess was occasionally interred in the same kurgan as the chieftain—but not necessarily in the same burial. The Bashkortostan archaeologist Vitaly Feodorovo told me that in an Early Sarmatian multiple burial near the city of Ufa in the western Urals, he found three skeletons lying outside the passage to the central tomb: two males and a young female, all with nearly identical holes at the base of the skull, indicating they had been dispatched as sacrificial victims. The men seem to have

---

3. The anklebones, or *astragali* in Latin, are used today, primarily for gaming.

4. The forest-steppe Hansi-Mansi tribes living northeast of Pokrovka incorporated Sauromatian spoons into their ritual of feeding bear cubs raised for sacrifice. The Sauromatians also incorporated nearly identical spoons into their cultic accoutrements.

been retainers of some kind; they had been buried with a few belongings, such as a whetstone, a quiver hook, and a spoon. The female, however, had a more impressive trove of offerings, including a small cultic vessel, an eye bead, gold and glass beads, a large bronze mirror incised with rosettes and geometric motifs, a small box containing various pigments, and a fragment of a leather cutout suggesting a composite griffin head and scroll motif. Clearly, she had been a priestess, valued so highly by her patron that he or she had wanted to be guaranteed of her services in the next world.

"The Lady of the Lake" stands on a small knoll overlooking a vast lake in western Mongolia. She wears a veiled pointed headdress and large beads, and holds a ritual cup. Stylistically this sculpture appears to date to the first millennium B.C.

One of my first studies on the Early Nomad societies was on the dramatic finds that the Russian archaeologist Sergei Rudenko had made in the 1940s and '50s, five large kurgans in the Altai Mountains of southern Siberia, belonging to an Early Iron Age nomadic tribe that resided in the Pazyryk region and, we know today, belonged to the Saka confederacy.[5] The bodies had been placed in double-walled log houses buried inside the kurgans, and when Rudenko opened the tombs, he found much of the organic material in remarkably good condition, a consequence

---

5. Rudenko excavated eight kurgans at Pazyryk; Kurgans 1 through 5 held the most significant cultural artifacts.

of both the Siberian permafrost and the holes cut by grave robbers not long after the interments, which had allowed water to seep in; it promptly froze and, therefore, preserved the contents. In one kurgan, a middle-aged woman was buried in a caftan lined in squirrel skin and decorated with a flourish of brightly colored felt appliqués in floral designs. Leather appliqués adorned her fur apron, and hundreds of tiny pyrite beads had been sewn on the soles of her soft leather boots. Her mortuary offerings included an elaborate headdress made from black colt's fur, amulets to ward off evil spirits, locks of hair and fingernail cuttings tucked into leather pouches, and a clutch of cowry shells, which have been associated with the female reproductive system and fertility since ancient times. But it was the assortment of mirrors that indicated to me she held priestess status.

Like the males in the burial, the women's bodies had been mummified, with some of their muscles removed and the cavities filled with grasses, anise, and other plants. Herodotus reported that some steppe tribes were said to mix the flesh of their revered dead with horse flesh and consume it in order to absorb the deceased's prowess and knowledge, and even some modern scientists have interpreted the tissue removal as evidence of endocannibalism (cannibalism within the tribe). However, the surgeries simply might have been part of the preservation process—Renate Rolle, working from ancient sources, notes that the Scythians considered the dead "living corpses" and didn't bury them for forty days, when the soul was believed to finally leave the body. Until that time, the corpses were regarded as sentient beings who retained ownership of their possessions and were even valid marriage partners. In fact, although she doesn't go into details, Rolle writes that "various factors" in the burials "indicate that even sexual acts cannot be ruled out as part of the funeral rites" (1980, 27, 29). In the past Herodotus was derided for his tales in which the corpses of chieftains were carted around from tribe to tribe for final farewells and honored at feasts before their interments, but even at Pokrovka it was clear that some corpses had been buried long after their death. The Altai tribes had become quite proficient at removing flesh and the use of fragrant herbs to make socializing with the corpses bearable.[6]

In many burials we found layers of gray ashy material over and under the skeletons, material that had wrapped the deceased for preservation and transport. The most compelling proof that a corpse was transported to summer pasture was a male skeleton in supine position, with the bones of a disarticulated lower leg, without evidence of trauma, off to one side. At the time of death, the body had been prepared for burial, wrapped in felt blankets supported by cane cut from nearby riverbanks. The bundle was hung in a tree to protect it from wild animals, and over winter it became desiccated.

In the Pazyryk burials, permafrost had preserved unusual and even spectacular objects, such as a delicate wooden chariot with nonfunctioning spoked wheels and a canopy bearing large, three-dimensional replicas of white swans made of felt. In nomadic iconography, birds were associated with access to the spirit world, so it seems that the chariot, symbolically borne on the wings of the felt swans, might have been intended to transport the occupants of the tomb to the realm of the afterlife. Another artifact from the burial crypt was a unique fifteen-by-twenty-three-foot wall hanging with six identical panels fashioned from multicolored felt, each panel depicting a seated woman who appears to be granting an audience to a mounted dignitary. The woman is rendered proportionately larger than the man, which indicates she is of a higher status. She is clad in a decorated robe and a large square-shaped head-dress; one hand is raised to her mouth as if she is speaking, while the other clutches a stylized Tree of Life, an icon of the fertility cult. Her only jewelry is an elaborate triple torque, a thick, twisted neckband of precious metal worn by people of high status. Her caller also is obviously a person of consequence, as he rides a fine horse and his ornamented caftan is accented by a flowing cape. He has come in peace, for

---

6. Aside from the usual forty-day mourning period, a burial could be greatly delayed if someone died during the winter, when the ground was frozen. Mummification would help preserve the body until it could be transported to a cemetery.

though he bears the quiver of a warrior, it is devoid of arrows. Rudenko and many international scholars have interpreted this famous and rare example of ancient nomadic textile art. One explanation is that a mortal is seeking the blessing of a goddess; another is that it represents an investiture scene in which the goddess bestows royal power upon the king. Some have also suggested that the rider's facial features, exuberant mustache, and long flow of wavy, black hair lend him a distinctly Iranian air. This contains a modicum of truth, because a knotted carpet from the same burial depicts nomads leading tribute horses to present to the great Achaemenid king.[7]

Regardless of the various interpretations, this woman's stately headdress and the fantastic Tree of Life she holds, its reaching branches drooping from the back of her royal seat, seem to me to mark her undeniably as a priestess. And the rider's tight pants, boots, and caftan, which closely resemble those worn by the mummies found in the frozen tombs, suggest to me that he was a Saka chieftain of significant status, while his expectant and respectful gaze implies that he has come to the priestess for counsel. Her final decision is vital before he sets upon some portentous event.

Artifacts found in other graves also indicate that such international connections weren't unusual for chieftains or high-ranking priestesses. As advisers, they surely would have had a hand in the nomads' lucrative Silk Road trade (See Chapter 6 for more on the Silk Road.) A middle-aged Late Sarmatian priestess in the Kobyakova kurgan in the lower Don River region of Russia was buried with a cast-gold torque that probably originated in northern Iraq, a mirror imported from the Han Dynasty in China, gold and turquoise bracelets with workmanship suggestive of Kazakstan, and a gold-stamped perfume bottle credited to the Greek

---

7. Other artifacts in the Pazyryk burials indicate the local nobility maintained commerce with the Achaemenid Persian Empire; it is assumed that they traded gold (probably nuggets that washed down during the spring melt) for sumptuary objects such as portable art or the knotted carpet.

workshops of master craftsmen in the Crimea's Bosporus Kingdom.[8] The unrobbed grave of another Sarmatian priestess in the Khokhlatch kurgan (also in the Don River region) contained an astonishing array of gold and silver mortuary offerings, many of which also seem to have originated in the Bosporus Kingdom, including a gold *kubok* (a special ritual cup with Animal Style handles).

This particularly wealthy Khokhlatch priestess also possessed an exquisitely worked gold crown studded with amethysts, garnets, turquoise, and coral. Although this was an unusually sumptuous example, distinctive headgear was an important part of every priestess's trappings (see Chapter 6 for more on headdresses). It is doubtful that such riches simply reflected the current fashion. The size and shape of the attachments could have been dictated by the wearer's cultic beliefs, but more likely it revealed her tribal status in the same way that nomads' belts have been worn through the ages to identify the owner's clan affiliation and rank.

Historical documents from the Achaemenid Empire specifically identify one group of nomads as the "Saka with pointed hat," but the concept of a large headdress as a status marker seems to have originated centuries earlier and much farther to the west. In Anatolia, priestesses—and goddesses depicted in religious reliefs and stele—wore a brimless high square headdress called a *polos,* a style that might have been assimilated by the Scythians as depicted on their gold plaques. The Kobyakova priestess was interred with a red leather diadem with gold-foil heraldic deer and eagles standing before a stylized Tree of Life. In contrast, a fifth-century-B.C. priestess from the Subashi cemetery in western China wore a high, pointed affair with a brim. I hardly think it a coincidence that the same headdress becomes the hallmark of the witch centuries later.

In June 1995, the Russian archaeologist Natalya Polosmak excavated a burial mound on the Ukok Plateau in southern Siberia that held a par-

8. The Bosporus Kingdom lay by the Bosporus Straits, which connects the Black Sea and the Sea of Marmara, the latter of which separates Asian Turkey (Anatolia) from European Turkey.

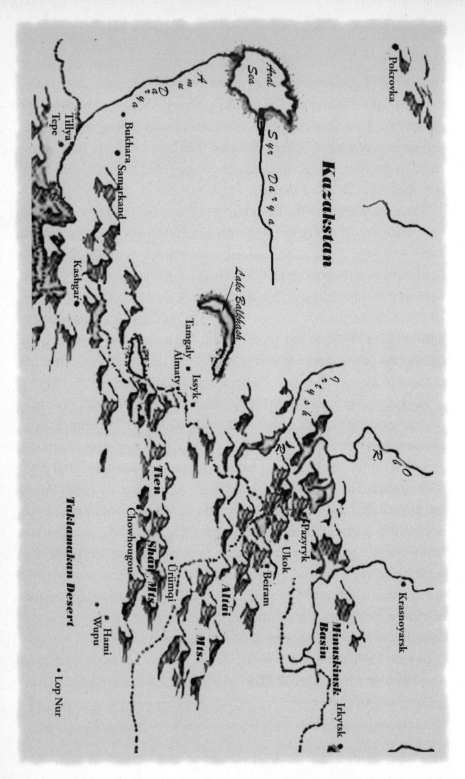

Map of Eurasia with the important archaeological sites of the first millennium B.C.

tially mummified fifth-century-B.C. Saka priestess who was about twenty-five years old when she was entombed. Once again, permafrost had preserved many organic materials in the burial chamber, including an impressive three-foot-high conical hat that commanded a full third of the hollowed-out fir log serving as the priestess's sarcophagus. This imposing headdress consisted of molded felt stretched over a wooden frame and was decorated with images of eight savage felines (probably Tien Shan snow leopards) and birds perched on the branches of a tree, all carved from wood and covered with gold foil.

This type of iconography, which has become known as Animal Style, is endemic to steppe art. In keeping with their reverence for nature, the ancient nomads celebrated animal life on everything from sarcophagi to tattoos. A few zoomorphic images might have been merely decorative, but many, such as deer and snow leopards, were particularly potent for priestesses; I believe that they functioned as protectors and as helpers. Other less intuitive wearers probably thought the animals served a forceful talismanic function and evoked their protection or sought to assume their strength, swiftness, or cunning. Many were creatures that the steppe dwellers actually encountered—eagles, deer, boars, mountain sheep, snow leopards—but in addition, fantastical animals such as griffins, which had the head of an eagle and the body of a lion, also entered the mix, inspired by religious beliefs and tribal legends (see Chapter 6 for more on the gold-guarding griffins.) Frequently, a leopard did not seem powerful enough for their purposes, and the ancient artists would blend the physical characteristics of several creatures to the most potent icons of all, which were reserved for high-ranking individuals. Hybrid zoomorphs found in priestess burials include the winged snow leopards on the Ukok priestess's torque and the tattooed deer with griffin heads at the end of its antlers, a vivid design that graced her left arm.

From the equine corpses and artifacts preserved at Pazyryk and other sites, we know that occasionally the nomads created mythical hybrids using their own prized horses by outfitting them before they were sacri-

The slate walls at Tamgaly, which has served as a cultic site for three thousand years. A horned (masked) horse and rider are to the right of Warren Matthew's hand.

ficed with intricate headdresses that incorporated representations of antlers of the mighty elk. Evidence of this practice is also found at Tamgaly, an ancient cultic site in southern Kazakstan that remains one of the most magical places I've ever been privileged to visit.

Along with a small group of other scientists, I was introduced to this ancient wonder in 1989 by Serjhan Akhinjanov of the Kazak Institute of History, Ethnography, and Archaeology. We had driven for hours—we *always* drive for hours on the steppes—finally stopping before an immense scattering of black rocks that jutted above the surface of the sun-scorched plains to form giant staircases. Serjhan gestured past the grimy windshield of our Jeep and offered a single word: "Tamgaly." The archaeologist spoke with a mixture of pride and awe, as if just uttering the name might evoke the spirits that were long believed to inhabit this otherworldly place. His reverence was understandable. For more than three thousand years, these slate outcroppings, about a hundred miles northwest of Almaty, have served as a major cultic site for a variety of peoples, from settled Bronze Age tribes to Iron Age nomads to medieval warriors astride armored horses to modern Muslims. The earliest supplicants interred parts of their dead in symbolic burials, sometimes they offered sacrifices, and often they peppered the smooth, dark surfaces of the rocks with petroglyphs that called down blessings from the gods and recorded their spiritual quests.

Serjhan noted that we could gauge the relative age of the etchings by their color; the new petroglyphs are a milky gray, while the relics of the Bronze Age have turned so dark that they are just barely distinguishable from the slate background, which has been baked to an almost jet-black by the sun over the millennia. The rocks are famous for this phenomenon, and once while we were excavating at Issyk our white-haired, deeply tanned Kazak archaeologist, Beken Nurapiesov, good-naturedly remarked to one of my volunteers, a Madagascan of Indian descent, "Oh, Michael, we're just like the rocks at Tamgaly—the longer we're in the sun, the blacker we get."

Our little group of scientists wandered from formation to formation, amazed at the abundance and variety of the images, and the way they revealed an intimacy with nature. Even when I study photographs of the Tamgaly petroglyphs now, I am continually amazed that ancient artists could have expressed such complex ideology in stone silhouette, using only the most primitive of stone or bronze tools. Twenty-one Bronze Age sun gods march across

One of the twenty-one anthropomorphic sun gods at Tamgaly, here seen riding on the back of a horse or possibly a kulan (type of an ass also known as an onager).

one slate face, all striking slightly different poses, their stick-figure bodies capped by outsize round heads sprouting solar rays.[9] Several centuries later, religious convictions had changed. The resulting images focused on potent horses, wearing masks reminiscent of those found in the Pazyryk horse burials, including the long, curving horns.[10] Some of the horses were drawn with masked and horned foals in their bellies, emphasizing the nomads' preoccupation with fertility. Still later during the first millennium B.C., a menagerie of stylized deer, mountain goats, horses, and camels became the dominant images, along with an occasional archer. I'm not sure which century a line of dancers holding hands like paper-doll cutouts belongs to, but it remains a striking image. (See Chapter 9 for sophisticated petroglyphs of dancers.) Aside from the natural evolution that transforms every religion over time, the changes in the belief systems of the steppes would have been influenced by the extensive trade network in the region. Over the course of centuries, missionaries as well as merchants traveled the Silk Road, and devout laymen argued the merits of faiths as diverse as Greek and Roman polytheism, Christianity, Buddhism, Judaism, and Islam beside caravansary fires.

Yet another change in religious practices is evident in one of my favorite petroglyphs at Tamgaly: several human figures wearing costumes, probably made from complete sheepskins, that seem to hunch over their backs and encircle their heads. These figures clutch coiled rattles and are bent in concentration as they perform a ritual dance. These may be the first representations of Central Asian shamans, spiritual leaders who originated among the forest tribes in Siberia and, as their influence spread south, coexisted with and then displaced the priestesses. No one is sure exactly

9. In ancient times, seven was considered a magical number, so the artist(s) may have deliberately rendered a multiple of seven.
10. I had always thought these ithyphallic (erect-penis) images were bovine, yet the bull was an animal not found in steppe art. Recently, however, a group of French and Kazak archaeologists studying these petroglyphs made a very astute observation: Because the penises of the animals came from between the hind legs, they were equine; if they had been bovine, penises would have extended from the center of the belly. See Francfort et al. 1997.

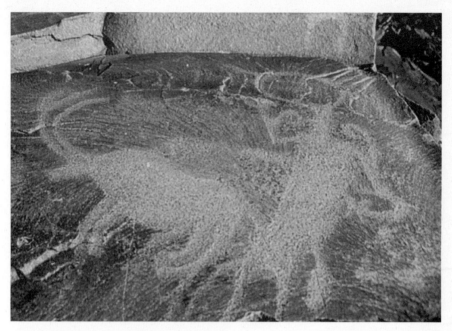

A shaman ritually inseminates a horned (masked) horse. One of the petroglyphs at Tamgaly illustrating the fertility rituals among the Bronze Age and Early Iron Age people.

when or why this transition occurred, but the petroglyphs at Tamgaly suggest that shamanism was becoming an important fixture in the religious life of nomads in the Early Iron Age in the first millennium B.C.

As the writhing figures on the black rocks suggest, the ability to enter into an ecstatic trance was an important weapon in the shamans' arsenal of magic, allowing their souls to fly through the skies to seek the counsel of spirits or visit the dead in the underworld. These out-of-body experiences were also crucial to their powers of healing; the nomads believed illness was caused when a person's soul strayed or was abducted to the spirit world, so the shamans would pursue the wanderer and secure his or her return to the land of the living, thus effecting a cure. Most had spirit helpers, such as birds or powerful felines, who would aid them in their quests.

Shamans might inherit their gifts, be selected by the tribe, or decide to pursue the vocation on their own. The manifestation of a nervous disorder such as epilepsy was considered one of the signs of shamanic powers—it was believed to facilitate the necessary ecstatic trances—and, in contrast to the priestesses, who were considered among the elite, shamans were often tribal misfits who lived apart. But like them, they underwent extensive training, used cultic mirrors, and wore distinctive costumes when performing their mysterious rites. In the shamans' case, these adornments included feathered headdresses and strands of colored rags woven through their hair. We know that shamans from the seventeenth century on credited iron with magical properties and affixed metal disks to long strips of cloth anchored to their jackets; even the ancient figures at Tamgaly have such accoutrements attached to their guise. These disks, which might have represented the sun or the moon, would have clattered and glinted as the shamans danced or fell into ecstatic trances (Eliade 1964).

The Russian ethnographers, who were among the first to study the Siberian peoples, maintain that the first shamans were women, but as shamanism displaced the priestess cults and assumed greater influence in tribal affairs, men began to dominate the profession in Siberia and Central Asia.[11] As the twentieth century dawned, the Bolsheviks and later the Soviets took a dim view of shamanism and suppressed it with the same brutal force they applied to other religions, including Buddhism, Judaism, Orthodox Christianity, and Islam.

The sociologist Marjorie Mandelstam Balzer (1997) reports that in the Siberian Far East, some shamans were reputed to have escaped persecution by simply turning into birds and flying away from their would-be captors. Another trio of enterprising shamans were set free after they induced an entire roomful of Soviet bureaucrats to believe that they saw wild bears and snow falling inside a Young Communist League hall. Balzer also tells of the legendary female shaman Alykhardaakh, who bested the authori-

---

11. The word *shaman* comes from the Evenki, one of the Siberian tribes speaking a Tungusic language. Shamanism was and is practiced by many different peoples, including North American Indians, tribes in the South American rain forest, Southeast Asians, and Tibetans. Their methods may differ, but they share certain fundamental beliefs, such as animism and the shamans' ability to induce their own souls to leave their bodies to travel to the spirit world and the land of the dead. See Eliade 1964.

ties after inviting them to her cabin for a seance. "After dancing and drumming herself into a trance," Balzer writes, "she called forth water, and the men's ankles were submerged. Then she called forth a large fish, which she caught in her hands. Finally, she asked the officials to remove their pants and hold their male organs. The men, caught in this embarrassing position when she emerged from her trance [thus breaking their spell as well], vowed never to bother her again."

Only a few shamans, of course, were as clever or lucky. Many were killed; others were labeled madmen and institutionalized or given drugs to still the voices in their heads. The ones who continued to practice took to conducting their rituals at night, with guards posted to warn worshippers of approaching government henchmen.

Lately, however, there's been a resurgence of these ancient practices, as I learned firsthand on a trip to western Mongolia in 1996 to visit some Kazaks at their summer camps. When I mentioned my interest in shamanism, a kindly older gent commented that he had met a practicing shaman living at a nearby Tuvan Mongol encampment the previous summer.[12] Hoping she had returned to the area this year, I set off with Aigul, who was my Kazak translator, and Bayer, our guide. There are no roads in this vast, rugged section of the country; fortunately, Bayer knew the territory well. We were forced to follow

Marjan, wearing the traditional Mongol *deel*, is one of the few remaining shamans in the high Altai Mountains of western Mongolia; a small glacier is visible in the background.

12. Only a few Mongols live in the Altai Mountains; the Tuvans, the Derbets, and the Arianghais predominate.

The Archaeologist in the *Deel*

Seeing Marjan in her *deel* reminded me of the first time I tried on one of these attractive traditional costumes. In 1992, as a member of the UNESCO (United Nations Educational, Scientific, and Cultural Organization) Silk Road Dialogue program, I was one of fifty international scholars who traveled for a month by Jeep from western Mongolia to Ulan Bator, the capital city. During the final days of the conference that capped off our research, Matt met me in the city, where we were guests at the presidential palace, a large and sprawling complex dramatically perched in a canyon on the outskirts of the city. We were invited to a banquet one evening, and when we arrived, we found a long table set with traditional wares for sale, including a selection of *deels*. I had long admired these comfortable unisex robes, which feature a row of buttons across the shoulder and under the left arm, and a high mandarin collar; I eagerly went into the dressing room to don a fetching red brocade number lined in pink silk. I buttoned the *deel*, but didn't bother to wind the nine-foot-long gold sash around my waist. Rather pleased with the effect, I stepped into the reception room filled with scholars from around the world and Mongolian diplomats and asked, "How does this look?"

To my bewilderment, the faces of our Mongolian hosts wore expressions of horror. "Put on your belt quickly," one of the women muttered in my ear, hustling me back into the dressing room. There, quite scandalized, she explained that only a woman of loose morals failed to belt her *deel*—to saunter forth without one's sash was the Mongolian equivalent of parading around on street corners in hot pants and a halter top. She helped me tie the sash properly, and I was able to resume my place with the delegation, virtue restored.

only animals' trails and slight impressions in the earth. Directions are given in terms like "Go west at the mountain's foot, then upward until you reach the forest, then along the forest until you come near the edge of the glacier." We drove through a series of mountain passes, stopping once to ask the way from an Arianghai Mongol who was staking a yellow marmot pelt to cure in the sun. Like nearly every nomad I've ever encountered, he was hospitable and gladly gave us directions, all the time offering us cups of *arke,* a distilled, very alcoholic milk (awful stuff!), which, judging by his merry demeanor, he had already amply sampled. We climbed ever higher, finally reaching well beyond the nine-thousand-foot level before we spotted a small cluster of *gers* (yurts) above a grove of fir trees and cooled by breezes passing over an adjacent glacier. A handsome young man, who turned out to be the shaman's grandson, directed us to the *ger* of a spry woman in her mid-sixties named Marjan, who had a flat, round face graced by high cheekbones and a shock of reddish brown hair that peeked out from her kerchief. She stood about five feet tall and was so roly-poly in her *deel* (pronounced "dell," the belted robe that is the traditional Mongolian costume for both men and women) that she resembled a colorful snowwoman brought to life. She invited us in, offered us bowls of salt tea (tea boiled over an open fire with a handful of salt and sheep's milk added), and told us that her mother had been a respected shaman whose jerky movements and bizarre mutterings during trances had alarmed Marjan as a child. "She would hold a bird's wing in her right hand and a World Tree [a representation of the Tree of Life] in the other," she recalled. "Sometimes she would get so wild I was afraid she would hurt someone." Later, her mother tried to pass on her expertise to her daughter, but the Soviet system had taken hold in Mongolia by this time and Marjan was terrified they would be sent to the gulag in Siberia if they were exposed as shamans. She burned her mother's costume, buried their mirror and bell, even threw some of the paraphernalia into the river, and the pair stopped practicing. Even before her mother died in 1987, Marjan had gradually lost the incantations and rituals as the years took their toll.

After the collapse of the Soviet Union, however, like many other former shamans she was anxious to revive the old spiritual traditions. "Today Gyn, the sky god, comes to me and tells me things," she said. "With his help, I try to help sick people." She explained that shamans can practice only on the ninth, nineteenth, and twenty-ninth day of the lunar calendar, and then only at night. I noted a hesitation as Marjan continued, and when I asked specific questions she told me she was still trying to relearn the old ways, because she was so young when shamanism was outlawed and she hadn't yet assembled her necessary cultic items. She did, however, confide that another shaman named Khagan living next door had recently joined Marjan's extended family and seemed to be better established in the shamanic arts. I asked to meet Khagan.

When we arrived at Khagan's *ger,* and announced our mission, the middle-aged woman studied us with distrust. She admitted that her mother had been a shaman, but emphatically denied practicing herself. Then she turned to Marjan. "This is something you should not talk about," she harshly chided in a dialect that combined Tuvan Mongol and Kazak, her dark eyes unfriendly and her tone stern. "You should not tell *anyone* that we are shamans." Although I was a bit taken aback by the animosity in Khagan's voice, I understood that we were treading in delicate territory, so I thanked her and we left immediately. Once again I was saddened by the deep wounds from the years of Soviet oppression.

Not all shamans, of course, are as reticent as Khagan. Scholars at the Academy of Science in Almaty have determined that there has been a resurgence of all religions in the wake of the fall of the Soviet Union, but they have found that it is shamanism, combined with the worship of nature gods, that is making the strongest comeback. Even when they profess other faiths, nomads still incorporate elements of these beliefs into their rites. I observed this phenomenon many times. When I asked a Kazak or Mongol if he was a Muslim, for example, he'd reply yes and then would invite me to a ceremony in which the purported religion incorporated an array of the old nature gods and some shamanic rituals, rendering the rites a true hybrid.

In 1999, I was invited to a Derbet Mongol ceremony in the eastern Altai Mountains by people who were Buddhists. The summer had been extremely dry, and the Mongols were desperate for rain to relieve their parched herds, who were still feeding only on scant, sere winter grasses. A lama (a Buddhist monk or priest) presided over the men's events at the top of a small mountain, while the women had their own gathering partway up the slope. As a married woman, I was forbidden to attend the men's rituals, but the women were insistent that I join theirs. As they circled their *oovo* (a cultic site composed of piled stones), they chanted and sang, tossing bits of dried cheese and boiled sheep ribs as offerings into the roaring fire built on the stone heap. They libated the *oovo* with drops of milk, and occasionally two or three of the women stopped and, facing the fire, bent low from the waist, making a special offering or request before continuing in the procession. I wondered whether elements of these rites had originated in the days of the priestesses, but nothing that I had discovered in my digs gave me a clue. Later, at the bottom of the mountain, we all continued to celebrate the ceremony with tiny ritual shots of vodka and *airag* (the Mongol equivalent of koumiss). The gods seem to have been pleased by the ceremony, for rain began to fall after the horse races and just as the wrestling matches were finishing.

Earlier that year, I had had a chance to talk about this religious revival with Tsayangiin Baatar, the dapper governor of Uvs aimak (province) in western Mongolia. I needed to secure his permission for an expedition I was planning in his territory, and he turned out to be welcoming and extremely curious about archaeology. He invited our group to dinner at the old Communist Party headquarters, and over a meal of ground mutton wrapped in homemade pasta, the talk turned to the resurgence of religion in Mongolia. In recent years, he explained, shamans and lamas had brought back the elaborate festivals celebrating the seasons and honoring specific deities or the spirits that inhabit lakes and rivers. One such ceremony held in the summer pays homage to Khan Bukha-noion, the most important patron of the mountains. Worshippers climb to the foot of Ulyasta, a sacred peak in the high Altai known as the White Rock. The governor continued, "The path is strewn with boulders and passes over glacier fields, and the difficult journey must be made on foot or by horse or camel. Once they arrive at a particular glacier-fed stream, the shamans sprinkle offerings of white liquids at the site (considered the color of purity), hoping to ensure prosperity for their followers. After some time they sacrifice a sheep, and then cook it in cauldrons over an open fire, and after it's eaten, the men climb the White Rock and leave butter, pastry, sweets, and milk vodka to further appease Khan Bukha-noion, the great mountain spirit."

Although women are forbidden to climb to the top—probably because of the hybridization of the Mongols' rituals in which the men hold special religious powers—they have a ceremony all their own that they hold in the shadow of another mountain to mollify the revengeful spirit of Khoito teebi, or Northern Granny. The Mongols believe she was an ancient shaman who was shunned by her tribe and wasn't allowed to be buried in the local graveyard. The spirit of the angry shaman retaliates to this day, rendering the local women barren unless they offer sacrifices in her honor.

Conversely, ethnographer Alma Kunenbaeva told me that a Kazak woman who *doesn't* want to have a child may also enlist the services of a shaman. In ceremonies shrouded in secrecy, the shaman encourages the woman to drink or smoke special herbs, or mixes a "magical" substance into heated oil. The woman then sits in the warm oil mixture, and a miscarriage results. When I asked what happened to the fetus and the afterbirth, Kunenbaeva replied with finality, "It just disappears."

The more I learned from Governor Baatar and other sources about current shamanic practices, the more I was reminded of Kunenbaeva's observation that steppe culture "pushes for the old tradition." The libations of koumiss and other white liquids, the sacrifice and consumption of cultic foods, and the worship of nature gods are remarkably reminiscent of the days when Sauro-Sarmatian priestesses presided over the spiritual life of their people. Modern-day shamans still use mirrors to heal; they wear headdresses and costumes when performing their mysterious rites;

they still observe a religious hierarchy, with different levels presiding over the concerns of families, clans, and tribes.

Even customs that seem wholly secular bear the imprint of the ancient religious beliefs. The reverence for the hearth, on which the Sauro-Sarmatians and Scythians swore their ancient oaths, is obvious in many domestic rites. When a Kazak woman goes into labor, the men of the aul gather outside her yurt, yelling to scare off any evil spirits that might be lurking. Inside, the mother-to-be stands upright, holding on to ropes suspended from a pole that is positioned horizontally across the yurt and represents the male organ. Her female attendants light the hearth and prepare a special soup from many different grains, all of which symbolize fertility. Custom dictates that the child should be born by the time the soup is done, a process that takes several hours. If the baby isn't obliging enough to make its appearance by then, water representing the mother's amniotic fluid is poured into the soup, which is believed to hasten the little one into the world.

The hearth also plays a significant role in bridal ceremonies. When a new wife arrives at her husband's yurt, she must build a fire in his hearth and pour oil on the flames to make them jump higher. As the flames consume the oil, the spirits of the tribe are said to enter the yurt to welcome the bride. Careful not to let the fire die, she places her hands as near as she dares to the dancing flames so they become covered with soot, which she then rubs on her face. The soot is supposed to make her "soft" so that she'll be better able to adapt to the changes in her life. Another of her duties is to prepare tea for the elders of her husband's clan. Every step is ritualized and carefully scrutinized, and tension fills the air—if the bride fails to make and serve the tea in the prescribed fashion, it is considered a bad omen for the marriage.

Other remnants of ancient ways can be found in everything from the amuletic designs woven into yurt decorations to the horsemeat and koumiss that remain ritual foods reserved for special occasions. Headgear continues to feature significantly in Kazak customs (see page 38): brides wear tall, conical headdresses bearing gold and silver ornaments, and premature babies are tucked into their grandfathers' fur-lined winter hats until they die or reach their scheduled birthdates, when they are symbolically delivered a second time. Vestigates of ancestor worship are obvious in other customs, such as a child born a year after the death of a close relative being hailed as the rebirth of a great-great-grandparent. The child is considered lucky and is given that ancestor's name. Birds continue to be associated with fertility and protection—an influential, educated family of Kazaks I visited in western Mongolia still cling closely enough to ancient customs to hang owl feathers over their baby's cradle to keep her safe and presented me with an owl's claw amulet to protect me in my travels. (See "Lilith: She-Demon or Independent Woman?," page 93.)

These might be considered secular customs, because no shaman or other religious figure is involved, and no obvious mention is made of a god or goddess during their practice. But despite the nearly six decades of religious repression that has drained the overt religiosity from these ancient traditions, it is apparent that the ways of the priestesses continue to have a profound influence on the lives of the peoples of the steppes—and beyond. The extensive trade connections that so colored Eurasian religious traditions also allowed elements of the priestess cults and shamanism to seep into foreign faiths and folklore. The ecstatic trances of the steppe shamans, for example, have been credited with inspiring the whirling dervishes of Sufism, an Islamic mystical tradition still practiced in central Turkey. And the use of birds as emblems of fertility, which became an important element of steppe rituals, probably originated in European folklore. The souls of young women who died before giving birth were believed to turn into *vily*, shape-shifters who could assume the form of a maiden or a swan (Barber 1997). If properly entreated, their unspent fertility could be used to benefit the fields, the herds, or women longing for children. To harness this power, young girls in some Eastern European villages dressed in snowy white blouses with long, flowing sleeves and full skirts to dance at an annual festival. As they performed, they'd flap their arms like the wings of a swan to ensure their fruitfulness after they married.

Lilith: She-Demon or Independent Woman?

The owl feathers that Kazaks hang over an infant's cradle always put me in mind of the legends of Lilith, one of the more interesting examples of how a female image that started out as a benign deity was transmuted into a symbol of terrifying evil in patriarchal societies.

Lilith seems to have originated as a Mesopotamian goddess around 2000 B.C., when her long-haired, nude image was rendered in red and black clay reliefs and placed in temples and shrines; smaller versions were honored on home altars. Endowed with the wings, legs, and talons of a powerful bird, Lilith stands on a lion flanked by owls and another lion. A backdrop of mountain symbols proclaims her divinity, which is also indicated by her conical headdress adorned with bovine horns. Scholars speculate that she may have been associated with the moon and primal female sexuality, and was regarded as a protectress of pregnant women, mothers, and children. She also may have been affiliated with justice, as she clutches a ring and staff in her upstretched hands.

Around 1600 B.C., however, when Semitic people from the Levant entered Babylonia (northern Mesopotamia or modern-day Iraq), Lilith's image underwent an unfortunate conversion. Both texts and artwork reveal that her overt sexuality was now seen as threatening; she became known as the "Bringer of Death," a winged monster with the face of a beautiful woman who preyed on newborns and stole the nocturnal emissions of men to breed a race of demons. The sole mention of Lilith in the Bible is a passage in the Old Testament: "Wildcats shall meet with hyenas, goat-demons shall call to each other; there too Lilith shall repose, and find a place to rest. There shall the owl nest and lay and hatch and brood in its shadow" (Isaiah 34:14–15, New Revised Standard Version). Biblical scholars are divided over exactly how to interpret this description, but it confirms Lilith's traditional association with owls (symbols of night and death) and fertility—and places her firmly in the company of goat-demons and other unsavory types.

Lilith also earned a prominent place in Judaic folklore, where she usually was portrayed as a thoroughly unpleasant character, still snatching babies from their cradles, tempting men, and spawning her little devils. However, some Talmudic sources paint a more sympathetic picture of Lilith, suggesting she might have had some provocation for her assaults on children. In their version, Lilith had been Adam's original wife, whom God formed out of the earth, as he did the first man. Adam's delight in his new companion quickly faded, however, for Lilith proved to be an independent-minded lass who refused to assume the supine position during sexual intercourse. In a rabbinical commentary known as *The Alphabet of Ben Sira*, Adam and Lilith's quarrel is described thus: "She said, 'I will not lie below you.' He said, 'I will not lie below you, but above you. For you are fit to be below and I above you.' She responded, 'We are both equal because we both come from the earth.' Neither listened to the other. When Lilith realized what was happening, she pronounced the Ineffable Name of GOD and flew into the air."

Adam begged God to retrieve his runaway bride, and God dispatched three angels to track her down. When they confronted Lilith near the Red Sea, the angels threatened that "one hundred of her children will die every day" if she didn't return to Paradise and behave. Still she refused, and in return for her punishment, she vowed to exact eternal vengeance against the children of Adam (who had promptly settled down with the more docile Eve, fashioned from his rib). Lilith's only concession was to promise not to attack any infant wearing an amulet inscribed with the names or images of the three angels.

Many other cultures have their own versions of the Lilith myth. The Persians warned against "the evil Lilith who causes the hearts of men to go astray," the

English derided the "Devil's Dame," and the Germans named her as Satan's grandmother. She has been linked with the Queen of Sheba, another powerful and lusty woman, who in traditional Arabic and Judaic folklore was rumored to have been a seductive, child-snatching jinn (half human, half demon). The particulars may vary, but in each case, Lilith's or her counterpart's unbridled sexuality, independent nature, and wanton nakedness seem to be deplored as much as her propensity for murdering babies.

Lilith the fertile and protective mother, Lilith the child-killer—both are long-lived images embedded in the prayers and nightmares of many lands. Even though her legacy is so complex and contradictory, those owl feathers suspended over the cradle are certainly intended to protect the Kazak child from the talons of a wrathful she-demon and to invoke the spirit of the benevolent goddess.

The arts of the priestesses were paramount in maintaining tribal rites of passage and the spiritual life of the tribes, and the rituals of mummification, tattooing, and horse sacrifice as well as their mortuary offerings allow us a glimpse into their world. Their petroglyphs, painstakingly carved by a proliferation of artists, are an ancient library where the most portentous events or rituals were recorded. The nomads began with the worship of a small pantheon of nature gods and in some places the beliefs and rituals of the nomads have come full circle today. Many nomads have become more isolated from the influences of modern settled societies than they were in the time of Herodotus and today they climb mountains, light fires, and make libations to their nature gods, calling upon them for plentiful rains, for healthy baby animals, and for healthy baby people.

CHAPTER SIX

RICH LEGENDS:
FROM GOLD MAN TO GRIFFIN

When people hear of the golden artifacts concealed in some of the priestesses' graves, they often ask whether I've ever encountered such spectacular hoards in my own excavations. My answer is "No, thank goodness," for I've learned from hard experience what a mixed blessing these rich troves can be. The modest residents of our Pokrovka kurgans didn't possess a great deal of finery, but we did discover some precious objects, including three hundred small gold disks, a grand belt embellished with heavy gold foil from a Late Sarmatian male's grave, and gold temple pendants and ornamental Animal Style plaques in a Sauromatian priestess's grave. On such occasions, the camp was thrown into red alert, for we knew that we risked robbery or, at the very least, the trampling of the excavation site if the local populace learned of our find. Anyone who had to go into the surrounding villages for supplies was pledged to secrecy with the most solemn and creative oaths we could muster, while Leonid Yablonsky and another worker spent a fitful night in near-freezing temperatures sleeping in our Jeep at the site until we could finish the exca-

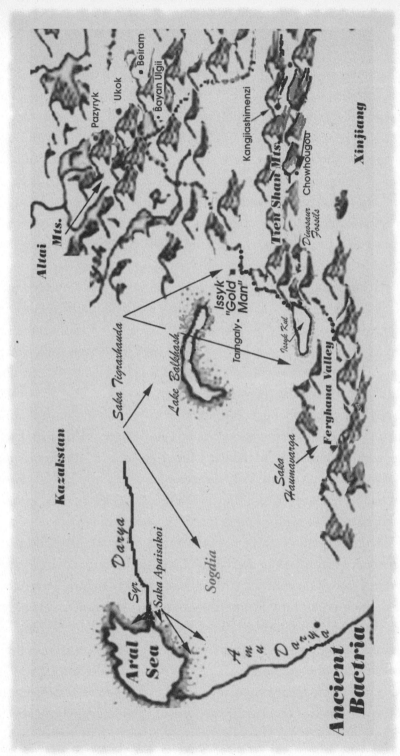

Location of the Issyk kurgan, the gold-producing regions during the Early Iron Age in eastern Eurasia, and dinosaur fossils that probably were the foundation of the gold-guarding-griffin legends.

vation and transport the gold to the relative safety of the camp.

I learned about the perils of golden windfalls during my first joint project with the Kazak Institute of History, Ethnography, and Archaeology in 1990. Karl Baipakov, the head of the institute, had paired me with Beken Nurapiesov, the Kazak archaeologist who was so taken with the dark rocks of Tamgaly. Once a promising Ph.D. candidate, Beken hates the formalities of academia and never finished his doctorate, but he is a respected expert in kurgan archaeology and had assisted at many notable surveys and excavations in southern and eastern Kazakstan. We were about to explore together the fifth-century-B.C. Saka kurgans near the village of Issyk in southern Kazakstan, the home of the famous Gold Man.

Issyk lies about forty miles east of Almaty in the Semirechiye (meaning seven rivers), a region fed by a multitude of rivers that flow from the Tien Shan Mountains and disappear into the steppes. A relatively mild climate, ample water, and fertile soil have made the land hospitable to agriculture for millennia, and today thriving collective farms produce grain, tobacco, and hay. The unusually high concentration of kurgans in the area—more than a thousand have been discovered to date—suggests that it attracted a large population of Saka in the Early Iron Age, some of whom may have forsaken their nomadic ways and turned to farming. The presence of some extremely large kurgans also implies that Issyk and its environs served as the burial grounds for the confederacy's great chieftains.

Whether strictly nomadic or partially sedentary, the Saka in this area undeniably had amassed a great deal of wealth through trade, tribute, or warfare. A goodly quantity of the Issyk kurgans were massive "czar" structures, which stood thirty feet or more over the plains and may have harbored intricate log-reinforced chambers. These were all robbed and subsequently have never been properly excavated. Russian archaeologists have harvested the smaller kurgans in the burial grounds since the 1950s, but no unmolested graves were discovered in the giant czar kurgans until 1969, when an observant farmer saw something glinting in the furrow left by his plow.

The Saka Confederacy

From a few textual sources and an increasing number of archaeological excavations over the past half-century, we are beginning to understand who the people of the Saka confederacy were and where they practiced their nomadic way of life. Previously referred to as "Scythians" or "Scytho-Siberians" (because the Scythians have a similar culture), these Indo-Iranian Caucasoids had developed a complex federation of tribes. Some wandered in the high intermountain valleys of the Altai and Tien Shan mountains, while others may have carried on rudimentary agriculture in the lower valleys and along the rivers that flow from the mountains and disappear into the steppes. The Pazyryk's burials in the southern Siberian Altai Mountains were preserved by permafrost and yielded unprecedented artifacts revealing far-reaching contacts into Iran. The Saka sphere, with burials that resemble those of Pazyryk, also extended to Early Iron Age tribes in the southern Altai Mountains in Mongolia, the western Altai in eastern Kazakstan, and the lower alluvial plains of southern Kazakstan. Saka chieftains were also entombed in massive kurgans that dot the verdant pastures in the high (now Chinese) Tien Shan Mountains, and in this region their sphere of influence extended southward to the edge of the Taklamakan desert as well as into the Ferghana Valley. From writings belonging to the era of Darius I, the great Achaemenid king, we learn the names of what may have been the three largest and most important Saka tribes in the confederacy: the Haumavarga in the fertile Ferghana Valley, who were becoming sedentary; the Tigraxhauda, who occupied Sogdia, beyond the Syr Darya (in Uzbekistan and western Kazakstan) and the Semirechiye of southern Kazakstan; in the Syr Darya delta the Apaisakoi engaged in agriculture, fishing, and crafts. The Massagetae, whose queen Tomyris so vengefully did away with the great Persian king Cyrus, may have ruled a sub-tribe of the Tigraxhauda, for her mobile legions were said to be along the Syr Darya. All Saka shared aspects of their culture and lifestyle; they had similar burial rituals, and in all likelihood worshipped goddesses and gods in common. Each also had three items in their repertoire that became the hallmark of Eurasian nomadism in the first millennium B.C. The first encompasses horse bridles and harnessing, while the second are their tri-lobed (and deadly) arrowheads. The third commonality is Animal Style, although each tribe seems to have possessed its rather definitive stylization. The most impressive stylization of their animals worked in nearly every media imaginable—the snow leopard and probably other large felines, deer, and elk, as well as bears, and occasionally horses—were those that present twisted upward hindquarters. Unfortunately, we cannot be sure of their motive for taking such artistic license.

Pushing aside the dark, loamy soil with his boot, the farmer exposed a small piece of worked gold, which he dutifully reported to the local authorities. The Kazak Institute mounted an expedition to the site, led by the renowned Kemal Akishev, and the crew soon uncovered the Holy Grail of every burial archaeologist: an unrobbed noble tomb. A large chamber, roughly twelve by seventeen feet and more than eight feet deep, constructed from fir logs had been tucked into the side of the mound, escaping detection by thieves when they plundered the central burial pit centuries before. The log top of the sarcophagus had rotted away—no permafrost in this area to preserve organic remains—and the skeleton housed inside had been badly crushed under tons of dirt. But time had been kinder to the artifacts buried with the body, and workers quickly uncovered four thousand small gold plaques and ornaments in near-mint condition and still arranged in their original positions (Akishev 1978).

Beken Nurapiesov had led Akishev's crew, and he told Matt and me the story of the tomb's thrilling discovery as we drove to the site nearly three decades later. "The skeleton had been cleaned and all the gold plaques were in full view in the pit. Dusk was falling. What were we to do? We didn't have time to finish recording and remove the thousands of objects before dark, and we couldn't leave the skeleton and all that gold alone overnight, so we hired two local men as guards."

Beken paused and pushed his thick white hair back from his forehead. He turned to me and asked, "Do you know what happened next, after the crew left?" Still a bit of a novice when it came to excavating in the Soviet Union, I had no idea, although today I might have guessed.

"Well," he said with a mirthless laugh, "those guards weren't about to spend the night in the cold by an open grave without a little liquid courage. They went into town to buy a bottle or two of vodka, and while they were gone, someone came and scooped up the gold pieces that were on the boots and even took the bones of both feet and one lower leg." He shook his head ruefully at the memory. "Of course, the thieves would have melted down the gold. The plaques are gone. Gone forever."

Despite this loss, the treasure that remained was enough to make it among the most remarkable finds in the annals of Saka archaeology. The figure in the fir sarcophagus had been only five-foot-three and slight of build; the riches coupled with the weapons in the burial led Akishev to assume the skeleton was that of a young chieftain. The body had been clad in leather trousers and a caftan embellished with some 2,400 arrow-shaped gold plaques, each one about an inch long, as well as a parade of small gold plaques bearing stylized lion heads along the jacket's piping. A similar cascade of gold plaques had adorned the missing boots, and his belt had been accented with thirteen stylized gold deer heads and three gold plaques depicting moose with upturned legs in the Pazyryk style, and deer with griffin heads extending from the coils on their shoulders. These spectacular ornaments, which clearly signaled the deceased's exalted rank, were made in the ancient tradition of lost-wax casting.[1] A gold torque whose

---

1. In this process, the design for each plaque was carefully fashioned in wax and then covered with clay, which, when dry, was fired to make a mold. The wax melted (and thus was lost), and molten gold was poured into the clay mold.

One of the three gold plaques from the Issyk young personage's belt. Dating to about 400 B.C., it was made using the lost wax process. A couchant deer with a long rack of horns over its back is embellished with several griffin heads that flow from scrolls. One griffin becomes the animal's ear, another extends from its back, and a third is incorporated into its muzzle.

terminals ended in snarling snow leopards encircled the youth's neck, and two gold rings adorned his hands. A whip had been placed near his head, and a ceremonial iron dagger and long sword, both decorated with scenes of parading embossed gold animals along the blades, were encased in ornate, gold-encrusted scabbards and placed at his side. The designs on the cover plaques on the sheaths were of a horse and a moose, each with the oddly twisted hindquarters indicative of the Pazyryk style.

The Gold "Man" with golden ornaments. The gold torque is clearly visible just below the skull that was crushed when the top of the sarcophagus gave way allowing tons of dirt to fall on the skeleton.

102

Most striking of all was the corpse's conical headdress, which had stood about twenty-five inches tall and was constructed of wool felt stretched over a wooden frame. A small gold ram had been affixed to its tip, and what Akishev took to be four arrows flanked by long pairs of feathers were superimposed over a pair of heraldic steeds resplendent with ibex horns, creatures that repeated the mystical theme found on the Tamgaly petroglyphs and in the horse burials at Pazyryk. On the neck flap and back of the headdress, fantastical winged and twisted snow leopards again mirrored Pazyryk iconography and revealed the close connections that Issyk must have had with the nomads at Pazyryk.

A local woman in the Pazyryk region in southern Siberia, wearing a costume similar to those worn by the first millennium B.C. Ukok priestess and the Issyk warrior priestess.

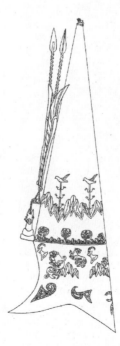

Reconstruction of the Issyk personage's headdress. In the top register, small birds perch in Trees of Life that spring from mountain symbols. In some Eurasian cultures, birds represent souls waiting to be born. Around the neck flap, mountain goat protomas and the twisted Tien Shan snow leopard snarls above mountain symbols. On the front of the headdress, Tree of Life symbols project above horned horse protomas. All the ornaments were fashioned from heavy gold foil.

103

Drawing on reliefs depicting Saka nobles on the Achaemenian Persian palaces at Persepolis in what is now southern Iran, Akishev reconstructed the headdress and clothing. The fabulous costume of the Issyk Gold Man, as Akishev had dubbed his find, quickly garnered much attention in archaeological circles and, twenty years later, became one of the main attractions in a traveling exhibition hosted by various museums in Asia and the United States.

A snow leopard with hindquarters twisted is associated with mountains. It was one of the symbols on the Issyk personage's hat.

Like thousands of other visitors, I was enthralled by the Gold Man when I first saw the exhibition, and I was privileged to examine and photograph the intricate plaques at the Archaeological Museum in Almaty a short time later. But over the years, as I became more familiar with the artifacts in this burial and the cultures of the Early Nomads, something about Akishev's analysis began to trouble me. That famous headdress, for one thing—while it is true that high-status nomads of both sexes wore pointed headdresses, the artistic motifs and exaggerated height of the Gold Man's were strongly suggestive of a fertility cult, particularly the birds perched in a series of stylized, symmetrical

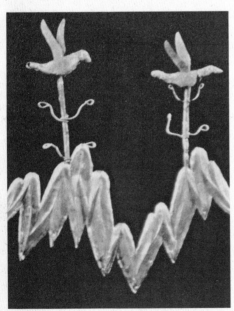

Ornaments depicting birds perched in Trees of Life sprouting from mountains were symbols of fertility and perhaps rebirth.

Trees of Life sprouting from mountain symbols. Even the popular interpretation of the headdress's ornamentation as arrows or spears was questionable: The arrows used by the Eurasian nomads of the time were tri-lobed, while the Gold Man's ornaments had only two barbs. I had observed similar designs on the felt carpet at Pazyryk, and believed that these clearly depicted cattails (local to the region), a floral motif, or another stylization of a Tree of Life—all fertility symbols—not weapons.

Other aspects of the burial offerings puzzled me. The Gold Man's jewelry included three gold and turquoise earrings and a set of carnelian and white beads, items never before found in an early nomadic male's burial, and the signet ring on the right hand bore an unusual design, the profile of a person wearing a feathered headdress suggestive of the images of shamans. The tomb also contained such telling artifacts as a gilded bronze mirror, a silver spoon with a bird's-head handle, and a koumiss beater—all of which have cultic significance. And then there's the matter of the skeleton's slight stature. Akishev had dealt with that by saying it

Issyk warrior-priestess, reconstructed as a male. Her headdress, caftan, and boots are undoubtedly correct, but she may have worn a skirt, as have other excavated Saka women.

had belonged to a youthful chieftain, but, given the weapons and the other burial offerings, wasn't it more likely that the Gold Man was really a warrior-priestess, a Gold *Woman* of some importance?

After I came to the conclusion that the Gold Man probably had been a female, I had butterflies in my stomach caused by both dread and anticipation. I felt a moral imperative to publish my interpretation—while we might never be able to prove unequivocally that the skeleton was female, so much evidence pointed to this conclusion, I believed it simply would be wrong to let the present, widespread interpretation stand unchallenged—but I was well aware that I could be considered an interloper by some colleagues, especially those in the former Soviet Union. Suggesting a change in the sex of the skeleton also might be perceived as a feminist attempt to rewrite history or challenge the male-oriented Soviet archaeological system. Still, I was confident that those who knew me would understand that an objective analysis of scientific data was always paramount to my work and that I would never skew evidence to fit a personal agenda.

So, in the September/October 1997 issue of *Archaeology* magazine, I published an article titled "Chieftain or Warrior-Priestess?" outlining the reasons I believed that the richly accoutred Issyk skeleton had belonged to a high-ranking warrior-priestess. Then I waited. To my surprise and relief, although the occasional colleague refused to consider such a switch in sex, others readily came forward to support me. Beken Nurapiesov, for one, told me that the members of the original excavation crew had remarked on the similarity of the Gold Man's headdress to the traditional hats worn by Kazak brides, and a French archaeologist confided he had heard rumors at the Kazak Institute that the archaeologists had thought it was a female in the burial. Even Orazak Ismagulov, the physical anthropologist who had examined the skeletal remains at the institute, admitted that he never examined them *in situ* and hadn't been able to make a positive sexual identification. "The bones were very small and could have belonged to a female," he said during a phone conversation. "It was probably the prestigious artifacts, particularly the sword and dagger, that made Akishev think the skeleton had been a male chieftain."

I told Ismagulov that I had contacted some Israeli scientists who had perfected a method for determining sex from ancient DNA and asked whether any samples of the Gold Man's remains might be made available for testing. He agreed to look, but when I called back a few days later, his daughter and fellow anthropologist, Ainagul Ismagulova, had some disappointing news. "Our original laboratory was moved to another building after you were here," she said, "and I can't find any of the Issyk skeletal material. However, if we ever do find any, I'll let you know."

A number of years have passed, and not a single Issyk bone has surfaced—which is no surprise, given what I know about the Soviet archaeological modus operandi. Consumed with taking cranial measurements, the scientists tend to save only well-preserved skulls and discard the other bones. In the Gold Man's case, the skull was crushed, so it's likely that no one bothered to gather up the pieces to be repaired in the laboratory. This was an enormously frustrating turn of events, and one that ensures, at least for now, that the Issyk figure's sexual identity will remain one of the mysteries of the steppes.

As the thousands of precious artifacts found in the Issyk kurgan suggest, the Saka had a taste for gold and the means to indulge it. It was a passion shared by other steppe nomads, whose graves provided a dazzling display of wealth, including intricately fashioned solid-gold vessels, phalerae (round gold ornaments to decorate their horses' heads and chests), jewelry, and headdress and clothing decorations. During the seventeenth century, the Russians collected many such treasures looted from Siberian tombs, some of which are currently on display in the Hermitage museum in St. Petersburg. Originally they all were ascribed to the Scythians, because that was the only ancient nomadic tribe known at the time, but today we know that these riches from Siberia had actually belonged to either the Sarmatians or the Saka.

The treasure trove of golden artifacts associated with the Gold "Man" and the caches of the Saka could never have been preserved were it not for centuries of protection. But under whose watch? Legend has it that

Roads of Gold, Roads of Silk

Romantic myths of griffins and dragons notwith-
standing, the gold amassed by the nomads was quite real
and, as had happened millennia earlier when the
demands for obsidian (to fabricate knives and arrowheads), amber (for personal adornment), and tin (to mix
with copper to make bronze) had spurred the development of trade routes across vast distances, gold found its
way across the steppes along early Silk Roads. Some
trade routes had been established as early as the
Neolithic period, but the area truly became a conduit for
international commerce around 200 B.C. during the
Roman expansion, when wealthy Europeans and
Persians developed an insatiable appetite for the fine,
luminous silk cloth wrought by Chinese artisans. An
unprecedented number of caravans of camels, horses,
and donkeys began to travel along a series of Eurasian
routes (including a sea route along China's coast and
around India) that became known collectively as the
Silk Road, eventually connecting China, India, Iran, and
Europe. Silks, rugs, porcelains, spices, jade, precious
metals, and Chinese coins were among the luxuries that
were conveyed westward, while the Chinese clamored
for the steeds that Chinese historians called Heavenly
Horses from the Ferghana Valley because of their superi-
ority and beauty. Technological innovations—gunpowder, compasses, paper money, and printing techniques—
continued to flow westward in medieval times.

Steppe nomads such as the Saka, the Sauro-
Sarmatians, and, later, the Parthians, Huns, Alans, and
Mongols found many ways to profit from the caravans.
They served as guides and guards; sold them horses, cattle, fodder, and other supplies; and—the most profitable
of all—exacted tribute for permission to travel through
their territories. They also set up caravansaries, inns
where wayfarers could rest, eat, and safely store their
cargo and livestock for the night; some, such as

Samarkand and Bukhara in Uzbekistan and Merv (now known as Mary) in Turkmenistan, eventually grew into great cities that served as centers of learning and culture.

For centuries, the Silk Road remained a source of pride and profit for the peoples of the steppes, but tribal warfare eventually undermined the security of the route and greedy chieftains' tribute demands grew exorbitant. When a sea passage between Europe and India was discovered in the fifteenth century, it quickly displaced the Silk Road as the preferred regional trade route.

A depiction in felt of a griffin attacking a ram, from the Pazyryk excavations.

the infamous griffins of mythology were the guardians of the gold.

According to the Greeks, the Arimaspians, a race of one-eyed people, tried to wrest golden nuggets from foul-tempered griffins in the eastern regions of the steppes. What appears to be a fanciful concoction rests on a logical foundation, according to the folklorist Adrienne Mayor (2000). She postulates that the griffin myth could have arisen from sightings of dinosaur nests, eggs, and bones protruding from rock formations that yielded gold nuggets. She also writes that in ancient times on the southern side of the Tien Shan Mountains from Issyk, Chinese historians assigned to document military movement along the rim of the Taklamakan desert feared the "heaps of bright white stones like bones" they encountered. *I Ching,* which was compiled around the time of Homer but drawn from earlier myths, warned peasants to be aware of "dragons in the field." In the second century A.D., chroniclers in this region contributed to the myths by writing about dragons inhabiting the land of the Issodonians, a Saka tribe who lived near Lop Nur, the now-dry lake bed in the eastern Taklamakan desert (see map page 78).

During the ensuing centuries, the Chinese harvested "dragon" parts for use in folk remedies; mindful of this practice, Europeans in the 1800s flocked to the Chinese "drugstores" searching for dinosaur teeth and bones. In 1920, the well-known naturalist and author Roy Chapman Andrews, who later served as director of the American Museum of Natural History, came upon an unexpected windfall in the Flaming Hills of Turkestan: hundreds of dinosaur nests, eggs, and skeletons that were anywhere from 65 million to 100 million years old. Most of the animals were either a protoceratops, a lion-size beast with a set of vicious teeth and a birdlike profile, or a psittacosaurus, a similar-size creature that sported a parrotlike beak. Around 400 B.C., the Greek physician Ctesias noted that these creatures resembled a race of four-legged birds—an observation that dovetails nicely with the renderings of griffins, with their leonine bodies and bird-of-prey heads, in Scythian and Saka art (and this, in turn, dovetails nicely with the current evolutionary theory linking dinosaurs with birds). In 1986, Canadian and Chinese paleontologists exploring the ancient Issodonian lands and the Tien Shan foothills found additional psittacosaurus nests, eggs, and skeletons. The scientists agreed that the nomads would often have come across fully articulated skeletons of beaked dinosaurs in fossil beds close to gold deposits, which probably led them to conclude that these fearful creatures were guardians of the precious metal. The fossilized remains of psittacosaurus have even been spotted as far west along the Silk Road as western Uzbekistan's Kyzyl Kum desert.

Although I was never deep enough into the desert to see them, in Xinjiang the fossils are so close to the surface that even amateur paleontologists have excavated dinosaur skeletons, some of which were found in an upright position, apparently buried as they stood waiting out one of the horrific Black Storms of wind and sand that pummel these lands. Protoceratops fossils have been found both in a four-legged stance and balancing on two legs, poses very much like the depictions of griffins in nomadic art that show a bird-headed, winged lion with a long tail. In fact, these ancient griffin images more faithfully resemble the actual dinosaurs than some artistic attempts by scientists in the nineteenth and early twentieth centuries.

In my own exploration of the area, visions of griffins came to mind as we drove down a steep trail in the Altai Mountains after visiting Marjan, the Tuvan shaman. Part of the road was bordered by the wide and swiftly flowing Hovd River, and as we followed it downstream, our guide Bayer pointed out two small operational gold mines high on the cliffs above the opposite bank. I was eager to visit a mine, but, much to my chagrin, there wasn't a bridge for many miles in this remote area, so I was cheated out of the chance to visit the fabled province of miserly griffins, whose legends also might have inspired the dragons I had so often admired on Chinese bronzes.

CHAPTER SEVEN

THE ADVENT OF THE AMAZONS

In the Louvre's enviable collection of Greek antiquities, there's a curious piece of Attic Black Figure pottery shaped like an elongated bell with one side cut away. Dating to the early fifth century B.C., this epinetron, as the device is called, was used when carding wool: a seated woman would settle the hollowed-out section over her lower thigh and rub the wool over the scales incised on the upper surface to separate the fibers before placing them on a distaff. Decorative as it was useful, the epinetron is capped by the molded relief of a woman's delicate veiled head, while two long painted panels run down its sides. One panel, appropriately enough, depicts a group of willowy, upper-class Greek ladies contentedly working wool and chatting; the other side showcases a trio of grim-faced and muscular female warriors preparing for battle. These very different portraits of womanhood would represent a striking contrast in any cultural context, but their juxtaposition is even more remarkable given the status of women in Classical Greece. To the cultured Athenians of the time, the two panels represented nothing less than the Athenian feminine ideal and

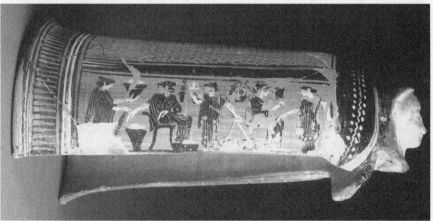

Epinetron from the early fifth century B.C. depicting Amazons in battle (top) and Greek women
preparing wool for weaving (bottom).

its antithesis, a cautionary tale of the horrors that would be unleashed if
the natural and proper social order were disturbed.

The women warriors portrayed on the Louvre epinetron are Amazons,
whose images began to appear on Greek ceramics in the seventh century B. C. During the Classical age (about 500 to 323 B.C.), the motif became
so popular, it was given its own name—*amazonomachy*—and could be
found on architectural friezes, jewelry, and ceramics of every description. Centuries later, these artworks still hold a fascination for anyone

113

interested in the roles of women in the ancient world, and they hold a special allure for me because Herodotus identified the Amazons, along with the Scythians, as the progenitors of the Sauromatians.

Even though I never gave a thought to excavating Amazons—or any warrior women—when Leonid Yablonsky invited me to join him at Pokrovka (these legendary creatures were rumored to have lived in Anatolia or Greece), one of my motives for joining this Russian archaeologist was the opportunity to see firsthand how the Sauro-Sarmatian cultures and art compared (or contrasted) with those of the much-better-known Scythians. Subsequently over the years, I studied amazonomachies in many venues, from the elegant Victoria and Albert Museum in London to the worn marble sarcophagi in Konya, Turkey, to the quaint collection of the museum in Rostov-na-Donu (Rostov on the Don) on the north coast of the Black Sea in Russia, always wondering whether these scenes held some clue to the veracity of the legends that surround these most famous of women warriors. Yet I was haunted by the knowledge that these representations did not do justice to the Amazons' capabilities.

The krater (left), used for mixing wine and water, shows an Amazon dressed in Asian costume—long, tight-fitting pants and caftan—holding the reins of her horse in her right hand, a war axe in her left. On the lekythos, or lecythus (right), which held oils or ointments, are three Amazons (only one is completely visible here) on horseback.

Some artistic representations depict the Amazons in peaceful, domestic pursuits, such as taming horses or bathing, but most show them engaged in battle with Greek troops or mythological heroes—

and usually getting the worst of it. Many of the poses have the quality of a dance, with serene-faced warriors locked in graceful combat; some seem more erotic than bellicose. The Greek men are often portrayed nude (sometimes ithyphallic), and although the Amazons manage to keep their clothes on during battle, occasionally a breast or shapely leg will erupt from a well-placed gap in their garments. The style of those garments, in fact, serves as a barometer of Greece's political climate: In the early pieces, the women are usually outfitted in the crested helmets and short tunics typical of Greek soldiers, but after the Greeks bested the Persians in the Battle of Marathon in 490 B.C., their female foes begin to appear in Middle Eastern or Asian garb, including the caftan, tight trousers, high boots, and tall, pointed hats of the steppe nomads.

This pelike showing Amazons in combat is from the Five Brother kurgans of Elizavetovskoye in the north Black Sea region of Russia.

One of the most popular legends depicted in Classical Greek art is the Twelve Labors of Hercules, the heroic, half-mortal son of Zeus. In the ninth of these adventures, Hercules is commanded by Eurastheus, and urged on by Hera to capture the Amazon queen Hippolyte's sacred girdle, a gift from Ares, the god of war, whom the tribe revered.[1] The queen isn't about to surrender this treasure without a fight, and many of her company die in hand-to-hand combat before Hippolyte herself is slain by Hercules. (In some versions of the myth, she is raped instead of killed, or Theseus and Hippolyte's sister Antiope square

---

1. A girdle was an elaborate sash made from leather, metal, or cloth. In Classical Greece, it was a symbol of chastity; to remove a woman's girdle was to render her defenseless against sexual advances.

off instead of Hercules and Hippolyte.) The Amazons retaliate by invading Attica[2] and setting siege to the Acropolis—unsuccessfully, of course.

Greek literature, as well as art, abounds with tales of these fierce women warriors, beginning in the eighth century B.C. when Homer and Arctinus of Miletus composed their epic poems about the Trojan War, the legendary siege of Troy by the Greeks under Agamemnon in the twelfth century B.C. In the *Iliad,* Homer called the Amazons "the equal of men" who fought on the side of the Trojans, and Arctinus described their hopeful arrival in Troy, led by their brave and lovely queen Penthesilea. Later authors, such as Quintus of Smyrna, picked up the story from there. In most versions, the Amazons initially seem to be winning the battle, but then the Greek soldiers, with their superior manly strength, begin decimating them. Finally, Ajax and Achilles arrive on the scene, and Penthesilea futilely hurls her last two spears at them. Achilles strides over to the Amazon queen and impales her on her horse with a single thrust of his spear. As she lies dying, he removes her helmet so he can see the face of his enemy, only to be smitten by her beauty. In many versions of the tale, the love-struck hero is taunted by one of his sidekicks; maddened by grief, Achilles flings the soldier to the ground so hard that he is killed.

Throughout the Classical and Hellenistic (322–30 B.C.) ages, a host of Greek poets, playwrights, philosophers, and historians continued to write about the Amazons' exploits, seasoning their accounts with a mixture of admiration and contempt. Plato praised them (as well as Sauromatian women) for their readiness to fight in defense of their nation, and Aeschylus proclaimed them "virgins fearless in battle," though the latter's declaration of their chasteness seems to be a minority opinion—most Greek authors stressed the women's sexual freedom as much as their boldness on the battlefield, claiming that the women, who usually lived separately from men, dallied with the opposite sex with wild abandon once a year to ensure the propagation of more little Amazons. Upon invading

---

2. In ancient times, Attica was a region of east-central Greece that included the city of Athens.

Central Asia, Alexander the Great was said to have spent a fortnight with the Amazon queen Thalestris, hunting lions by day and making love by night. Unfortunately, the queen was killed shortly after this amorous interlude, so the mighty girl-child she may have conceived was never born.

Although he didn't mean to be complimentary, I am especially fond of the words of the renowned fifth-century-B.C. Athenian author and orator Lysias, who noted that "the daughters of Ares" were the first in their region to be "armed with iron, and they were the first of all to mount horses, with which, owing to the inexperience of their foes, they surprised them and either caught those who fled or outstripped those who pursued. They are accounted as men for their high courage, rather than as women for their sex; so much more did they seem to excel men in their spirit."

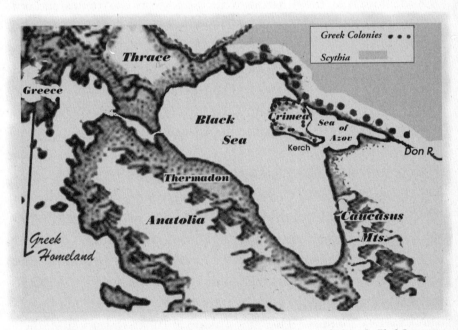

In the seventh and sixth centuries B.C., the Greeks established colonies north along the Black Sea coast where they soon interacted with the Scythians who inhabited the steppes beyond the coast. Legends of Amazons fighting with Greeks, who had previously settled around 1200 B.C. in northern Anatolia, were recorded by Herodotus. After overtaking the Greeks' ship, the Amazons shipwrecked on the northern coast where they encountered the Scythians.

The authors of antiquity also delighted in recalling the Amazons' savagery and failings. Amazon mothers were said to either return their male infants to the children's fathers or to kill them at birth. The women were also reputed to sear or cut off the right breasts of their female children so they could better shoot a bow—indeed, pundits including Herodotus insisted that the word *Amazon* stemmed from two Greek words meaning "without a breast" (*a* = without; *mazos* = breast). But Amazons were never depicted with one breast in artistic renderings, and some modern linguists seem to agree that the word *Amazon* actually comes from a Proto-Indo- European term meaning "no-husband one."[3] I had always thought that Herodotus's definition was suspect, but when I saw today's full-busted Mongol women archers taking fine aim and marking the bull's-eye, I knew there was certainly no need to remove a breast.

Aside from Ares, the Amazons were said to worship Artemis, and not always the spirited but demure virgin huntress revered by cultured Greeks. The Amazons were often linked with a darker and more ancient version of the deity, a cold-hearted, all-powerful mother goddess who demanded blood sacrifices (both of animals and human males) and unsavory orgiastic rituals (see "The Goddess of Many Guises," page 119). Every account stressed that no matter how brave or skilled the Amazons were in battle, they were no match for male Greek warriors. Lysias, for example, in his *Funeral Oration* recounts with great relish the Amazons' inevitable downfall. He describes how the warlike women weren't content with conquering the nations in the immediate vicinity of their reputed homeland (which he ascribed to Anatolia, the west coast and central part of modern-day Turkey), but dared to march against Athens. This time the foolish and greedy women "met with valiant men" and "found their spirit now was like their sex"—that is, they suffered an ignominious loss. Nor was defeat in battle their only humiliation. Lysias continues, "They stood alone in failing to learn from their mistakes, and so be better advised in their future actions; they would not

---

3. Martin Schwartz and Martin Huld

The Goddess of Many Guises

Although Lysias hailed them as the "daughters of Ares," the Amazons surely would have found Artemis—the hunter, the warrior, the independent female—a most appealing deity. The daughter of Zeus and Leto, Artemis was the twin sister of Apollo, the god of the sun and music. Like most Greek gods, Artemis possessed many sides to her character, some of which seemed rather contradictory. She was the goddess of the hunt, equipped with silver arrows that brought a swift and painless death, yet she also was "Mistress of Animals," charged with protecting wild beasts. Along with Athena (goddess of wisdom) and Hestia (goddess of the hearth), she was a virgin goddess, impervious to Aphrodite's wiles or the arrows of Eros, but she also watched over women in the throes of childbirth. She defended the young and the guileless, yet she had a fierce temper and an irrational pride that claimed many an innocent victim. Actaeon and Callisto come to mind: Artemis turned the former into a stag so he would be torn apart by his own hounds after he accidentally witnessed her bathing, and she hunted the latter, a nymph who had been one of the goddess's companions, for the crime of surrendering her chastity to Zeus (the god saved Callisto by spiriting her to the sky, where she remains today as the constellation Ursa Major).

Fickle Artemis also could be merciful, as when she spared the life of Iphigenia, the daughter of Agamemnon, the commander of the Greek forces during the Trojan War. He decided to sacrifice his comely child to the goddess to ensure favorable winds for his armada, but Artemis substituted a deer in her place and spirited her to Tauris (now Tabriz, in Iran) where she became one of her priestesses. And when Artemis's brother Apollo cast his lustful eye on another nymph, Daphne, the goddess saved her from being raped by transforming her into a laurel tree.

The worship of the goddess is further complicated by

the apparent induction of several older cults into the Greek religion. As a goddess of the moon, Artemis became associated with stories and rites originally ascribed to Phoebe, one of the mighty Titans who gave birth to the gods, and Selene, another moon goddess. She also became linked with Hecate, the dreaded goddess of the underworld, and Ma, the ancient fertility goddess worshipped in Anatolia first by the Hittites and then by the Phrygians. Because of these different guises, the rites honoring Artemis could take many forms, from the festive initiation ceremonies in Brauron to the gory human sacrifices demanded by the Tauric Artemis.

---

return home and report their own misfortune and our ancestors' valor; for they perished on the spot, and were punished for their folly, thus making our city's memory imperishable for its valor; while owing to their disaster in this region they rendered their own country nameless."

Note that Lysias seems to bemoan the Amazons' demise only because it robs the Greeks of a chance for their praises to be sung by a vanquished enemy. The last part of his quote is also intriguing because although the Greeks, and later the Romans, devoted tale after tale to these formidable warriors, the accounts are maddeningly vague and contradictory when it comes to pinpointing their homeland. Separated by time and distance and lacking any reliable methods of reportage, it's no wonder that ancient authors proffered differing accounts, but Lysias's words suggest that the Amazons' land of origin might have been deliberately obscured by historians as punishment for their headstrong and ignoble actions.

While that's admittedly speculation on my part, there's no dispute that various Greek and Roman sources have placed the Amazons' point of origin in locales as diverse as the shores of North Africa, of the Aegean, the Black Sea coast of modern-day Turkey, the Caucasus, and the steppes of southern Russia. They were rumored to have been nomads, but they were credited with building the great temple of Artemis at Ephesus and founding a variety of outposts on the Aegean Sea, including the town of Mytilene on the Greek island of Lesbos; and the Turkish port of Smyrna.

Much to the frustration of modern-day Amazon buffs, however, no solid and convincing archaeological evidence has been unearthed to back up any of these claims—no lost cities dominated by female artifacts, no ancient cemeteries devoted entirely to warrior women, no caches of artwork portraying the Amazonian point of view. Just ask Lyn Webster Wilde, a British journalist who spent several years trying to assess the veracity of the Amazon legend for her book *On the Trail of the Women Warriors.* In the course of her research, Wilde came to interview me during a 1997 excavation in Moldova (the former Moldavian Soviet Socialist Republic), seeking information about the women warriors of Pokrovka. Over a cup of tea in an outdoor café in the capital city of Kishinev, we discussed how female warriors certainly existed in the Iron Age. But, like most scholars, I was compelled to stress that there simply is no physical scientific evidence to date that a tribe of women warriors ever lived separately from men and engaged in the exploits celebrated in Greek, and later Roman, art and literature. The evidence from our Pokrovka excavations points out that even the Sauromatians, whom Herodotus claimed were the Amazons' direct descendants, lived in a society in which men and women happily cohabited. While we have archaeological documentation for the Sauromatians and their reputed Scythian forefathers, if their Amazonian foremothers existed they failed to leave behind the same kind of tangible legacy. Lyn agreed it was unlikely a race of women ever existed that exactly mirrored Herodotus's description, and I agree with her conviction that the components of the Amazonian myths existed in many different times and places.

This lack of hard proof has led many historians to speculate that tales of the Amazons may have been fabricated by the Greeks to help keep their own women in line. One of the paradoxes of Greece's Golden Age is that while democracy was being born, the rights of women were eroding, under the influence of the Dorians, a patriarchal people who had arrived in west-central Greece sometime between 1200 and 900 B.C. The Dorians gradually restructured the old priestess-led, Great Goddess—

worshipping cultures into a masculine-dominated form and stripped women of many of the rights, both religious and otherwise, that they had enjoyed in the Heroic Age (1600 through 1100 B.C.).[4] The result in Classical Greece was a society in which women were completely subjugated to men and confined to a life that most modern observers would characterize as stupefyingly dull, isolated, and demeaning.

In Athens, the much-heralded cradle of democracy, women were accorded the legal status of minors and depended on the protection and patronage of their husband or a male relative for everything from shelter to respectability. They were living in one of the most dynamic, exciting times in history—an era when the arts and sciences were flourishing as never before—yet they were forbidden to participate in many of their society's pleasures and privileges. Upper-class Greek men spent most of their time away from home, exercising in gymnasiums, trysting with lovers, or debating politics or philosophy in public forums; well-born Greek women were largely confined to their houses, toiling at domestic tasks, surrounded only by children, slaves, and female relatives. Even when their husbands entertained at home, wives were restricted to the second-floor women's quarters unless the male guests were close relatives. Theater was emerging as a magnificent art form, but the only women likely to be in attendance were the *hetairai,* the refined and glamorous courtesans who arrived on the arms of their wealthy patrons.[5] Democracy was being born, yet women were excluded from participating in politics or public life. In

---

4. Apparently, women were extremely reluctant to surrender their religious roles and continued to conduct secret rituals for centuries. In his advice to a newly married couple in the second century A.D., Plutarch felt compelled to remind them that "no god can be pleased by stealthy and surreptitious rites performed by a woman." For more on mother-goddess cults, see Chapter 10.

5. Wilde (2000, 17) describes how the most celebrated woman in fifth-century B.C. Athens was Aspasia, the companion of Pericles, the so-called Tyrant of Athens. "She started life as a *hetaira* and ended it as a madam, but was widely respected: Socrates visited her and brought along pupils. Pericles cherished Aspasia and would kiss her on leaving and returning home," an extremely unusual public display of affection for the times. For more on the *hetairai,* see "The 'Painted Women of Joy,'" page 123.

The "Painted Women of Joy"

In Greece's ancient age, the world of the prostitute encompassed both the apex and the nadir of society. At the top reigned the *hetairai*, whom George Ryley Scott summed up in his *The History of Prostitution* as "women of beauty, education, culture, and attraction, outshining in every respect the virtuous wives who were engaged in breeding and rearing the children of the race." These "painted women of joy," as they were known, attended the theater and lavish banquets, conversed with men on nearly equal terms, and rode about freely through the streets of Athens. They dallied with the brightest and most powerful men of their time, and, supported by their wealthy patrons, ran large and luxurious households with an independent hand. Although they were forbidden to participate in religious festivals and their children could never be citizens, they enjoyed a measure of honor, freedom, and privilege that respectable women could only dream of as they went about their menial chores, confined to their homes.

Farther down the social ladder were the *auletridi*, the flute-playing dancing girls who entertained at banquets and festivals. Genteel, educated, and elegantly dressed, they gratified the sexual wishes of the well-heeled Athenians who attended these events. Less prominent citizens had to content themselves with the *dicteriadi*, or common prostitutes, who plied their trade primarily at temples or brothels. The first public brothel on record, in fact, was established in Athens in the sixth century B.C. by Solon, the famous wit and legislator who framed the democratic laws of Athens. It was run by the state and staffed by slaves, who surrendered their meager earnings to the government. Even after the brothels became private enterprises that employed freewomen, they still had to pay a hefty tax to the state.

Sold by their families or forced into prostitution by poverty, the *dicteriadi* eked out a miserable existence.

Dressed in wretched clothing and always close to starving, they were treated poorly by both the brothel owners and their clients. Yet like upper-class Greek women, who were expected to bear their dull lives and their husbands' flagrant infidelities with uncomplaining grace, prostitutes were compelled to act content with their lot. As one fourth-century-B.C. observer commented: "If [a prostitute] doesn't like laughing, she spends the day inside, like the meat at the butcher's when goats' heads are on sale; she keeps a thin slip of myrtle wood propped up between her lips, so that in time she will grin, whether she wants to or not."

---

many cases, their education was confined to the domestic arts, and not only their minds but their bodies were neglected, as they were forbidden to exercise or eat the best foods. They couldn't own property, and while a husband could divorce his wife by simply evicting her from the house, a woman seeking divorce had to enlist one of her male relatives to petition the courts on her behalf—a drastic action that was seldom taken.

Sold to the highest bidder or to secure a valuable alliance for the family, Athenian girls were married around age fourteen (the ones who were allowed to live, that is; it was a common custom to let female infants die of exposure). Their husbands usually were twice their age or older, and this large age gap left young widows suspect—they were thought to be at risk of succumbing to unseemly sexual temptation and were promptly placed under the stern guardianship of a male relative and urged to remarry as soon as possible, often according to the dictates of their husbands' will. Older widows were considered less susceptible to erotic impulses and so were accorded a little more freedom.

First-time brides were required to be virgins,[5] but their grooms were expected to have amassed a wealth of sexual experience with prostitutes, slaves, or other men. Homoeroticism, in fact, was considered to be the

---

6. If a freeborn or noble woman was proved to have engaged in fornication or adultery, she was considered damaged goods and her husband or male guardian could sell her into slavery.

highest and purest form of love, ranking far above affection between men and women. (Lesbian love wasn't quite elevated to this pedestal, although with men absent from home so much of the time, women were encouraged to take female lovers or to masturbate; the joy of dildos was celebrated in artwork and even in a play by Aristophanes.)

Perhaps surprisingly, women were accorded more liberty and respect in that bastion of he-man military aggression, Sparta. This wasn't due to any high-minded principle of egalitarianism; the Spartans, who were always in need of fresh recruits to take the place of fallen soldiers, simply recognized that strong, healthy mothers tend to breed strong, healthy sons. Thus Spartan girls were well nourished and engaged in regular exercise, as Plutarch observed: "[The Spartans] took particular care about the women as the men . . . [and] made the young women exercise their bodies by running and wrestling and throwing the discus and the javelin, so that their offspring would have a sound start by taking root in sound bodies and grow stronger, and the women themselves would be able to use their strength to withstand childbearing and wrestle with labor pains."[7] Another toning secret was imparted in Aristophanes's play *Lysistrata,* in which a Spartan woman declares that her strong, shapely figure is due to her habit of vigorously kicking herself in the buttocks when she dances. I doubt that buttocks-kicking was a featured event, but women participated in athletic competitions from a young age, and unlike Athenian females, they were treated to a good diet and liberal doses of wine. This healthy regimen, coupled with the practice of postponing marriage and childbirth until age eighteen or so, helped reduce the mortality rate for young women (their Athenian counterparts tended to die in their mid-thirties, ten years earlier than males).

The genteel Athenians expected their women to be chaste and diffident, but the Spartans preferred saucy, outspoken females and winked at their adulterous affairs—after all, husbands were often away at war for

---

7. Plutarch, *Life of Lycurgus,* 14.2, second century A.D.

prolonged periods of time, and stocking the pool of ready soldiers was of prime importance, regardless of the parentage. Plutarch noted that occasionally an older Spartan man would invite one of his strapping young friends to sleep with his wife to produce hardier offspring, and if a man fancied the attractive and fertile wife of another, he might persuade the husband to "let him sleep with her, so that he could plant his seed in a good garden plot and beget good children."[8] But Spartan custom held that it was disgraceful for a husband to be seen visiting his own wife for amorous purposes, and men had to sneak in and out of their spouses' boudoir at night. The aura of danger and illicitness was believed to spice up a couple's love life, and so keep them happily procreating longer.[9]

Despite the relative advantages enjoyed by Spartan women, they still were second-class citizens subject to the will and whim of their men. The only time Athenian women were truly allowed to cut loose was during religious festivals. Many of these festivals were reserved for women only, a vestige of their former power. Dedicated to Dionysus, Demeter, Artemis, and other deities, the festivals often featured bizarre symbolic rites that harked back to the old Great Goddess–worshipping era. They lasted anywhere from three to ten days, with the women (and sometimes girls) going off on their own to sacred sites. There they would appease the gods and ensure their own fertility by drinking wine, dancing, and telling lewd jokes and stories. They offered sacrifices: a human, an animal, or perhaps, as thanksgiving, fruit, honey, and vegetables. During the day they would partake of a joyful meal, but after nightfall their somber ceremonies were to placate malevolent powers that came from the dark underground.

---

8. Ibid., 15.6. To ensure that "good children" were indeed produced, all fathers were expected to present their newborns to a committee of elders, who would examine them. If a child was deemed strong and well formed, it was allowed to live; if it seemed sickly, it was left to die in a pit. Mothers also tested their babies by washing them in wine instead of water. Wine was reputed to induce convulsions in weak babies while tempering the strength of healthy ones.
9. Spartan couples also began their married lives in a lively way, engaging in a nude wrestling match before the ceremony for the entertainment of their guests.

Blood Rites and She-Bears

Two of the Athenians' most significant religious festivals were the consecration of prepubescent girls to Artemis and the mysterious celebration of the Thesmophoria. In the former, girls between the ages of nine and twelve were brought to Brauron (Vravrona), a sacred site on the east coast of Attica. The *arktoi* ("little bears"), as the young initiates were called, donned yellow tunics that supposedly looked like the golden bear fur and they imitated lumbering she-bears as they entered an opening in the rocks to a hidden shrine. There they made offerings to Artemis, whose duties included protecting innocent children, virgins, and women during childbirth. After making their obeisance to the goddess, the *arktoi* walked through a long, narrow passageway—a symbolic representation of the birth canal—and emerged reborn as women. Over the next several days, they slept in a dormitory, danced, played games, and learned about womanly arts, such as weaving and cooking. As Lyn Webster Wilde comments in *On the Trail of the Women Warriors*, it must have been a pleasant interlude for the girls, but "they were actually being symbolically divested of their childish wildness (their bear-nature) and tamed and domesticated ready to serve in adult female life."

The Thesmophoria, an annual festival held in honor of the fertility goddess Demeter, was reserved for married women. The Athenian version lasted three days and took place just before the fall planting. Sworn to secrecy regarding the rites they were about to witness, the women climbed up Pnyx hill to the Thesmophorion, a sanctuary sacred to Demeter, bearing food, wine, and other ritual accoutrements. They built crude huts in which to live, elected a pair of officials, and may even have consumed plants to suppress their sex drive so they would remain chaste during the festival.

Then they began the rites, which recalled Demeter's search for her daughter, Persephone (or Kore), after the latter was kidnapped by Hades, the god of the underworld. On the second day, the women sat on mats made from willow branches and fasted in memory of the distraught goddess's grief. They hurled ritual insults at each other and told lewd stories and jokes, mimicking the antics of Iambe, Peresphone's nurse, who tried to raise Demeter's spirits during her long quest. The highlight of the festival occurred when certain women called bailers, or *antleriai*, climbed down into a deep chamber called a megaron, which represented the underworld. While the other women clapped and shouted to drive away the guardian snakes lurking in the dark depths, the bailers retrieved the remains of piglets that had been tossed into the pits days earlier. When the bailers emerged from the trenches, they placed their finds on the altars of Demeter and Persephone, alongside fertility symbols fashioned from dough. The women broke these offerings apart and mixed them with seed, creating a magical concoction that later would be spread on the fields to ensure a good harvest.

The last day of the Thesmophoria was dedicated to "fair birth," and celebrates Demeter's reunion with her daughter and the divine compromise that allows her to spend part of each year with her. When Persephone is consigned to Hades's gloomy kingdom, Demeter mourns and winter seizes the earth, but during the season the girl is allowed to be with her mother, crops burst into bloom, the herds multiply, and the sun shines brightly. Festival-goers honored this happy time by preparing a feast and calling for the goddess's blessing on their herds and fields. They also celebrated human fertility by passing around cakes in the shape of penises and worshipping representations of female genitalia.

As wild as this festival may seem to modern sensibilities, it was actually fairly tame compared with some other Greek religious celebrations, especially the ones dedicated to Dionysus, the god of wine and fertility, during which the female worshippers were said to have engaged in drunken orgies and torn live animals apart in frenzied sacrifice. These were regarded as rather scandalous activities, but the Thesmophoria was considered completely proper for the gentlewomen of Athens, and so important to ensuring the city's prosperity that the wealthy men of the city happily bore its considerable cost.

Men were strictly forbidden to participate or even view these cere-monies; there were dire tales of transgressors' being castrated, blinded, or killed by outraged female celebrants. An escape from controlling men, time off from endless chores, freedom from social constraints, plenty to eat and drink, and the feeling that they were participating in important communal rites—these occasions must have seemed like paradise to the repressed Greek women. (See "Blood Rites and She-Bears," page 127.)

Although these infrequent festivals offered some release, it's difficult for a modern observer to believe that Greek women didn't resent their second-class treatment and yearn for more freedom, just as it's incon-ceivable that the same gifted, freethinking men who conjured up such noble concepts as rationalism and democracy didn't realize they were giv-ing the fair sex a decidedly unfair deal. Some justification was needed to make women compliant and men complacent, some explanation why this male-dominated social order was right and just. And that's where the legend of the Amazons might have come into play. Myths were power-ful tools in Greek society, accepted as fact and used to justify societal con-ventions as well as to explain natural phenomena and the meaning of life. Tales of the Amazons demonstrated what would happen if women did the unthinkable and threw off the tempering hand of man. Women who were athletic and strong, traveled around freely, and shunned male soci-ety became a band of bloodthirsty, headstrong, promiscuous vixens who were forever aligning themselves with enemies of the Greeks. They also were fatally flawed, for though the Amazons might enjoy a few moments of glory, these unnatural beings ultimately could never triumph over stal-wart Greek men on the battlefield—myth after myth proved that this was so. Reflecting on these stories, even the most liberal-minded Athenian man might feel justified in keeping his spouse and daughters under strict control, while an Athenian woman's gentle nature would recoil at the thought of emulating these she-devils.

Or at least that was how the myths were supposed to work. There are glimmers that suggest even these powerful myths couldn't completely resign Greek women to their lot, and that some men recognized the inequity of this repressive social system. Accounts of the Trojan War often mention how the Trojan women were inspired by the Amazons and clamored to join in the fight alongside their courageous female allies. And Sophocles must have been speaking for many Greek women when he wrote this speech for the tragic female character Procne:

> But now outside my father's house, I am nothing, yes often I have looked on women's nature in this regard, that we are nothing. . . . When we reach puberty and can understand, we are thrust out and sold away from our ancestral gods and from our parents. Some go to strange men's homes, others to foreigners', some to joyless houses, some to hostile. And all this once the first night has yoked us to our husband, we are forced to praise and to say that all is well.[10]

When I look at the amazonomachy on the epinetron mentioned at the start of this chapter, I can't help believing that, despite all her social conditioning, an Athenian woman gazing at those free-roaming warriors must have felt at least a twinge of envy as she sat and worked her wool.

The legend of the Amazons didn't die with the decline of the Greek empire. The Romans, always in thrall to the Greeks, also embraced these stirring tales and embellished them freely. Diodorus of Sicily, a first-century-B.C. historian, claimed he was shown the graves of Amazon generals during his travels in northern and western Africa (to this day, a

---

10. In Greek legend Procne's husband, Tereus, rapes her sister, Philomela, and tries to silence his victim by cutting out her tongue. Philomela, however, weaves her story into a tapestry and sends it to her sister. Procne retaliates by killing their son and serving him up as a dish to his father. Tereus attempts revenge, but the sisters escape by turning into a swallow and a nightingale.

number of so-called Amazon tombs are pointed out to visitors in certain parts of Greece). He said many tribes of warlike women had lived in the area, including one that fought the Gorgons and conquered Atlantis, only to be ousted by an allied force of Scythians and Thracians. Pliny the Younger claimed that the Amazons founded Ephesus, the most important Ionian city on the Aegean coast of Turkey, and erected its famous temple of Artemis, one of the Seven Wonders of the Ancient World.

Some of these legends persisted through the ages and surfaced in other countries. In the fifteenth century, a Spaniard named Ruy González de Clavijo served as diplomat to the court of Tamerlane and reported:

> Fifteen days' journey from the city of Samarcand, in the direction of China, there is a land inhabited by Amazons, and to this day they continue the custom of having no men with them, except at one time of the year, when they are permitted, by their leaders to go . . . to the nearest settlements and have communication with men, each taking the one who pleases her the most . . . They are of the lineage of the Amazons who were at Troy, when it was destroyed by the Greeks (quoted in Wilde 2000, 179).

Later populations' fascination with Greek and Roman myth has done much to keep the myth of the Amazons alive and well today.

CHINA'S MYSTERIOUS MUMMIES

One of the least enviable aspects of an archaeologist's lot is having to deal with the assorted governmental, academic, and commercial bureaucracies necessary to conduct research or excavate in a given area. This was particularly true in the former Soviet Union—just securing permission to travel in certain remote or politically sensitive regions resulted in an avalanche of red tape that threatened to bury all but the most dogged explorer. Even armed with all the required documents and contacts, I have been interrogated for hours by airport security personnel convinced that I was planning to use the expedition's cash or equipment for some nefarious purpose. I have had my phone tapped, been shadowed by none-too-subtle government agents, and been grilled by the KGB. Being an American didn't help, of course; Ronald Reagan's "evil empire" remark didn't do much for diplomacy, and I can't say that I blame the Russians for bristling at such a blanket indictment of their culture. Nor did being a woman endear me to my hosts—I've sat in several gloomy, overheated backrooms in Russian airports trying to convince skeptical guards that, yes, while a female, I was indeed a professional archaeologist in charge of a bona fide expedition bound for some remote corner of their country. Still, even after more than a decade of excavating in the former Soviet Union, I wasn't quite prepared for the adventures in paranoia, deception, and bureaucratic chaos that our crew was to experience in China during the making of a *Nova* documentary.

The project started pleasantly enough, with a dinner at a Berkeley restaurant in late 1996 at the invitation of Howard Reid, an English documentary filmmaker whose current project focused on Chinese mummies. Howard had heard about my work with the ancient nomads who might have interacted with "the mummy people," and I had been helping him with his research and script preparation for some time via e-mail. His script called for an archaeologist and a biological anthropologist to appear on camera as they explored the origins of the mummy people, and our correspondence had convinced Howard that I might fit the bill for the former. While I didn't profess to be an expert on the Chinese mummies, I had studied them several years earlier in a museum in Xinjiang, and thought that these exceptionally well preserved relics of the Bronze Age and Early Iron Age would be an excellent topic for a documentary. I also was very much taken with Howard, an affable and amusing man who had spent two years in an Amazon jungle to earn his credentials as an ethnographer.

I agreed to join the crew and, a few months later, flew to Beijing for the "recce" (pronounced *RECK-ee*; British jargon for a reconnaissance mission) to select locations for filming and to make arrangements with government officials. There Howard and I met Shu, a highly educated and charming Han Chinese woman married to an English professor. Shu, who spoke flawless English, was our translator, and also our "fixer," an invaluable assistant who spent endless hours negotiating with the Ministers of Culture in Beijing and Xinjiang so we could research and shoot the necessary materials and sites. Savvy and quick-witted, she also kept me out of trouble when I impulsively aimed my tiny digital camera at some forbidden object.

We flew west to Ürümqi, the capital of Xinjiang, China's largest independent territory, where we headed directly for the historical museum. Rich in oil, coal, and iron, this sparsely populated region in northwestern China is ringed by some of the loftiest mountain ranges in the world: the Altai, the Pamirs, and the Tien Shan. Almost a fifth of Xinjiang is consumed by Asia's most arid desert, the Taklamakan, where the mummies we were to film had been excavated two decades ago by Chinese archaeologists. (See "Excavating in the Taklamakan," page 135.)

During the flight, I thought about the first time I had visited the area. In 1991, the American anthropologist Nancy Peterson, who had been teaching at a university in Ürümqi, arranged for Matt and me to undertake a cultural tour of the territory, in exchange for our hosting a similar trip to Kazakstan. I had accepted her invitation eagerly, as I was studying the Saka who had lived in the northern Tien Shan and wanted to check my supposition that they also had practiced a nomadism similar to the Saka's in what is now Xinjiang or engaged in trade with the local, sedentary population. We hit pay dirt right away: The Ürümqi historical museum to my delight contained displays of bronze horse bits, cauldrons, and ritual bronze altars ornamented around the edges with small cast-bronze animal scenes, many identical to the Saka artifacts displayed in the Kazakstan museums. Clearly, these artifacts were evidence of Saka presence in this region during the Early Iron Age. All this was exciting enough, but when I made my way to the large cases that held the mummies recovered from graveyards in the Taklamakan, my pulse quickened and my curiosity intensified.

I knew that the Chinese had dated some of the mummies recovered from this vast desert, with its postcard-perfect golden dunes and daytime temperatures that often top 130 degrees Fahrenheit, to around 2000 B.C., an age that rivals the earliest Egyptian mummies'.[1] Unlike their pharaon-

---

1. Some caution is advised when accepting the age of the mummies, as Chinese scientists are continuing to revise the dating.

Excavating in the Taklamakan

Nestled in the heart of the Tarim Basin, the Taklamakan is the greatest desert of Central Asia and one of the largest sandy deserts in the world. It stretches 600 miles east to west and 260 miles north to south at its widest points, and its ever-shifting dunes can form thousand-foot-high pyramids of sand. Only 0.4 to 1.5 inches of rain fall annually on this parched land, where temperatures can easily reach 130 degrees Fahrenheit during summer days and plunge to 15 degrees below on winter nights. Several Silk Road routes skirt its perimeter, but few humans ventured into the interior of the Taklamakan until the 1900s, when explorers such as Sven Anders Hedin from Sweden, Albert von Le Coq from Germany, and the Hungarian-born Sir Aurel Stein became intrigued with mentions of lost cities in ancient Chinese texts and the writings of Marco Polo. They were amply rewarded with finds of military outposts, cemeteries, and cities that could date to the second millennium B.C. They also discovered the remnants of many now-dry lake beds, including Lop Nur, that had dotted the northern part of the desert, indicating that this land was once much more hospitable to humans.

On the southern rim of the Taklamakan, the French archaeologist Corinne Debaine-Francfort discovered the lost city of Kelia, which thrived in the second to fifth centuries A.D. and was one of the sites that so tantalized Stein. To date, her crew has discovered a monastery and excavated twenty tombs. In a grueling undertaking, Debaine-Francfort must transport all her supplies, and even the water they need for survival, via camel caravan—a feat made even more challenging when she was seven months pregnant. An ambitious Sino-Japanese project has yielded some spectacular results, including many preserved Caucasoid mummies, old commercial documents, some impressive statuary, and huge quantities of silks and woolen textiles, all so beautifully preserved they appear almost new.

A stone-carved priestess holding a cup (perhaps a *kubok*) wears little more than a tall pointed hat and large beads. This sculpture was found near Azov in the north Black Sea region but is also stylistically related to the first-millennium-B.C. mummified priestesses excavated in Xinjiang, China.

ic counterparts, however, these corpses weren't royalty, and they didn't have all the mummy swaddlings that indicated they had been deliberately preserved. The extreme dry heat of the desert had quickly desiccated the bodies that had been buried in the summer, thwarting the growth of bacteria and resulting in a remarkable, inadvertent state of preservation; burial during the cold winter would have freeze-dried the corpses.[2]

I was immediately drawn to a woman recovered from a tomb near Chärchär, which lies on the southeastern rim of the Taklamakan.[3] Roughly 2,500 years old, she was clad in a still-vivid rust-colored dress, felt stockings, and pale deerskin boots. She rested on her back with her knees propped up with sticks and a pillow cradling her head. Neatly manicured hands rested on her abdomen, her wrists tied together with a braided woolen cord. A chin strap had been secured over the top of her head

to keep her jaw shut, but it had grown slack over time and now her mouth gaped open, revealing a set of well-worn teeth and a shriveled tongue. Spirals had been painted or tattooed on her face, instantly calling to mind the designs used by the ancient nomads to embellish animal

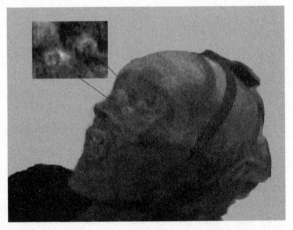

Caucasoid woman mummy excavated from the Chärchär cemetery, now in the Ürümqi historical museum. Spirals across her face are enlarged in the inset.

2. While most of the corpses owe their mummification solely to desiccation, the American textile expert Elizabeth Wayland Barber (1999, 31), who investigated the textiles worn by the mummies, reports that one of their Chinese conservators discovered a strange yellow dust on the skin of some of the later mummies that seems to have further preserved them. This may have been an animal fat painted on the skin, which seems to have kept it more supple.

3. Three women were recovered from this burial; the other two were less well preserved. For a more complete description, see Kamberi 1994 and Mallory and Mair 2000.

plaques. I hadn't begun my Sauro-Sarmatian excavations at this point, but later, of course, I realized that these scrolling designs, seen so often on steppe art, probably indicated her status as a priestess.

In fact, as I studied her features intently during that first visit, I realized with a start that instead of Asian features as I might have expected in China, the woman had many Caucasoid characteristics. Her face was long, the bridge of her nose was high, and the well-defined sockets suggested her eyes had been large and round. Her hair was reddish brown shot through with gray, and she had stood more than six feet tall. I moved from case to case, my excitement growing as I saw that other mummies also appeared to be Caucasoids, including a six-and-a-half-foot-tall man with a dark-red mustache and beard who had been wrapped in an intricately woven mantle of maroon wool.

What a shock these tall, auburn-haired mummies with their European appearance must have given the Chinese who first took them from their desert tombs! The Han Chinese (what we usually think of as ethnic Chinese) arrived in the Taklamakan region only around 120 B.C., when they established military outposts, so no one would expect to find roughly four-thousand-year-old corpses with classic Chinese features in this region; still, as Elizabeth Barber (1999, 19) notes, the prevailing wisdom in China was that "Mongol-type peoples had 'always' inhabited this entire area, ever since the spread of *Homo sapiens* around the globe at the end of the Ice Age ten to twelve thousand years ago. . . . To find Caucasians was a surprise."

And indeed it was, although I later discovered that a handful of Western explorers had long been aware of the Europoid appearance of these Chinese mummies—their reports had been published in scholarly journals starting in the late 1800s, but nothing appeared in the popular American press until April 1994, when *Discover* magazine ran an article titled "The Mummies of Xinjiang," three years after my first visit to Ürümqi. So why had it taken so long for word to get out?

In many ways, this question mirrors the situation I faced with the women warriors of the Eurasian steppes. As I mentioned earlier, Russian

scientists had known about their existence for decades before my expedition lifted our first warrior-priestess out of her Pokrovka tomb. But
they had done little with this knowledge, because it didn't fit into the
established mode of thinking about these peoples as strictly male-
dominated bands of ruthless marauders. To include in their calculations
these women of power—the priestesses, warriors, and high-ranking hearth
women—seemed either inconvenient or inconsequential to most Russian
authorities, so their story was largely brushed aside.

But inconvenient women aren't the only ones who get conveniently
overlooked by the men in charge; in the case of the Caucasoid mummies,
the same dynamic was at work with an entire people. Chinese tradition
has always maintained that the nation had developed its glorious civilization in relative isolation, free from outside influences. What they don't
always recall from their own ancient sources is that the first Caucasoids
had lived in the Tarim Basin (which contains the Taklamakan desert) for
many centuries before the arrival of the Han Chinese. But then these both-
ersome mummies, with their light-colored hair, round eyes, and second-
and first-millennium birthdates, kept popping up in the Chinese desert.

In the late 1800s and early 1900s, adventurers such as Sven Anders
Hedin, a Swedish writer and geographer, and Sir Aurel Stein, a Hungarian-
born explorer in service to the British Empire, ventured into the
Taklamakan. They mapped the region, discovered long-forgotten cities,
and excavated hundreds of desiccated mummies, many with Caucasoid
features. They reported their finds in archaeological journals and books,
but since the corpses were left to deteriorate at the excavation site, interest in them proved to be transitory. In 1978, the Chinese archaeologist
Wang Bing-Hua, who headed the Xinjiang Institute of Archaeology,
launched a systematic and fruitful search for more such mummies, but
while his and other Chinese archaeologists' efforts have yielded at least several hundred to date, the Beijing government hasn't exactly welcomed
their discoveries. With few exceptions, the mummies were reburied or
dispatched to obscure regional museums, where many were poorly con-

served and displayed without much explanation. (That is, when they were displayed at all—in one museum, I was shown mummies stacked like cordwood in a small closet; in another, they were stashed unprotected in unsanitary storage rooms where dirt and automobile pollution had covered them with powdery black dust.)

While Eastern politics can certainly be an obstacle for Eastern archaeologists, Westerners must be doubly careful not to offend the sensibilities of the history-proud Chinese. Up until the *Discover* article was published in 1994, European and American scientists who had viewed the Ürümqi mummies were discreet about these finds; we knew that to make much of a hullabaloo about something that went counter to the stance of the Chinese government would jeopardize our chances for further research in the country. And even after the Caucasian mummies were publicized, the central government remained extremely touchy about the issue, a lesson our film crew learned well during the making of the *Nova* documentary. We were constantly accompanied by Sa Sha and Zhu Jun, two young officials from the News and Culture Department of the Foreign Affairs Office, who reported to Wang Guowang, the senior official in charge of the propaganda unit of the People's Republic Army. In addition to making contacts and introducing us to the proper authorities in each town, these two young men were charged with our safety, and with ensuring that we didn't go anywhere or film anything that might offend the sensibilities of the Chinese government, an objective that turned out to be as easy as pinning a tail on a donkey.

During the recce, our director, Howard Reid, and I had met with Jacob,[4] the Uygur director of the museum in the city of Hami, who told us that, while there was an official moratorium on archaeological digs in Xinjiang province, "in the spirit of international cooperation" we would be granted the rare privilege of excavating a virgin grave for the film. It was time to make good on that promise.

---

4. Uygurs, Kazaks, and Mongols traditionally don't use last names.

Accompanied by the film crew, along with Victor Mair, professor of Chinese studies at the University of Pennsylvania, and Charlotte Roberts, a biological anthropologist from Bradford University in England, we crossed the Tien Shan and dropped into the dusty-white alkaline haze of the Taklamakan. In the museum in Hami, an ancient Silk Road city about 376 miles southeast of Ürümqi, we filmed a collection of perfectly preserved artifacts, such as pottery containers and a huge wooden cart wheel, and a pair of mummies—an old man and a young girl—on display. All had been discovered at a Bronze and Iron Age cemetery outside the nearby oasis town of Wupu, the site of our promised excavation.

The next morning, we made the hour's drive to Wupu, but instead of proceeding directly to the cemetery, we were ushered into the house of the most prosperous man in the village for a meal with his extended family. Although appreciative of their hospitality, I grew restless as the festivities stretched on; I asked several times when we might begin our excavation, but our hosts' answers were evasive. Finally, around 2:00 P.M., we were allowed to go to the cemetery, where we were greeted warmly by Jacob, who led us to a spot where two Chinese men were leaning on shovels, and explained that his crew had located a burial and they would excavate while the camera crew filmed the activities.

The men soon cleared away a patch of soft earth, uncovering a series of logs laid on top of the burial pit. "That's odd," Victor said, pointing out that the logs were placed upside down from their normal configuration, and that the usual layer of protective reeds was missing. When the excavators removed the logs, they revealed an empty pit about six feet deep. I knew something was very wrong; it should have been filled with the dirt that would have filtered in through the centuries. I sat next to the edge and leaned forward as one of the men began shoveling out dirt from the bottom of the pit. In the dim light, I could make out the mummy's rib cage, but, to my surprise, I didn't see any pottery or wooden artifacts like the ones we had just filmed at the Hami museum.

"Can you see the head?" I asked Charlotte, who was also peering intently into the chamber. "No, not yet," she replied. I was now completely baffled because the head, being the thickest part of a skeleton, is always the part that emerges first during the excavation of a normal burial. The workers brushed away more dirt, revealing the rest of the body and the limbs. I stared in disbelief. The corpse was headless.

As our eyes grew accustomed to the gloom of the pit, we could see black fungal growth on the body—unusual in a desert burial, but identical to the fungus I had observed on the poorly conserved mummies in a storage closet in the Hami museum. Charlotte and I exchanged glances, but said nothing as the excavators handed us tiny bits of fabric and fragments of wooden artifacts, which we dutifully examined for the camera's benefit. After the shoot, everything was put back into the grave and the workers replaced the logs before sprinkling a token amount of dirt on top. While walking back to our van, Charlotte nudged me—there was a set of tire tracks leading from the cemetery's gate to the excavated pit. The mystery was solved: Our hosts had borrowed a mummy from the Hami museum's storage and reburied it in the cemetery. And it's a fair bet that just before doing that, they had removed the head so there'd be no chance of filming any of those Caucasoid features the government found so vexing.

Did it really matter to our Chinese keepers if the Western world knew that Caucasoids had lived in Xinjiang more than a couple of millennia ago? In retrospect, I don't think that was the motive behind their unscrupulous ruse. I really believe it was predicated on financial gain. A string of other production companies were lining up to film mummies, and the Chinese knew they had better save fresh material for any ensuing documentaries. The most sought after artifact in the Western world was a mummy with a Caucasoid head. And the next camera crew that came through reached their objective in the same Wupu cemetery.

Realizing that what we had captured on film was far from the promised "virgin" excavation, we pinned our hopes on getting some exciting footage of mummies in the Ürümqi museum, where, as Shu had told Howard during the recce, we were cleared to shoot. But now, as we drove west along the edge of the Taklamakan toward the next archaeological site on our schedule, Wang Guowang informed us that we wouldn't be allowed to film the mummies of Ürümqi but might be able to shoot some in the Korla museum, about 370 miles to the southwest. Knowing we had no choice, Howard agreed, but when we arrived in the bustling oil city after several hot and exhausting days of driving, we were told that there were problems with this site as well.

While Howard engaged in long, tense negotiations with Wang Guowang and He Dexiu, the Chinese archaeologist who served as director of the Korla museum, the rest of the crew roamed around town, sipped tea in the lobby of the hotel, and worked in our rooms. At one point, Howard called us together and said, "The negotiations aren't going well." I could tell that beneath his cool demeanor, he was frantic that he would not get enough footage to make a viable film. More money poured into the right hands might beget permission, but then again, it might not, and our coffers weren't exactly limitless. We also knew that no matter how frustrated we became, we had to maintain a diplomatic facade—if we provoked the authorities, Beijing might elect to confiscate any footage we had before we left the country.

Finally, at eight that night, Howard phoned to say that he had struck a deal. Two hours later, after gathering up the crew and loading the van with the camera equipment, we set off through darkened city streets still teeming with people looking for nightlife or a meal at one of the outdoor restaurants that sprawled onto the sidewalks.

When we arrived at the museum, we each grabbed as much equipment as we could carry and gingerly felt our way in total darkness up the five flights of stairs to the mummy floor. Sweaty from the exertion and a bit unnerved, we discovered that the college-student guard who was supposed to be on duty was nowhere to be seen—nor was his bicycle or the key to the mummy gallery. We sat contemplatively in the dark, drinking warmed-over coffee provided by He Dexiu from a pot in his office. At 11:30, Victor howled to quit, but Howard ignored him, and fifteen minutes later the guard returned, without an explanation or an apology. (Later, we learned that he had been visiting his girlfriend.)

Our irritation melted as we entered the gallery and gazed at the mummies, which none of us had seen before. Each was displayed in a separate case, and we were amazed at their excellent condition. Charlotte commented that one woman had an unusually broad, flat face, and when He Dexiu came into the gallery, he told us that this woman had died during or shortly following a cesarean section. "There is an incision on her stomach neatly pulled together with horsehair thread," he said, "and there's something between her legs." This piqued my interest, and I asked him if we could remove the mantle that covered the mummy's body so we could examine her more closely, but the director just smiled and muttered, "Oh my, no." Frustrated but knowing better than to press the matter, Charlotte and I turned our attention to the other specimens.

A couple of Chinese workers appeared from the dark corridor and removed the glass covers shielding two of the cases. As the cinematographers set up their camera and lights, Ian Charleton, our assistant producer, and I began to shoot a few pictures with our digital cameras. Suddenly He Dexiu's irate voice echoed throughout the chamber: "Stop! Turn off your cameras! It is forbidden." Apparently filming the mummies with big professional cameras was okay, but shooting with small digital ones was verboten; they assumed that since we had contracted to shoot with one big camera, the small digital ones just weren't included in the bargain.

He Dexiu, who had led the crew that had unearthed the mummies in 1989, proudly escorted us to the next glass-enclosed cases. I was particularly interested in how the group from Tomb 2 in the Zaghanluq cemetery near Chärchär had been buried. At a depth of about a foot from current ground level, the first mummy, an adult female wearing an orange-colored chenille-weave dress, had been found on a layer of reeds, in startling condition. Her eyes appeared to have been gouged out, and her legs and arms seem to have been ripped from her body. At the very top in the same tomb was a male child who had been around a year old when he died. Well nourished and endowed with golden-brown hair, the baby had been carefully wrapped in swaddling and placed headfirst into the grave, feet sticking straight up. This was unheard of, and observing the dried tears and mucus crusted on his face, Charlotte and I speculated that the poor child might have been buried alive. His remarkable state of preservation underscored the horror of his death, his mouth stretched open in an eternal silent scream, tiny fists clenched at his sides. A second baby had also been found lying near the surface, but it had crumbled into dust when exposed to fresh air.

About two feet below this trio, separated by layers of sand, reed mats, and a sturdy wooden lid, the main burial chamber had been found. As in the case of the baby boy, the intense desert heat had done its job well, and we were amazed at the lifelike appearance of the 2,500-year-old mummy, a woman who had been around 40 years old when she died. She had been discovered neatly positioned on her back, her knees propped up with reeds and her left hand raised in what looked for all the world like a graceful gesture of benediction. Her long, heavy fall of reddish brown hair was bound in neat braids, and little tufts of colored wool had been placed in each nostril.[5] No wrinkles marred the smooth surface of her face, and thick black lashes rimmed her eyes. She was about five feet nine inches tall, slender and shapely in build. Charlotte commented that her face was flat but long, and I noticed that her prominent and narrow nose didn't fit the Mongol mold. Tattooed or painted designs, especially the spirals that covered parts of her hands and face, were reminiscent of those found on the Ürümqi mummies.[6] I knew by this time these designs meant that she had been a priestess, an assumption that was borne out by her burial artifacts, which included an altar, cultic spoons, and white wool squares

5. We're not sure why the mummy people inserted these woolen tufts, but we do know that other cultures plugged facial orifices to keep evil spirits from entering the body after death or to prevent leakage of bodily fluids.

6. These mummies came from the same cemetery as the Ürümqi mummies and date to the same time period, about 450–400 B.C. The burial artifacts of the two women have much in common indicating they shared the same social status.

painted with repeating red scroll designs. I'm sure she had been quite lovely in life, but I was startled by the degree of He Dexiu's admiration. "During the excavation," the archaeologist declared passionately, "I realized that I was holding the most beautiful woman in the world. If she were alive today, or I was alive then, I would certainly have made her my wife." (The Korla priestess isn't the only mummy to inspire such adoration; a tall, auburn-haired, four-thousand-year-old temptress in the Ürümqi museum so enraptured the local populace that she was dubbed "the Beauty of Loulan," and portraits of how she might have appeared when alive were featured on posters and CD covers.)

While the crew filmed the mummies from every conceivable angle, He Dexiu speculated that the dismembered woman and the babies had been sacrifices for the beautiful priestess, but Charlotte and I later agreed we hadn't seen any evidence to bear out this theory. Even though the condition of the dismembered woman was unusual, her body was so close to the surface that anything could have happened in the 2,500 years she lay there. He Dexiu had allowed us to examine her remains, and we saw that there wasn't any damage to her shoulder sockets or hip joints, but that her entire arm and leg bones were missing, leading us to believe that her limbs had been removed long after death.

Finally, at 4:00 A.M., Howard called it a wrap, and we gathered up our equipment and felt our way down the dark steps to the waiting van. It had been extremely hot in the museum, and I looked forward to a nice shower back at the hotel. Alas, it was not to be—

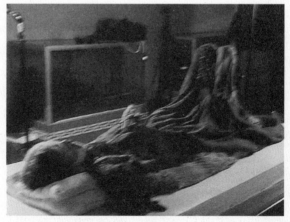

A priestess who died around 450–400 B.C. and was recovered from a Chärchär tomb, is exquisitely preserved.

145

the water had been shut off for some unexplained reason, not an unusual occurrence in the lands where I travel. I fell into a fitful sleep, haunted by the sad fate of the frightened baby and wishing that I could have seen the stunning priestess as she practiced her rites.

Even when the authorities weren't trying to outwit us or confuse us with contradictory decisions, the political climate made filming in Xinjiang a tricky business. Han Chinese, along with pockets of mostly nomadic Kazaks and Mongols, were until recently the minorities in this northwestern territory; the majority of residents are Uygurs, a Turkic-speaking mixture of Europoid and Mongoloid agriculturists who have dominated the region since the eighth century A.D. The Chinese government had promised the Uygurs their autonomy, but in the past few decades Beijing has sent millions of Han Chinese soldiers and their families into Xinjiang to clear land that they then farm as immigrants. Now a full one-third of the population of Xinjiang province is Han Chinese, and increasing at an astonishing rate, a situation that infuriates the Uygurs. They have demanded their independence, but the huge oil fields in the Taklamakan ensure that China will never surrender this lucrative territory. Uprisings are common, and the government keeps a close watch on the populace.

We witnessed evidence of this political tension firsthand on several occasions. Once during the recce, we had stopped in a village near Kuqa to service our van. The continual blasting of a public address system from a nearby kiosk was maddening, and I asked Shu to translate. "They are saying that nine of each ten public officials must leave their offices and go into the countryside to interrogate all the people. Each citizen must have a letter signed by ten people that he or she is loyal to the government. If they don't have this letter, they will go to jail."

Another time, we were detained at a roadblock on the way to Korla by police brandishing machine guns as they checked our travel papers. Shu explained that the officers were inspecting all vehicles to make sure they weren't harboring Uygur prisoners who had escaped from a nearby labor camp located in the mountains to the north. And just as we were to start filming, we were delayed several days because a BBC film crew had illegally crossed the Chinese border from Kazakstan to report on a bombing by Uygur dissidents that had killed a number of Han Chinese in Beijing. The journalists were soon discovered and deported, but all doors were slammed shut to British reporters—especially crews with cameras, including ours. It was nearly a week before our producer, working frantically in London, was able to convince the Chinese embassy that we had absolutely no ties to the BBC.

As we followed the northern Silk Road from Ürümqi on our way to Hami, one of our young escorts from the Foreign Affairs Office pointed out a series of tall red-brick towers and recounted their place in Xinjiang's history. As he spoke, I envisioned the recurring scene from two thousand years ago: A Chinese sentry, upon seeing a fire beginning to blaze on the tower to the west, knew that it signaled a nomadic Hsiung-nu raiding party quickly moving toward him. He clambered up his tower, kindled a fire, and, as the flames grew high, he turned to the east; against the silhouette of the fading sunset a new fire was beginning to flicker on the next tower.

Today Kazaks make their home on this scrubby, rolling pastureland. While some remain nomadic, others have turned to a sedentary life, peddling yogurt and felt rugs to tourists and offering rides on near-dead ponies. Mrs. Su, the dynamic cultural minister from Hami, who had driven miles over the most miserable of washboard roads to meet us, later explained with pride how her office had improved the lot of these Kazaks. "They didn't know how to sell their yogurt or charge to ride their horses," she told me as we walked toward a yurt. "We taught them tourism." Though she was charming, I couldn't quite bring myself to believe that her office had actually improved Kazak life.

Despite our assorted complications, I was able to study significant artifacts belonging to the mysterious mummy people who had inhabited this Silk Road corridor long before the first Western merchants were supposed to have set foot in the area. Even though the Europid features and strapping physiques of the well-preserved mummies clearly testify to their Western origins, a critical examination of their mortuary offerings provided additional and powerful clues toward pinning down their genesis.

The four-thousand-year-old Beauty of Loulan, for example, carried wheat and a winnowing tray with her into the next world. Wheat didn't exist in China proper at this time, so the Loulan people had to have brought it with them when they migrated from the West, where it had been domesticated much earlier. Xinjiang had no wheel-making technology during this era, yet a spoked wheel of an unusual design, like one incised on a silver bowl from northern Afghanistan, was among the artifacts coming from the Wupu cemetery. Another clue appeared as I mused over the displays of pottery containers in the Hami museum. I was astounded that they bore a close resemblance to gray-burnished pottery vessels and bronze cup shapes (called situlae—"buckets" in Latin) popular in northeastern Iran around 1200 B.C. For me there was little doubt that at least one wave of Caucasoid peoples had migrated from—or via—northeastern Iran, stopping off in the northern Afghanistan oases where they gleaned wheel-making technology.

The Xinjiang mummy people appear to have interacted with people from as far away as what is now Central Europe and Siberia. Some of the older, very simple knives and axes found in the Tarim Basin are rendered in the style and technique of those from the Minusinsk Valley in southern Siberia, where the earliest specimens predate any known Chinese bronze. This suggests that Siberian traders had come south through the Altai and Tien Shan mountains on horseback, bartering precious bronze knives for grains and perhaps other food delicacies; we know from other excavations that some traders stayed on in the region.

The wealth of woolen goods that clothed the Wupu and Chärchär mummies is also a wonderful clue. Elizabeth Barber (1999) observes that plaid twills found on the mummies bear "an uncanny resemblance to a series of textiles of the same age from Central Europe, woven by ancestors of the Celts." It's fascinating how closely their patterns, colors, and weave mimic those of modern Scottish tartans—a highland lassie would be right at home sporting one of these plaids worn by an ancient Central Asian oasis dweller.

Indo-European linguists, who study the ancient and now-dead Proto-Indo-European language, indicate that the mummy people were connected to Proto-Celtic people. This evidence comes from a series of texts discovered in the 1890s at various sites ringing the Taklamakan. Tocharian, a language dating from the sixth to eighth centuries A.D. in which the desert texts were written, is closely related to the ancient forms of Celtic. Because of this connection, the linguists believe that these languages developed simultaneously in populations more or less isolated from other Indo-European speakers. Then, at some unknown time in the shadowy past, the people in these two groups separated, and the Tocharian speakers migrated into the Tarim Basin.

In the foothills west of Korla, we found a short Tocharian inscription, a person's name, on the wall of a seventh-century cave that we had filmed. Much more interesting and significant to my ethnographer's mind, however, are the portraits in that and many other caves of burly Caucasoid men with green or blue eyes and red or blond hair and beards, dressed in costumes remarkably like those worn by the Sassanian nobles from Iran.[7]

The linguistic evidence has tempted scholars to conclude that the mummy people might have been the ancestors of the Tocharians although the languages of the earlier people probably were Iranian, and were related to their Central European predecessors. Han Chinese historians, however, steadfastly identify the nomadic Yüeh Chih as the Tocharians who ranged over western China in the fifth century B.C. (See Chapter 10 for more on the Yüeh Chih in northern Afghanistan.)

---

7. The Sassanians, who followed the Parthians (200 B.C.–A.D. 200) in controlling the Silk Road through greater Iran and Mesopotamia, remained in power until they were replaced by Islamic invaders in the seventh century.

Changing Lifestyles in the Tarim Basin

I originally came to Xinjiang in search of archaeological evidence of a Saka presence in the territory and clues to their relationship with the Saka in Kazakstan. A multitude of artifacts found in museums and burial sites satisfied that quest, and I began to picture how these adventurous nomads might have affected the sedentary peoples they encountered.

It would seem that around 2000 B.C., a Caucasoid people came from the West and settled on the edge of the Taklamakan desert, relying on agriculture and the domestication of a few animals, including donkeys and sheep, for their subsistence. As we stood in one of the cemeteries of the Chowhougou people that lie between the northern Taklamakan rim and the Tien Shan Mountains, the archaeologist Lui EnGou pointed out that artifacts from the burials reveal that around 900 B.C., people came on horseback, riding down the southern slopes of the Tien Shan into the oasis villages. They probably traded sheep or mutton for wheat, woven woolen fabrics for felted textiles, maybe even bronzes for brides. Over the centuries as the clans needed more pastures, they began herding in the rich high Tien Shan pastures, but they continued to visit the southern lowlands to exchange commodities, innovations, and techniques with the oasis dwellers. We know that by 750 B.C. a good portion of the sedentary people had embraced the nomadic lifestyle, for at this time we begin to see distinct changes in burial patterns and mortuary offerings. Horse hooves and hides as well as bridle bits were found in special votive pits dug adjacent to the burial pits. Equally revealing is the fact that instead of one or two skeletons in fetal position in a single burial pit, now up to nineteen skeletons were laid out on their back, indicating that the now-nomadic Chowhougou people brought their deceased from the high mountain summer pastures to bury them near their winter home, a custom similar to our Sauro-Sarmatians', except the seasonal patterns are reversed.

As I stood in a Chowhougou cemetery, only a few miles to the north the canyons drew dark smudges on the Tien Shan foothills. They also provided passages to the high intermountain pastures where we had recently encountered some Mongol herders. I instantly conjured the scene about 2,700 years ago: A myriad of young village men, rebelling against the plow, took up the reins of their horses and rode up those canyons. They had become nomadic herders—a much easier and more romantic way of life than following a donkey down long furrows and weeding rows of plants in the hot summer sun.

But some of these interpretations aren't so clear cut. For starters, there's about a thousand-year gap between the last of the Iron Age mummies (300 B.C.) and the first evidence of the Tocharian language (A.D. 700), a gap that most historians are reluctant to cross. My investigations have further widened the field and the evidence points to influences from several cultural regions (see "Changing Lifestyles in the Tarim Basin," page 150) and farther back in time (see Chapter 9, which reveals other European connections with the Tarim Basin). For now, we are all left to ponder that red hair, those distinctive plaids, those sister languages, and now the distinguishing pottery and wheels from the burials.

No one can be exactly sure what kind of interactions took place between the mummy people and the nomads, who were Caucasoids and spoke related Indo-Iranian languages so many thousands of years ago. The scrolling tattoos and plaited reddish-brown hair of the Caucasoid mummies, features that are so foreign in China today, only lead my imagination to further ideas about these ancient travelers. We can but speculate about the route of their journey and their reasons for coming to this hot and dry landscape. What we do know for certain is the beauty of the resulting culture. The mummies of Ürümqi inspired not only a generation of protective scholars, but myself as well. My biggest regret is that I couldn't examine them more closely. What might I have discovered if He

Dexiu had lifted the sheet and allowed me to examine the mummy with the cesarean section? What would we have unearthed if we'd excavated a burial mound ourselves? Such questions continue to burn in my mind, as the mummy people remain obscured by time and bureaucracy.

CHAPTER NINE

ANCIENT FERTILITY RITUALS
IN THE TIEN SHAN

The aptly titled *Mysterious Mummies of China*, the *Nova* documentary that resulted from our adventures in Xinjiang, provides an all-too-brief glimpse of a petroglyph site that sheds some light on some of the mummy people's origins. It also reveals a fascinating component of the ancients' fertility rituals.

In 1991 during my first visit to Xinjiang, Wang Bing-Hua, then director of the Institute of Archaeology in Ürümqi, introduced me to a grotto of carved art with the difficult-to-pronounce Chinese name of Kangjiashimenzi. After showing me the mummies and their artifacts in his earnest and formal way, Wang Bing-Hua abruptly asked if I would like to see his petroglyphs. From the sudden eagerness of his tone and the sparkle in his dark eyes, I knew that they had to be something unusual and nodded my assent. He pulled a slim, hardbound volume out of a cluttered bookcase and opened the cover, pointing to a schematic drawing of human dancers, gleaming silver figures that snaked across the cinnamon-colored endpapers. He then revealed the color plates in the book, and my astonishment mounted as he turned each page. By this time, I had seen thousands of prehistoric petroglyphs, but never before had I witnessed such a large crowd of well-executed human figures portrayed on a stone surface in Central Asia. Wang Bing-Hua chuckled with pleasure at my enthusiasm and volunteered to make arrangements for me to see these wonders in person.

Only long afterward did I realize how many strings my helpful colleague must have pulled to arrange a visit to a site that was in an area completely closed to foreigners because of its proximity to military outposts and political prisons. But pull he did, and a few days later, Matt and I found ourselves following the most northern of the old Silk Roads: a serpentine path along the Tien Shan, once frequented by merchants in camel caravans, nomadic herders and raiders, and throngs of other travelers. After a two-hour drive, we stopped at Hutubei to collect the local archaeologist whom Wang Bing-Hua had directed to guide us. A quiet backwater in 1991, this small city was mainly populated by Han Chinese tradespeople and bureaucrats serving the peasant farmers transplanted from the nation's interior. Soon we turned off the paved highway, jostling along in our Jeep on a dirt road leading to an intermountain valley of the Tien Shan, toward the site, which is only about sixty miles southwest of Ürümqi. Along the road were walled compounds, shaded by rows of poplar trees where the Han Chinese had settled. Each family received a twelve-acre plot to farm, and I saw women winnowing wheat cut by hand with scythes, tossing the grain into the air from large, flat baskets, letting the chaff swirl away in the wind.

It was captivating to watch a Bronze Age technique in action, but farming small acreages without modern equipment is largely inefficient; the families were barely ekeing out a living. Muddy puddles at the edge of the yards hinted they were not blessed with modern plumbing and drew their water by buckets from hand-dug wells. Later I was told that occasionally a clever Han Chinese would lease his neighbors' plots, buy a tractor and harvester, and with skillful management became a productive farmer. Still, it was obvious that the government had little interest in modernizing the Xinjiang agricultural industry.

Beyond the compounds, we began to climb to higher elevations in the Tien Shan, motoring past small adobe houses where Kazak nomads wintered. Though it was summer, I did glimpse a few older grandparents who had remained to mind the younger children and tend to small garden plots. Higher up, we stopped to watch a solitary herder urge a string of Bactrian camels to the summer pasturelands. Our guide pointed out our destination, an incredibly massive dark-red sandstone rock that had weathered over the eons. It was visible across several valleys, jutting hundreds of feet above the softer green rolling hills. Wang Bing-Hua had described this distinctive formation as a "castle," but its intricate folds of stone reminded me of a Gothic cathedral, while the total effect was of a great fortress. Our road ended far below the base, so we parked and hiked up a steep hill to the monolith's grotto that housed the much-anticipated petroglyphs.

Through no fault of the photographer, the images that Wang Bing-Hua had shown me didn't begin to capture the magnitude of the bas-relief carvings. They ran from under the sloping grotto roof on the back wall, to a point graduating in size toward the ground, probably ten feet in length. But no sun could reach this protected area to rake the light across the scene that was so necessary to bring out their form and beauty on the flesh-colored stone. I was

Kangjiashimezi petroglyph sandstone cliff in Xinjiang, China. The grotto where the petroglyphs were carved is at the base toward the left in the illustration.

155

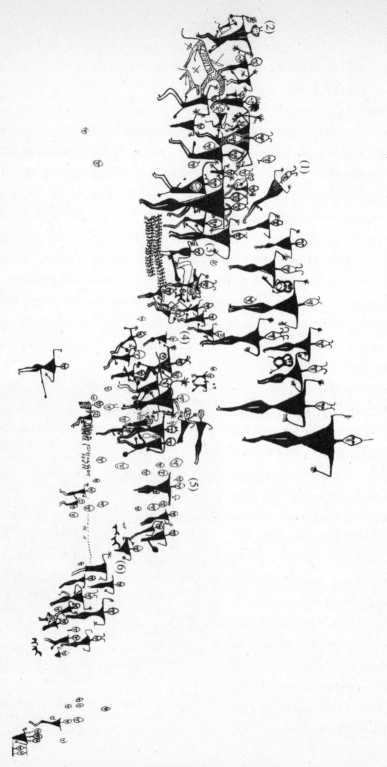

Schematic of the Kangjiashimenzi petroglyphs.

completely amazed at the scale and sophistication of the tableau before me. More than sixty figures were arrayed along the walls, ranging from larger-than-life-size humans to rows of diminutive people with their arms linked around each other's shoulders as if they were a chorus line of pre-historic Rockettes. Most of the figures are dancing, knees bent, fingers splayed, their upper arms extending straight in line with their shoulders, the right forearm bent up, the left turned down. Several sets of bows and arrows, traditional symbols of power and hunting magic, are sprinkled throughout. Although there are half a dozen or so dogs meandering through one group or another, plus two sets of heraldic animals that I took to be goats, and two large, striped felines, probably tigers, carved amid the humans, this could not be mistaken for an Animal Style scene, since the vast majority of the characters are human. As the tableau progresses to the right, not all of the humans are fully drawn, a few of the smaller ones in the bottom tiers lack heads, and, curiously, many disembodied heads float through the mix.

A specific canon of art certainly dictated the style in which the males and females were portrayed, and nearly all the figures appear to be naked, a condition emphasized by the enormous erect phalluses displayed on the men. The women, whose images (contrary to average human sizes) are much larger than the men's, are indicated by flattened conical-shaped headdresses, embellished with tiny antennae projecting upward and outward. The women's bodies are also uniquely portrayed: They have large inverted-triangle torsos, while prominent hips and thighs form a second, smaller triangle. The men's heads contrast with the women's as they are oval (apparently hatless), and their torsos are trapezoid, with sticklike legs.

For a long time, we just let the intricacy and scope of the images sink in. I tried to connect them with the hundreds of other petroglyphs I had studied through the years, but no similar art came to mind—these carvings are truly unique. Once, I glanced over at Matt, knowing full well that my husband, ever the engineer, was captivated by the sheer logistical marvel the project represented. The lowest scene was a good ten feet above

Double-headed female dancing image flanked by other dancers in the Kangjiashimenzi petroglyphs of Xinjiang, China.

the current ground level—and this distance would have been greater in antiquity than today—and he repeatedly shook his head in admiration as he pondered the scaffolding requirements for such an ongoing job.

But soon the questions emerged. When were the images on this majestic piece of rock art carved? Who were their creators? And could there be a connection with the mummies in the Xinjiang museums that I had seen only a few days before?

With all the technological tools at a scientist's disposal today, you might think that the first question, at least, would be easy to answer. But petroglyphs are notoriously tricky to date—carbon 14 dating requires organic material and none is available on stone, and studying micromorphological changes in the rocks is still a fledgling technique. Thus archaeologists usually depend on stylistic, ethnographic, or historical comparisons made with other reliably dated artifacts. Wang Bing-Hua had a few well-considered theories concerning the age of the Kangjiashimenzi petroglyphs, but I needed to make my own determinations.

Clearly, the petroglyphs aren't modern—recent carvings have a bright appearance and sharp edges, while these are muted and soft. They certainly weren't the work of ancient nomads who, although concerned with fertility, depict the concept in zoomorphic terms and didn't represent their own fecundity, concentrating instead on depictions of domestic, indigenous wild, and fantastic animals (thus the term "Animal Style"). When the Bronze Age or Iron Age people did render a human form, it was in the stick-figure style, representing anthropomorphized sun gods, a few paper-doll dancers, or the occasional shamanlike image found at Tamgaly—light-years away from these expressive and well-realized characters.

Since nomads dominated this region from around 750 B.C., that seems to eliminate both the Iron Age and the medieval period for their dating. Nor do they seem to belong to the Neolithic period; the sophistication of the art, as well as the technology and the leadership, required to construct this 29.5-foot-high and 45.93-foot-long tableau rules out that earlier era.[1] That leaves us with the Bronze Age, an estimation with which I knew Wang Bing-Hua concurred.

Stylistic considerations aside, other clues to the origins of the petroglyphs may be gleaned from their subject matter. While many interpretations of art rest on the well-known and generally accepted iconography backed by religious and secular writings—for example, in medieval Europe, a unicorn symbolized purity; a lion meant bravery—divining the meaning of prehistoric art must be based on comparisons of style, iconography, and cultural affinities. This is especially true for the Kangjiashimenzi petroglyphs, and I began to look for some well-established conventions.

The long, narrow faces of the humans in the tableau, with their pro-

---

1. In China, the Neolithic period (Stone Age) began in the sixth millennium B.C. In the middle of the third millennium B.C., many Chalcolithic (copper-stone) sites reveal that craftspeople were hammering raw copper while still chipping stone tools. The true metal casting of the Bronze Age began in the second millennium B.C. and lasted until iron was introduced around 750 B.C., heralding the arrival of the Iron Age. In the realm of the nomads, the beginning of the early medieval period occurred around A.D. 300.

nounced brow ridges, oval eyes, and prominent noses, indicate that they are Caucasoids—and obviously these artists would have represented their own people. Most likely, they belonged to one of the migrating groups that came to the Tarim Basin. They could even have been some of the mummy people. But from where? I was stumped, unable to identify any parallels in the vast arena of Iranian and Mesopotamian art that would provide a clue to the artists' (and therefore to the culture's) precise roots.

Back at my desk in Berkeley, I began to analyze the details in the tableau to interpret the artists' motivations. The tableau seemed to be separated into several smaller scenes, probably representing an evolution over time, and indicating a shift in the emphasis of the rituals. Several images had unique characteristics that caught my attention. The most unusual figure seemed to be masked, with big ears, antennae protruding from the top of its head, red (probably ochre coloring) "suspenders and bib," and projections dangling from its posterior. This combination of motifs, particularly the mask and dangling accoutrements, added up to "shaman." And it was about to impregnate a small image with splayed legs and a distinctive triangle in the pubic area (in ancient art the pubic triangle represents the fecundity of the female). Another group of figures also stood out. On their chests they wore human heads, while their bodies combined both the male and the female attributes: the double-triangular body and large headdress of the female, erect penis of the male.

As I compiled a checklist of the iconography, I could see that fertility symbols permeated the entire tableau: the hypnotic dance poses of the women, some of whom are about to fall while others have already collapsed into a deep trance; the erections as long as the men are tall; women lying with splayed legs, receptive to male partners. Even the felines and one pair of the small wild goats carved between the dancers have erections. As the tableau progresses to the right, we encounter lines of little progeny, marking the positive results of an inseminating ritual. And then there were the hermaphrodites—did they constitute ancient symbols to ensure fertilization, combining a gestating female with an inseminating male into a single image?[2] Whatever the symbolism, this preoccupation with fertility is easy to understand. In primitive societies with a horrifyingly high infant mortality rate and a comparative minuscule life expectancy, procreation was crucial for community survival.[3]

I also speculated as to why these ancient artists had spent so many precious resources on this project—such a masterpiece required innumerable hours traveling from their oasis village to this remote location—the mountainous climate is not suitable for agriculture—enormous time and energy to build the scaffolding, and then long sessions of patiently carving the rock art. Much as today, when people look for religious reassurance through building church spires and temple domes that reach for the heavens, so did these ancients choose an awe-inspiring structure. I also believe that the tableau held multilayered meanings. Annually (probably each spring), the priestesses and priests, who controlled the villages' fertility, made a pilgrimage to the mountain grotto to celebrate a vital rite, knowing that the carved representations of the dancers accentuated and perpetuated the power of the ceremony. It was choreography never to be forgotten by the ensuing generations.

In his book on Kangjiashimenzi, Wang Bing-Hua (1992, 43) writes that "the whole scene reflects a communal happiness in procreation, population increase, and the important role of a healthy, virile male." All these elements are present, of course, but this assessment gives remarkably short shrift to the female participants who dominate the tableau, not just in sheer numbers but in larger-than-life size and prominent placement. The biggest figures, some of which measure more than six and a half feet high, are women—the male figures are half these dimensions. The ladies stand in their graceful poses, top row and center, looming over the rest of the action. Nor are they mere breeding vessels waiting to be filled. Following the

---

2. Analogies from cultures such as the Early Nomads suggest these figures might represent transvestites, priestesses, or priests. See Chapter 10 for more on these statuses.

3. In the Early Iron Age cemeteries of Pokrovka, for example, roughly 33 percent of the burials were infants.

accepted iconography of the era, the shape of the heads announces the women are wearing headdresses, which in the ancient world were powerful emblems of high status; in light of other dominant characteristics, the circumstances strongly suggest that these were women of authority—that they were priestesses who maintained the fecundity of their people.

I also see a subtheme. In ancient European cultures, canines were often symbols of death, or guardians of the portals to the otherworld, and the dogs interspersed on this tableau may represent such a belief among these people. This concept seems to play into the symbology of the disembodied heads (representing ancestor worship?), some of which are displayed on the chests of the hermaphrodites. Perhaps these commingled personalities were the channel to communicate with, and to glean knowledge and power from, the ancestral spirits.

I thought about those elegant and purposeful Kangjiashimenzi dancers often, but I didn't have an opportunity to return to the petroglyph site until Howard Reid enlisted me for his *Nova* crew six years later. During the course of our speculations over the possible origins of the mummy people, I remembered the Europid appearance of the carved figures of Kangjiashimenzi, the majesty of the tableau, and suggested to Howard that they would make a worthy contribution to the documentary. He, too, was much taken with this highly unusual example of rock art. Though we couldn't be certain of the connection between the carving and the mummy people, we were both enraptured by the possibilities.

Three weeks after we finished filming the documentary, on a visit to the archaeological museum in Kishinev, Moldova, I stopped to admire the magnificent Cucuteni-Tripolye pottery vessels. These pieces were as tall as two feet, created by an influential agricultural society that dominated Romania, Moldova, and western Ukraine in 4000 to 3000 B.C.[4] Perhaps because

---

4. The Cucuteni people lived in Romania and Moldova, the Tripolye in western Ukraine. At first, scientists thought they were two different groups, but then later discovered that they were actually a single, homogenous culture.

nomads produced such poorly fired, undecorated pottery, the beauty and sophistication of these particular artifacts stopped me in my tracks. Painted on this storage vessel in dark ochre-red against a cream-colored background was an Eastern European woman who was the stylistic twin to the graceful dancers in the Xinjiang grotto. She had the same distinctive triangulated body and held her arms in the same unusual dance pose. Although no men are included in the scene and the woman is clothed, the Cucuteni-Tripolye figure must be associated with fertility, as she is rendered

Dancer, represented in the same style as the Kangjiashimenzi dancers were painted on Cucuteni-Tripolye pottery.

within an elliptical cowrie, a seashell that symbolizes the female reproductive system. And, just like her Far Eastern counterparts, the woman is accompanied by dogs, which are sketched in a similar manner.

I couldn't believe my luck, to have come directly from the Kangjiashimenzi petroglyphs only to find these stylistically identical Cucuteni-Tripolye dancers.[5] I had little doubt that a wave of migrants from Eastern Europe had arrived in the Tarim Basin, but could I find the evidence?

There was one major difference between the single pottery woman and the complex images, male and female, in the grotto tableau: the orgiastic factor. If the Cucuteni-Tripolye culture had spawned dancing females, somewhere along their journey to the East the original feminine ritual had incorporated erotic components involving men and overt procreation. Where could this have happened?

Three years passed before I found answers, in the work of Yuri

---

5. Later I found dancing women of the same style in the art of several other agricultural societies that were contemporaneous with the Cucuteni-Tripolye people. Also see Davis-Kimball, 2001b.

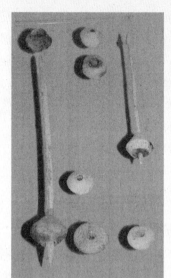

right:
Spindle whorls and spindles from Cucuteni-Tripolye settlement sites in Moldova.

far right:
Female figurines from Cucuteni-Trpiolye settlement sites in Moldova.

Rassamakin, a Russian archaeologist who had assembled an enormous collection of reports on excavations stretching from Eastern Europe to the north Black Sea (Levine et al. 1999). He was the Sherlock Holmes who followed the trail of the distinctive Cucuteni–Tripolye pottery shards, spindle whorls, and other artifacts from settlement site to settlement site. He discovered that after a schism in the culture, the Tripolye people migrated eastward into the northern Caucasus and the Don and Volga river regions. Their trail after this point is less clear, but we imagine that before the close of the second millennium B.C., they continued on to the oases of northern Afghanistan (or Bactria, as it was known in the ancient world),[6] where the orgiastic element that we see in the Kangjiashimenzi petroglyphs must have seeped into their rituals. (See Chapter 10 for the possible origin in ancient Bactria of the orgiastic rites associated with the goddess Cybele.) The demure dancers of the Cucuteni–Tripolye culture were about to shed their clothes and enter into a bacchanalian fertility

6. The people who lived in northern Afghanistan and southern Uzbekistan in the third millennium B.C. are now known as the Bactria–Margiana Archaeological Culture, or the BMAC (Ligabue 1988).

ritual, in which men played a contributing role. From Bactria, their descendants pressed on to the Tarim Basin, where they left one of the most imaginative and graphic representations in the entire history of art, the Kangjiashimenzi petroglyphs.

Another crucial clue in the petroglyphs to the origin of a possible second group who celebrated in the grotto is the depiction of pairs of rearing animals, necks arched and both front and rear feet touching their partners'. I immediately was reminded of the heraldic ibex (wild mountain goat) ubiquitously cast as Luristan bronzes, cultic artifacts that are associated with the Tree of Life and fecundity.[7] These small bronze statuettes were clandestine prizes from the burials in western Iran's Zagros Mountains (just west of Afghanistan). The ibex images on the petroglyphs, combined with the vessels in the Hami museum, only reinforce my theory that some worshippers had come from this region, and they were the ones who had organized the carving of the heraldic ibex pairs.

From style to semantics, the Kangjiashimenzi tableau yielded many secrets about the ancients' dependence on fertility rites to assure their lasting survival. The iconography allowed me to piece together the Tripolye populations' cross-continental journey from Eastern Europe to Afghanistan to the oases around the Taklamakan desert, which the tediously assembled archaeological details have verified. Those who trekked to this mountain fortress for the august ceremonies were the selected fortunates, the priestesses and priests who unquestionably commissioned this magnificent tableau.

---

7. Thousands of Luristan bronzes, dating from 1500–500 B.C. that were mostly clandestinely excavated, flooded the art market during the twentieth century. The bronzes included horse trappings, utensils, weapons, and jewelry, but the votive objects with heraldic goats and anthropomorphic images are unique in the art world. Named after the Lurs, the local residents in the Zagros Mountains in western Iran where they were buried, their origin is unknown—although they have been attributed to the Cimmerians or the early Medes and Persians, all of whom were nomadic tribes originating in Eurasia.

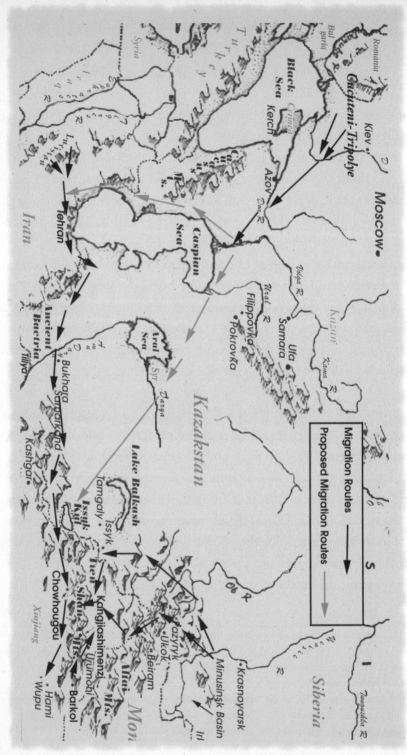

Archaeologically verified and proposed routes traveled by Chalcolithic and Early Bronze Age Cucuteni-Tripolye peoples from Europe to the Tarim Basin.

The Stone House at Barkol

Years ago, adjacent to the ancient Silk Road that follows the northern Tien Shan foothills toward the Gansu Corridor, a caravanserai bustled with activity upon the arrival of yet another string of camels laden with bolts of silk. Today a small Chinese village snuggles against the hillside above a small lake. Arriving in the evening, we overnighted there in order to hike the next morning to the base of the mountains where archaeologist Wang Bing-Hua had excavated the remains of one of four stone "houses" once occupied by a Bronze Age clan. This could have been the home of Kangjiashimenzi ritualizers as, although it would have taken a week or two to walk to the grotto, it was an ideal homesite for early agriculturists.

The remains of a Bronze Age stone house near Barkol, Xinjiang, China, with the Tien Shan Mountains in the background.

The house walls, constructed of carefully laid, huge granite stones, were still standing six to seven feet high. We entered the house through a wide, curving stone corridor that probably sheltered a few sheep and goats from the freezing winter cold. Circles of darker earth in the dirt floor signaled the placement of posts, long ago rotted away, revealing that the house had been roofed with a post-and-beam construction. I had noticed the same roofing on houses when we hiked through the village on our way to the stone house. Small branches had covered the space between the posts; then woven reed mats were laid on top before the surface was sealed with a mixture of mud and straw. Such an adobe roof indicated that rainfall was sparse on this side of the Tien Shan but probably adequate for dry-farm wheat, which is not irrigated.

Several large and well-worn stone mortars used for grinding grain lay on the floor, again the telltale sign of a settled society. I noticed that volunteer wheat still grew between the large stones that dotted the slopes and around the house. Perhaps these villagers had not even had to sow grain, as a new crop would have sprung from seeds lost during the previous harvest. Because the mortars were abandoned on the floor, I wondered if they had also turned to nomadism, leaving their heavy equipment behind.

But then our guide recounted an amazing sequence to the Bronze Age story. When Wang Bing-Hua excavated the house, he found about thirty skeletons lying on the floor and among the artifacts were two very large bronze cauldrons of the precise style used by the nomadic Yüeh Chih. This confederacy had occupied this region from the fifth to the third century B.C. before they were driven eastward by the Hsiung-nu, another powerful nomadic confederacy.

It would appear that the Yüeh Chih had taken shelter within the walls of this already ancient house and were then surprised by a fierce Hsiung-nu raiding party. I wondered if the thirty skeletons lying on the floor comprised the entire clan, or did a few survivors flee with their lives? If the latter were the case, the Hsiung-nu must have continued to hold the territory and the Yüeh Chih were never able to retrieve their dead, and as the centuries passed, the stone house filled with debris and dirt, as Wang Bing-Hua had found it.

CHAPTER TEN

MOTHER GODDESSES AND ENAREES

Before I had ever encountered the Kangjiashimenzi fecundity rituals, I came across a fertility-related feline in Bactria. At that time, I didn't know I would find the Tien Shan snow leopards in the Issyk warrior-priestess burial, or in the fertility rite petroglyphs, or that they might even be connected to the Great Mother Goddess in far-off Anatolia. I was in the Hermitage museum in St. Petersburg looking for the felt textiles preserved in the Pazyryk frozen burials when this ivory *akinakes* (sword shield) from Bactria waylaid me. Little did I realize the significance of that ancient land, now northern Afghanistan—that it must have been the major portal between East and West long before the Silk Road of the Chinese and Romans, or of Marco Polo and the Mongol Chinese emperor Kublai Khan.

It was 1985 and my fellow tourists, herded by our Intourist guide Natasha, had left me behind in the rear hallway of the Hermitage. Staying on schedule was sacred to these guides. A half-hour at this monument, twenty minutes' driving time, an hour at the next—their hapless charges

An ivory *akinakes* (nomadic sword) sheath carved from ivory. This was excavated from the Takht-I Sangin, a cultic site on the Oxus River (now the Amu Darya) in northern Afghanistan. The unusual iconography of a lion holding a spotted deer has been interpreted by some scholars as the domination of the Achaemenid kings over the nomadic tribes in this region. As the feline played such a prominent role among the ancient nomadic people, perhaps it had once been a prized possession of a warrior priestess or priest.

were lucky for a glimpse at each exhibit. On this occasion I stopped when I saw a display of children's artwork, and when I looked up, I could find no one from my group. I was panicky at first, but soon realized I knew the time our bus would leave and could meet up with the group then. So I set off in pursuit of the nomadic galleries that I really wanted to see.

Sounds easy. Not so! Gallery markers, if any, were in Russian, and I had just begun to study this difficult language, so I only knew such useful phrases such as "The cat fell off the bed." I found a KGB-looking guard, mustered my courage, and asked directions. We communicated via charades, and soon I was making my way up a long flight of stairs to transverse the czars' old Winter Palace, before descending several long flights to the basement galleries I sought. When I reached the top level, my path was blocked by exhibition cases extending into the passageway. As I walked around, I noted ancient coins and a few bronze pieces. Then I came to a sudden stop. I knew that I recognized the object lying on wine-colored velvet. But from where? I moved to a label and in my limited Russian I made out "Takht-i Sanguin." I remembered that Takht-i Sanguin had been a *tepe,* a mound that held the remains of a cultic temple on the Oxus River in Bactria.[1] Of course. This was a sheath for an *akinakes,* a Scythian dagger, carved and etched from ivory in the form of a feline—an upright lion on hind feet cradling a spotted deer.

The lion *akinakes* sheath seems to be a far-fetched link to what is often credited as the world's oldest religion, the worship of the Great Mother Goddess, which took many strange turns as it wound its way through a series of widespread cultures. It has never been my overt intent to research the Mother Goddess sources, yet if one studies the art and history of any of the ancient Near Eastern or Central Asian cultures, one immediately finds from the very beginning the strong presence of the Mother Goddess. So even though I preferred following nomads to remote pastures, the mystery of the Mother Goddess called to me. It wasn't long before I began piecing together her special symbols—the most dominant being in feline form.

Any study of ancient religions must begin in southern Turkey, where the earliest known archaeological evidence of human spiritual beliefs was discovered in the early 1960s by the Scottish archaeologist James Mellaart. There, in a thirty-two-acre mound known as Çatal Hüyük (*hüyük* is Turkish for "mound"), Mellaart unearthed the remnants of a city that has been radiocarbon-dated to approximately 6500–5800 B.C. The ornate decorations and suggestive iconography present in forty of the two hundred buildings he excavated led Mallaart to conclude that some rooms had been shrines, and that the Neolithic inhabitants of this ancient city had worshipped a Great Mother Goddess. The most famous artifact he excavated is a good-size terra-cotta sculpture of a full-figured woman in the process of giving birth while sitting between two massive leopards.

Mellaart's interpretations have come under fire from many, including

---

1. This temple, excavated by the Russian archaeologist Boris Litvinskii, was in the area where much of the famous Oxus Treasure, now in the British Museum, was recovered in the nineteenth century. The river is now the Amu Darya.

Ian Hodder, the British archaeologist who resumed Mellaart's work nearly thirty years after the Turkish government put an end to the older explorer's work in the country. As I found out firsthand in 1997 when I visited Çatal Hüyük at the request of a German film crew reporting on the current Mother Goddess movement, Hodder maintained that because almost all the female figures are tiny, they do not necessarily denote the existence of a Mother Goddess culture, and that the artwork might have celebrated mortal women's domestic roles, not a goddess's divinity. His remarks were published, and Mellaart rebuffed that contention testily, referring to the birthing female between two snarling felines:"It's obviously a goddess—no human being sits on two leopards!"[2]

Çatal Hüyük is a forty-five-minute drive south of Konya, a modern Islamic city in the heart of Turkey, and areas of the famed ancient settlement are being lovingly restored while excavations continue. These days the site even boasts up-to-date laboratories and its own Web site. Over the course of several days, I walked through the excavated remains, where once the dense maze of boxy mud-brick dwellings had no streets, and entrance to the living quarters was gained through roof-top openings. I examined the faint red traces of wall paintings from a newly excavated sector, and the remains of a bull's skull, that a team from UC Berkeley led by Ruth Tringham had just discovered in their newly opened sector.[3] Equally important, I talked with knowledgeable people on each side of the Mother Goddess controversy: Hodder weighed in with his cautious interpretations; and representatives of the Frauenmuseum (Women's Museum) in Munich, Germany, passionately and articulately defended the validity of viewing the site as proof of a Neolithic culture that worshipped the Mother Goddess.

---

2. Interviews with both Hodder and Mellaart appear in Robert Hunzig, "A Tale of Two Archeologists," *Discover* magazine, May 1999.

3. Although identified as a "bull's head," both cows and bulls of this breed of cattle had horns, so we can't rule out these remains belonging to a female animal.

Female riding a lion as depicted on a compartmentalized seal in the Bactrian culture in the 17th century B.C.

From an archaeological point of view, I was compelled to conclude that because the figurines were so tiny (some less than an inch high), and because they had been deliberately broken before they were placed in nonreligious or noncultic locales—such as building foundations, ovens, and grain bins—they were not Mother Goddess images. They do, it seems to me, have a fecundity connotation. Grain was a symbol of fertility. In fact, until only recently it was the staff of life.

The lady with the leopards, however, *is* suggestive of a powerful being, and although we don't know her status at Çatal Hüyük, the concept of the Great Mother Goddess controlling animals becomes well established in Mesopotamia, Anatolia, and Syria. In the early second millennium B.C., the Mistress of Animals, as this motif became known, appeared on the so-called compartmentalized seals in Bactria,[4] as well as in seventeen-century-B.C. artwork where she sits sidesaddle on a lion. A few centuries later she made her Anatolian debut displayed on intricate cylinder seal artwork.[5]

The Mistress of Animals is only one of the guises of the Great Mother Goddess, or Matar, who is mentioned in nearly a dozen Phrygian rock

---

4. Davis-Kimball 2000b. In the ancient Near East before around 2400 B.C., stamp seals in stone or bronze, with a round or square flat surface in which a design was carved, were pressed into soft clay to seal a container or mark an object. Later, stone cylinder seals with elaborate scenes of gods and goddesses on the surface were rolled over the soft-sealing clay. The larger round cast-bronze pieces from Bactria, with their fanciful geometric, floral, zoomorphic, and mythological designs have a surface resembling a cookie cutter, and thus were termed "compartmentalized" seals. Today they are considered amulets.

5. Specifically, the Mistress of Animals appears on cylinder seals dated from 1430 to 1360 B.C. from the Mitanni culture, which is said to have entered Anatolia (modern-day Turkey) from the Zagros Mountains in western Iran.

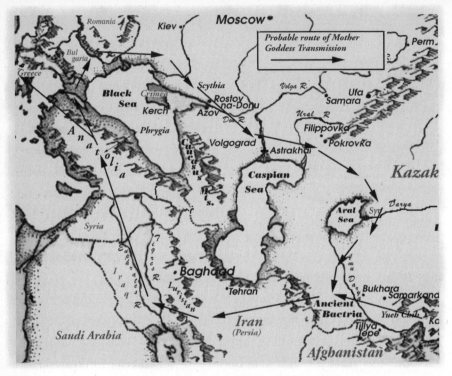

Probable transmission routes of the Female Riding a Feline.

inscriptions from the early first millennium B.C.[6] Aside from controlling wild nature, Matar was the mother of the gods, humans, and animals; she healed the sick and protected the faithful in times of war. She was associated with mountains and fertility, liberally bestowing fruitful harvests, prolific herds, and the blessings of many children (Roller 1999). In western Phrygia, reliefs depicted the goddess holding a lion cub and flanked by lions that placed their paws on her head. She was a sovereignty goddess, meaning that Phrygian kings probably had intercourse with her priestesses to guarantee their right to the throne. Like Lilith and other female deities, Matar started out as powerful yet benevolent. But as the centuries wore on and her legend rubbed shoulders with new and often

---

6. The ancient kingdom of Phrygia existed in west-central Anatolia. The Phrygian ruler Midas is renowned in popular mythology because of his golden touch, a legend that must have originated because of the quantities of precious-metal vessels that were placed in his crypt.

patriarchal societies, a darker and more complex portrait emerged. The kindly Matar seems to have evolved into the deity that became known as Cybele.

Through trade, migration, and military contacts, Cybele became venerated throughout Mesopotamia, Thrace, Anatolia, Elam, and Bactria; centuries later, she made her debut in Greece and then Rome.[7] As her ideology spread and transmuted, she remained a powerful goddess, but one who was unlucky in love, with some dire consequences for the mortals who served her. Different versions of her legend abounded, but after her adoption by the Greek and Roman worlds, most of the stories held that the divine Cybele had become enamored of a beautiful youth named Attis (who in many tales was her own son).[8] In some, the love of the goddess proved too potent for the mortal, and he went mad; in others, Cybele deliberately drove him insane to prevent him from marrying another woman or to punish him for dallying with a nymph. All the stories agree on one rather grisly feature: The crazed youth ended up castrating himself and dying days later of the injury.

At first, Attis was just a poor, doomed mortal, who, in some versions, was transformed into a pine tree upon his death, violets springing from his blood. But as the centuries passed, he began to assume more importance, and the myths took on a new slant: Attis had been resurrected, the legends now proclaimed, and awarded divine status by the gods, who hailed his bravery and beauty. Worshipped as the god of vegetation—his emasculating sacrifice was supposed to have lent fertility to the earth—he inspired his own cult, which was linked to Cybele's.

Even by ancient standards, the cults of Cybele and Attis involved some rather extreme orgiastic rites. The goddess was said to have loved the sound of cymbals, pipes, and drums, so her worshippers played madden-

---

7. Cybele was known by other names or merged with other goddesses, such as Dindymene, Ops, Pomona, Rhea, and the hermaphroditic Agdistis.
8. Attis was a common Phrygian name and may have been the name of one of their kings. However, he wasn't deemed a god in the Phrygian pantheon.

ingly loud, rhythmic music and danced themselves into a frenzy, imitating the Corybants, the wild, demonic creatures who were her attendants. Like the followers of Dionysus, Cybele's disciples drank wine liberally during their festivities and engaged in bawdy behavior, including sex acts. They offered animal and plant sacrifices and sometimes flagellated themselves, splattering the altars with their blood. At the height of their orgiastic ecstasy, when they were supposedly insensible to pain, some of the male initiates followed in the footsteps of Attis and, using stone or iron knives, castrated themselves. After making this sacrifice, they were eligible to become Cybele's eunuch priests, who, along with a bevy of priestesses, used their unique connection with the goddess to make prophecies and seek blessings for her followers. The eunuch priests were both revered and feared. They were often represented in art as beardless men with rounded bodies and soft, benign countenances; they were attired in the type of headdresses, long robes, and beads usually reserved for priestesses.

This eunuch business didn't sit too well with the Greeks, who were always a bit squeamish about any practice that threatened their manhood. The Cybele–Attis cult gained a foothold in the Hellenic world around the sixth century B.C., but the Greeks never cared for its Middle Eastern–Asiatic flavor, the loss of control over their women during the secret, nocturnal festivities, or the wild rituals (especially the awfulness of the emasculation component). Like the drunken revelries of Dionysus, it remained a disreputable subcult barely tolerated by the Greek establishment.

The cult of the Lady with the Lions also received a mixed reception in Scythia. Herodotus reported that an early-sixth-century B.C. Scythian sage named Anacharsis who encountered rituals performed in honor of Cybele during his travels in Greece and Anatolia was so smitten with the goddess that he brought her rites to his homeland. There's some evidence that the cult caught on in certain circles; pendants and plaques from Scythian burials feature women (or transvestites) dancing as they clutch weapons and the heads of beasts. Unfortunately for Anacharsis, Cybele's Scythian admirers didn't include the chieftain and his council—Anacharsis was charged with practicing unsavory foreign religious customs and put to death.

The seeds of the Cybele–Attis cult fell on much more fertile ground in Rome. Introduced around the beginning of the second century B.C., it gained great popularity when Cybele, whom the Romans officially gave the title Mater Deum Magna Idaea (Great Idaean Mother of the Gods, an honorary title identifying her with Rhea of the Cretan Mt. Ida), was credited both with stopping Hannibal's advance on the city and bestowing an unusually abundant harvest. The law, however, forbade even voluntary castration of Roman citizens, so the cult had to rely on priestesses and the *galli,* eunuch priests from Anatolia and other points east who wore female garb and anointed their long hair with aromatic unguents.[9] In the first century A.D., however, Attis began to assume almost as prominent a role as Mater Magna, and Emperor Claudius I decided to elevate the cult to official state status and permit self-castration so Roman men could become full-fledged initiates. Swept up by the popular cult, many availed themselves of this new privilege, especially on March 24, the annual Day of Blood, which commemorated Attis's sacrifice. Not all Romans were beguiled, however. In *Attis,* the first-century-B.C. Roman poet Catullus tells of one handsome, virile youth who castrates himself and persuades a group of his friends to do the same. Afterward, however, the initiate is filled with remorse over the loss of his manhood, and the miffed Cybele must command her lions to "mangle his brain with your claws" to turn him back into her devoted follower. The poem ends with a fervent prayer against falling under Cybele's spell: "Great goddess, spare me, never haunt my home—take others for your slaves, those creatures that you have driven mad and

---

9. The term *galli* (singular, *gallus*) may be Phrygian and inspired by the Gallus River, by whose banks Attis was supposed to have emasculated himself and whose waters were reputed to provoke religious frenzy. *Eunuch* comes from the Greek *eunouchos,* which means "in charge of the bed." Cybele wasn't the only deity to inspire sacrificial emasculation among her male worshippers. Eunuch priests served Hecate, the goddess of the moon, sorcery, and the underworld, in Caria, an ancient country in Anatolia.

those who in their madness wake again your passionate cruelty."

Herodotus wrote of the Scythian Enarees, who were affiliated with the orgiastic cult of a Near Eastern fertility goddess, Aphrodite Urania.[10] The Enarees came into being when a group of Scythian warriors pillaged Aphrodite's temple in Ascalon, Phoenicia, and the angry goddess retaliated by afflicting them "and all their descendants after them" with what Herodotus called "the 'female' sickness" (IV:67). The historian further explained that "the Enarees, who are epicene, say that Aphrodite gave them the art of divination," which they carried out through the use of willow wands. Herodotus didn't specify what he meant by "female sickness" or "epicene"—whether he meant castrated, transvestite, hermaphroditic, or merely effeminate. A pseudo-Hippocratic treatise noted the role of the Enarees: they were "eunuchs who belonged to the most powerful nobility, wore women's dresses, performed women's jobs, spoke like women, and enjoyed special respect because of the fear they inspired."

When it began to muster power in the first centuries A.D., the early Christian church singled out the Cybele–Attis cult as a particularly repugnant strain of paganism and did everything it could to discourage its practice. There's evidence, however, that some of the Christians' own rank and file also practiced self-castration in the name of their new Lord. In the New Testament, Matthew (19:12) wrote that "there are eunuchs who have made themselves eunuchs for the kingdom of heaven's sake," and self-castration to promote celibacy and religious devotion seems to have persisted for centuries, although it was never officially condoned by church leaders.[11]

---

10. UC Berkeley linguist Martin Schwartz interprets the meaning of the word *Enaree* as "effeminate," while Martin Huld from California State University at Los Angeles contends that it stems from the Old Iranian word for "unmanly."

11. The church seems to have made an exception to its general condemnation when it came to allowing young choirboys to be castrated to keep their soprano voices. This practice persisted until the late 1800s, when it was banned by Pope Leo XIII. The portraits of some monks in Christian illustrated manuscripts suggest that they too were eunuchs. In the Book of Kells, St. Stephen is portrayed with a bearded, masculine face, while an accompanying monk is soft and effeminate as well as smooth-faced.

To most contemporary observers, such self-sacrifice in the name of religion seems unthinkable, but we must keep historical context in mind. Eunuchs, whether voluntary or not, were common throughout the ancient world; many were slaves, but others were entrusted with positions of great power outside the spiritual realm. In the fourth century B.C., for example, a clever and power-hungry eunuch named Bagoas became the confidential minister of the Achaemenid Persian king Artaxerxes III. As commander-in-chief of the Persian forces during the conquest of Egypt, Bagoas amassed great wealth by selling back to Egyptian priests the sacred writings his forces looted from temples. After becoming the true power behind the throne, in 338 B.C. he murdered Artaxerxes and all his sons except Arses, whom he made king. Two years later, the cranky eunuch grew displeased with Arses and killed him, too, appointing Darius III the new regent. When Darius eventually tried to assert his independence, Bagoas planned yet another murder. The king, however, had been alerted to the plot and forced the unscrupulous eunuch to drink the poison himself.

Other eunuchs served with more honor. Persian kings and nobles used them as bodyguards and keepers of the royal harem, and by the time of Augustus Caesar in Rome (27 B.C.), eunuch chamberlains held a variety of influential government positions. Eunuch ministers were commonplace in the courts of the Byzantine emperors in Constantinople (A.D. 395–1453), as well as in the royal circles of China. The second emperor of the Ming Dynasty (1368–1644), for instance, employed a eunuch general of Muslim descent named Zheng He, who led his fleet to victories in Southeast Asia, Persia, Arabia, and eastern Africa.

When the impulsive acts of Cybele's followers are placed in this context—a world in which eunuchs were plentiful and many of them enjoyed positions of power in both secular and religious circles—the notion of self-castration seems more understandable.

Another factor contributing to the allure of emasculation for religious purposes was the widespread belief that possessing a feminine nature

The "Soft Men"

Religious transvestism has proven to be an enduring practice in many parts of the globe. Throughout modern-day Eurasia, India, Korea, Indonesia, Africa, and North and South America, some diviners and shamans wear women's clothing and embrace feminine mannerisms (Eliade 1972). These "soft men," as they're called by the Chukchi of northeastern Siberia, are inducted into the female realm through ritual sex changes or androgyny ceremonies. Depending on the culture, some live with women to absorb additional feminine power, while others become the brides of men. Like many Siberian shamans, many are regarded as curiosities and live apart from society, valued for their powers of healing and divination, but feared for their unusual habits and lifestyle.

---

would make one better suited for communing with the gods. This is one reason so many ancient religions placed women at the helm. Even if they didn't go so far as self-castration, male devotees in many cultures adopted the custom of cross-dressing, apparently in an attempt to become more intuitive and spiritual. Both eunuchs and transvestites proclaimed their gender switch by whitening their faces, wearing women's clothes and jewelry, and adopting feminine mannerisms, even sometimes marrying other men. But artifacts found in Bactria, Anatolia, and other lands reflect distinctions between the two statuses. While eunuchs are portrayed with soft bodies and rounded, feminine faces, other sculptures and reliefs depict another type of man: extremely virile-looking with rippling muscles and steely expression, yet still decked out in the flowing robes, jewelry, and long hair usually associated with women. The Kangjiashimenzi petroglyphs also hint at this practice: some of the human figures that have the headdresses and body types of females are equipped with substantial phalluses may have been hermaphrodites but more likely transvestites.

In the late 1970s, the Russian archaeologist Viktor Sarianidi discovered a remarkable example of what I believe must be religious transvestism, as well as evidence that the powerful Mistress of Animals cult, through the course of sixteen or seventeen centuries, had returned home to the land of its birth. During the 1978–79 season, Sarianidi excavated a mound known as Tillya Tepe (Gold Mound) in northern Afghanistan (ancient Bactria). Sarianidi's find was a veritable parfait of different cultures and religious practices, with layers of significant ruins and artifacts from the successive peoples who had lived in the area for more than a thousand years.

Among the earliest ruins was a fire temple initially built before 1000 B.C. Most likely associated with Zoroastrianism, the temple featured two column-flanked hallways and fortified towers at each corner, and was ringed by a high defensive wall. The centerpiece of the main room was an altar set on a twenty-foot-high brick platform, the site of sacred fires. To begin the fire ceremony, the priests lit some sandalwood twigs in a dish on a pedestal, allowed them to burn down, and then poured powdered incense on the embers to unleash a cloud of sweet fragrance. The priest then added more sandalwood to reignite the flames, and then, using a burning twig, transferred the fire to a large stack of wood that had been set at the main altar. In great temples, such as this one at Tillya Tepe, once the main fire was initiated it was supposed to burn continuously, as the fire itself was considered the personification of Ormuzd, called Ahura Mazda ("the good god"), the great winged Zoroastrian deity who was the spirit of light and goodness.

The temple enjoyed a long history, though not without mishap. Archaeological evidence reveals that it had been laid waste and then magnificently rebuilt in the middle of the first millennium B.C. Not long afterward, fire struck, and by the time Alexander the Great marched into the city around 328 B.C., he found only a pile of ruins where Ahura Mazda had once protected his followers from the forces of evil (Sarianidi 1985).

Some two hundred years later, Tillya Tepe once again was employed for religious purposes. In the mid-second century B.C., a new people had moved into the area: the Yüeh Chi, the confederacy of steppe nomads

A gold temple pendant worn by one of the warrior-priestesses at Tillya Tepe, dated to about 100 B.C. Although the stylization of the pendant is Greco-Bactrian and the iconography is Near Eastern, the winged fantastical animals twist in the Pazyryk style while the female is dressed like a Saka priestess (lost wax cast, one of a pair).

who had been forced out of the Tien Shan Mountains by the Hsiung-nu.[12] These nomads had crossed through what is now the republics of Uzbekistan and Tajikistan and entered the oases of Bactria, where they subjugated the local inhabitants and soon adopted a sedentary lifestyle. During the first century B.C., their descendants established a cemetery at Tillya Tepe around 100 B.C., an action consistent with the nomadic practice of reusing the holy places of earlier cultures (Rosenfield 1967).

They were evidently a wealthy people with extensive trading contacts, for Sarianidi's discovery yielded some twenty thousand elaborate gold pieces, many of which were encrusted with turquoise. Delicately wrought and exquisitely detailed, most were locally manufactured but bear the stylistic stamp of six different cultures: Bronze Age Bactrian, Greco-Bactrian, Greco-Roman, Iron Age Bactrian, Siberian-Altai, and Scytho-Sarmatian.

The artifacts strongly indicate that Sarianidi had stumbled upon a portion of the cemetery reserved for important religious leaders. Many of the materials and motifs are familiar from our Sauro-Sarmatian and Saka

---

12. Eventually, one of the Yüeh Chi tribes assimilated the other four and founded the widespread Kushan Empire and fostered the spread of Buddhism throughout Asia. Early images of Kushan Buddhist Bodhisattvas display all the Mother Goddess accoutrements, such as large headdresses and great strands of beads. In Buddhism, the historical Buddha, Gautama, was Bodhisattva prior to his Enlightenment. The term also refers to individuals who are destined to become buddhas, and is one whose essence is enlightenment.

burials: mirrors, colored organic materials, ceremonial weapons, and representations of birds and the Tree of Life. In addition, there is an ample amount of iconography on belt and shoe buckles, weapons, and jewelry related to the Bactrian and Greco-Roman beliefs, including eunuch priests, cupids, Aphrodite, and Athena. Sarianidi didn't express an opinion on the status of any of these individuals, but after analyzing the data, I concluded that the archaeologist had unearthed two priestesses, three warrior-priestesses, and a male whose burial offerings suggested that he had been a eunuch or a transvestite with duties similar to those of the priestesses and perhaps also similar to those of the Enarees.

This sole male had been about thirty years old at the time of his death. Like the priestesses, he had been attired in a long skirt and a V-necked caftan secured at the waist with a belt embellished with a series of gold plaques. His belongings included two daggers, a long sword adorned with animal combat scenes, two bows, a set of arrowheads, and two quivers, as well as the remains of his horse and a *kubok* (ceremonial cup). These artifacts were lavishly decorated with icons not usually found in male burials, such as a Tree of Life, a mountain goat with coiled horns, and eunuchs riding in a Far Eastern–style chariot drawn by fantastical leonine creatures. In life, the priest may have resembled a figure depicted on one of the women's belt fasteners: a strong, unbearded warrior with long, wavy hair streaming from underneath a pointed Bactrian helmet, wearing

One of the nine gold belt medallions worn by the only male in the Tillya Tepe. A female with her hair pulled back in a bun, wears a short skirt and sleeved bodice and boots while riding sidesaddle on a large feline. Note the textile shadrack (saddle blanket) strapped to the animal's back. Originally insets were in the heart-shaped depression around the edge of the medallion. This motif is one that seems to have originated in northern Afghanistan around the seventeenth century B.C.

One of a pair of belt fasteners worn by a
warrior-priestess buried at Tillya Tepe,
probably the depiction of an Enaree.

a flounced skirt, bearing an impressive array of weapons, and controlling a gathering of animals.

Most interesting to me were the priest's nine belt medallions, all of which portrayed the Mistress of Animals riding sidesaddle on a lion. Once again, we encounter the powerful symbol of Cybele in exactly the same guise that originally appeared on the Bactrian compartmentalized seals seventeen centuries earlier. After extending the influence of her orgiastic cult from the civilizations of Central Asia to Europe to a grotto in Xinjiang, the Great Goddess had come home.

As exciting as the finds of Tillya Tepe are, their story ends on a rather sobering note. Winter storms forced Viktor Sarianidi to abandon his efforts before he could explore the seventh grave that his crew had uncovered. We can assume that looters soon descended on the mound, for the spoils from an eighth rich burial—probably that of a priestess with a mirror—were sighted in the bazaars of Kabul. Before the next excavation season, the tragic war between Russia and Afghanistan was in progress and to date, neither Sarianidi nor any other archaeologist has been allowed to return to Tillya Tepe. Perhaps even more disturbing, the fate of the magnificent artifacts already unearthed is uncertain. Recently I met a Japanese scholar, the widow of the director of the Kabul museum where the Tillya Tepe gold pieces were entrusted, who said that after a militant group of Islamic fundamentalists captured Kabul in 1996, they closed the museum and stripped it of its holdings. No one in the international scholarly community seems to know the whereabouts of the Tillya Tepe gold, and we fear that these irreplaceable treasures were melted down to support the Taliban's oppressive regime.

✦✦

Worship of the Mother Goddess took many twists and turns over hundreds of centuries, as traders, raiders, and travelers introduced convictions and rituals into myriad cultures. Only an artistic record—depicting a female riding a powerful feline—notes her presence in Bactria during the early centuries of the second millennium B.C. Still in the guise of Mistress of Animals, the goddess resurfaces in Anatolia, where for the first time inscriptions define her as Magna Mater, the Great Mother, whose gentle nature looks over her worshippers. Within centuries, the Greeks enter Anatolia, and upon subsuming the Great Mother under their patriarchal influence, her character as Cybele undergoes a transformation, and no longer is she beneficent. Her religion takes on a dark mystical nature; her priests are involved in orgiastic rites and they sacrificially emasculate themselves in her honor. An inconceivable fascination with a perverse cult perseveres to be transmitted east to Scythia and west to Rome. Cybele rises to new heights, while her eunuchs acquire influence within certain political and religious systems.

By the first century B.C. the Mother Goddess had come full circle, returning to ancient Bactria, where she appears again riding a powerful feline beast, on the sacred belt of an elite nomadic Yüeh-chih priest, who may have been either a transvestite or a eunuch. The gold accoutrements in the Tillya Tepe burials reveal the high statuses of the deceased, while the iconography on these adornments indicates they were the keepers of the ancient Mother Goddess.

CHAPTER ELEVEN

IRISH WARRIOR QUEENS
AND THE DAMSELS OF DEATH

To the casual motorist trundling by on the A-3, Navan Fort near Armagh in Northern Ireland might not seem like a particularly note-worthy spot—it's a grassy mound atop a small hill; despite the name, no fort ever stood at the site. But aficionados of history and legend know that this once was the site of the fabled settlement of Emain Macha, the seat of the high kings of Ulster and the setting for some of Ireland's most stirring and famous epic poems.[1] Fierce Queen Medb, beauteous and insightful Deirdre, and Macha herself, the mythic heroine who imposed her name on the ancient capital—all were said to have walked these boggy green pastures in times long past.

Matt and I had come to Ireland in the winter of 1999 to follow the

---

1. Ulster, or ancient Ulaid, was one of the four original provinces of Ireland. It extended from the northeastern coast of the island south to what is now County Louth and west to County Donegal. The region was divided into nine counties in the early seventeenth century, and, in 1921, six of its counties became Northern Ireland, while the remaining three were incorporated into the Republic of Ireland.

Celtic trail we had first encountered on the steppes of Eurasia. Ever since my undergraduate days, I've been fascinated by the resemblance of the animals in Celtic art to the Animal Style of the Eurasian nomads; later the possible connections with the mummy people of Xinjiang further piqued my interest in the Celtic culture. These overlaps compelled me to explore how the women might have fared on this western arc of the Celtic migrations. Late Iron Age Celts known as the La Tène people had expanded from continental Europe into Ireland sometime around 300 B.C. and eventually dominated the isle.[2] Although an advanced culture in many ways, particularly where metallurgy was concerned, they lacked a true written language, and classical authors on the Continent failed to spill much ink on these islanders living on Europe's western fringe. In fact, few written reports existed to shed light on Irish history until the seventh century, when Christian monks writing in both Latin and Irish began producing copious documents. As a consequence, to study ancient Ireland is to study legend along with archaeology, which only seems appropriate in a land long celebrated for its literary accomplishments.

Scientists and historians are always reluctant to draw conclusions about a society from the murky world of mythology, and the Irish scholars we met on our trip were no exception. I found it telling, however, that even the most adamant scoffers who insisted there wasn't a word of truth in the old tales couldn't resist referring to them whenever the topic of women in prehistoric Ireland arose. And who could blame them? Female entities play a prominent and colorful role in Irish folklore, and these stories of conniving queens, mighty nature goddesses, and banshees with their doomsday wails are irresistible. Besides, I knew from studying the mythology of many cultures that despite their embellishments and leaps of imagination, legends often contain kernels of truth about actual events or about the beliefs and social structure of the people who created them.

---

2. The La Tène culture emerged among Celts living along the Rhine River in the mid–fifth century B.C. and spread throughout northern Europe and the British Isles.

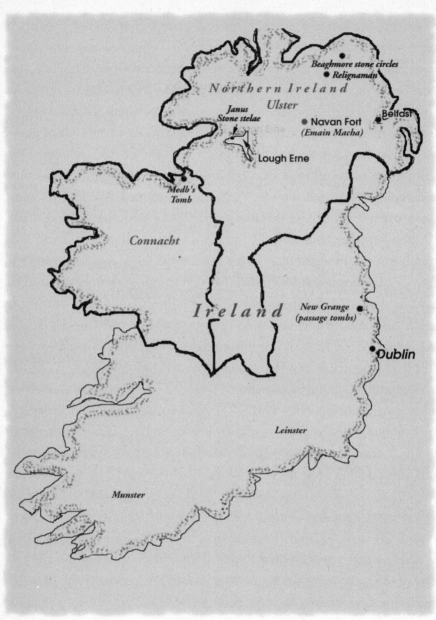

Location of archaeological sites in Ulster and Connacht in Ireland.

In Ireland's case, it takes the form of four cycles. The Tuatha Dé Danann were "the people of the Goddess Danu," a divine race who were said to have inhabited ancient Ireland, and the *Dindshenchas* relates how various Irish places got their names by linking them with mythical events. The Mythological Cycle chronicles a series of invasions by supernatural clans from before the time of the Great Flood to the arrival of the Celts. The Fenian Cycle, set primarily in the southern provinces of Leinster and Munster, features hero Finn mac Cumaill and his son Ossian; these sagas of romantic battles and battling romances are often cited as the inspiration for the Arthurian legends of medieval times. They are all interesting reading, but it is the myths of the Ulster Cycle, with its rousing tales of the valiant Cú Chulainn and its brash Irish heroines, that induced me to make the pilgrimage to the former site of Emain Macha on a blustery winter's day. The archaeology underscores the mythology, and the grassy mound with its ghosts of fearless Irish women added a third dimension to the epic stories.

Matt and I were accompanied on our trip by the Irish archaeologist Eileen Murphy, and having a native guide proved fortunate—the Navan Fort Interpretive Center is so cleverly disguised, I'm not sure we would have easily found it on our own. The parking lot is covered with a series of cement blocks punctuated with holes to let the grass grow through, providing a firm foundation in the boggy land while almost resembling an unspoiled green pasture; the Interpretive Center itself is discreetly tucked under the crest of the hill, preserving the sense of an open, timeless landscape, and visitors approaching from the main road won't see it until they're almost upon the entrance.

Inside the center, however, everything is high-tech, with an array of interactive displays, dioramas, and audiovisual presentations. We began by perusing the archaeological exhibits, which include artifacts dating to Neolithic times that reveal a relatively large group of agriculturists had settled here during the Bronze Age. One of the oldest finds is the King's Stables, an eerie, steep-sided artificial pool constructed around 1000 B.C., where prehistoric Ulster kings reputedly watered and stabled their horses.

It obviously had also been used for rather grisly ritual purposes, as the facial part of a young man's decapitated skull was found in the pond.[3] Around 700 B.C., agriculturists built the site's first substantial structure, a wooden house surrounded by a circular ditch and a fenced enclosure. Between 300 and 100 B.C., around the time the Celts entered Ireland from the Continent, the structure was rebuilt eleven times. The foundation of a house contained a most curious artifact: the skull of a Barbary ape, which was carbon-dated to the second century B.C. Its presence confirms that the Irish had diplomatic relations with North African and Mediterranean countries during the Iron Age.

Around 95 B.C., the Celts constructed an enormous circular wooden building upon the hill, one that stretched 130 feet in diameter and contained five rings of oak posts—273 in all—aligned around a great central pillar.[4] The Celts seemed to have used this imposing structure for rituals, for they filled the entire building with large limestone blocks hauled uphill from a nearby quarry and set the structure afire. Probably while the fire was still burning they covered the ruins with layers of clay and sod to create the earthen mound we see today. No one is certain of the religious beliefs that led to this grand conflagration, but Eileen's husband, the archaeologist Colm Donnelly (1997, 39–42), believes it was part of a Druid sacrifice to appease gods and goddesses.[5] Shortly afterward, perhaps during the first centuries A.D., the settlement became the capital of the Uluti, a

---

3. Evidence that the Celts practiced ritual decapitation includes representations in stone sculpture and metal repoussé artwork, and a significant number of decapitated heads deposited by Celtic peoples as sacrificial offerings, have been found in the peat bogs of England, Denmark, and Germany. Believing that the head was the repository of a person's power, the Celts, like the Scythians, made drinking cups from the skulls of their enemies.
4. The stump of the central pillar survived over the ages, and dendrochronology (the process of counting tree rings) allowed scientists to pinpoint the date of construction.
5. This ritual has parallels to one we found evidence of at Pokrovka, where the deceased was placed in a log house after a pit had been dug; the logs were set afire, but before the structure was consumed by flames it was covered with dirt, which formed the kurgan. We excavated the charcoaled logs and also found signs that a great ceremonial feast had taken place during the burial ceremony.

Celtic-speaking tribe whose name was transmuted through time, eventually becoming the foundation of the term "Ulsterman."

This ancient world came alive when we moved on to the center's theater to see films depicting some of the events related in *Táin Bó Cuáilnge* (*The Cattle Raid of Cooley*), the longest and best-known epic in the Ulster Cycle.

My favorite part is the prologue, which features Macha, a noblewoman of mysterious origins, who one day appeared at the manor of a wealthy Ulster widower named Crunniuc. Without a word of explanation, Macha insinuated herself into Crunniuc's household, preparing a fine meal, tending to the children, milking the cows, and slipping into the delighted widower's bed. The couple was soon married, and, in due course, Macha became pregnant.

Later that year, Crunniuc asked his wife if she'd like to attend the Ulster king's great festival. Macha declined, and cautioned him not to mention her at court. "If you do," she warned, "I will be lost to you." Crunniuc promised he wouldn't tell a soul about his lovely and accomplished wife and set off for the festival.

The celebrations lasted for several days, and Crunniuc managed to hold his tongue until the final chariot race. The king, racing a fine team of black horses, bested his competitors by several lengths and proclaimed, "None can run better than my horses. There are no better in the country." Without thinking, Crunniuc scoffed, "My wife can run faster than the king's horses," for fleetness of foot was among Macha's many gifts.

Bystanders reported Crunniuc's boast to the king, who furiously summoned the now-repentant Ulsterman and demanded that his wife be made to race the royal team. When Crunniuc explained that Macha was not present at the festival, the king had him thrown into chains and sent soldiers to fetch her. When they arrived at the manor, Macha asked for a postponement until she had given birth, as her time was imminent. The king's men, however, turned a deaf ear to her pleas and carried her off.

When she reached the court, she begged the king to wait until she had delivered her child, but he refused, saying, "If you do not race my horses now, your husband will be killed." She turned to the men of Ulster, pleading for them to take up her cause, but they merely jeered at the desperate mother-to-be. Macha then turned to the king and loudly proclaimed a dreadful curse. "I am Macha. I will race. But I swear to you that my name and the name of my heirs will mark this place forever! Ulstermen, each time your strength is most needed, you shall become helpless!"

Macha took her place beside the king's team and the race commenced. Just as her husband had predicted, Macha won easily, beating the king's steeds by seven lengths. But the exertion took its toll, for she arrived at the finish line in advanced labor and thereupon in anguish gave birth to twins, a boy and a girl. Afterward, Macha thundered at her tormentors: "All that heard me in my agony would know the pain I have had. The weakness will come upon you in your greatest hour of need when your enemies are closing in, and for five days and four nights each of you and your descendants for nine generations will suffer in the same way." After uttering this curse, Macha fell to the ground, dead.

From that day forth, the king's settlement was known as Emain Macha—"the twins of Macha" in Gaelic—and only the young boys and women of Ulster, along with the family of Cú Chulainn, the great court champion, who was not native to Ulster, were spared her curse. And as *Táin Bó Cuáilnge* recounts, for nine generations, every time Ulster came under attack, the king's men would experience the terrible pangs of childbirth just before engaging in battle, incapacitating them and leaving Cú Chulainn to fight alone (Kinsella 1970).

In some versions of the story, Macha isn't a mere noblewoman, she is a war goddess. This isn't surprising, given that the pantheon of Irish Celtic deities was dominated by goddesses, many of whom were associated with war, including Badb, Morrígan, and Nemain, whose terrible howl was said to cause a hundred warriors to die of fright. Anu was the Great Mother fertility goddess who seems to have evolved into Danu where she was celebrated at Newgrange, one of Ireland's most noteworthy Celtic archaeological sites. (See "The Passage Tomb of Newgrange," page 194.) When we visited the National Museum of Ireland in Dublin, we marveled at the piles of gold torques that had been tossed into bogs as offerings to water goddesses. In fact, when I asked Eamon Kelly, the museum's Keeper of Antiquities, about evidence indicating the status of women in ancient Ireland, he didn't point to the abundance of ancient gold jewelry in his collection; instead, he began reciting the names of goddesses. "Ireland herself is a goddess, you know," he said.

Given the prominent role of female deities, it's reasonable to expect that priestesses played an important role in the Celtic religious system, but, as with everything related to Irish prehistory, few artifacts and even fewer written accounts exist to corroborate this assumption. We know that Druids presided over Celtic religious rites, but the ancient Greek and Roman authors who wrote about them failed to mention the women who must have been included in this priestly class.[6] Some Roman authors, however, do refer to a caste of prophetesses known as *dryaden,* a word that might have been the feminine form of *druid.*

In "The Exile of the Sons of Uisliu," another story in the Ulster Cycle, it was a Druid adviser to King Conchobar who prophesied that the child born to the chief minstrel's wife would be one of the most beautiful in the land, but would bring great disaster to Ulster: "A woman with twisted yellow tresses/green-irised eyes of great beauty/and cheeks flushed like the foxglove/howled in the hollow of your womb . . . Ulster's chariot-warriors/will deal many a blow for her." Alarmed, the nobles demanded that the baby, Deirdre, be put to death, but the lusty king decided to raise her as his foster child so he might marry her when she came of age and avert the prophecy that way.

As she neared maturity, Deirdre happened upon a calf being butchered on a winter's day. She was much taken by the sight of the red

---

6. These authors include Julius Caesar and the Syrian-born Stoic philosopher Posidonius. For more on Druids, see Chapter 12.

The Passage Tomb of Newgrange

A few days before the winter solstice, a date laden with cultic significance for many societies both past and present, I was privileged to visit one of the premier archaeological sites in Ireland, the passage tomb of Newgrange. Constructed in Neolithic times, Newgrange is located atop a hillock at Brú na Bóinne (the Bend of the Boyne River), about twenty miles north of Dublin. It stands roughly 42 feet high and about 280 feet in diameter, and is the best-known of the three passage tombs found in this area peppered with prehistoric monuments—including more than thirty groups of stones standing on end, adjacent to the tomb, and barrows (heaps of earth or rocks marking ancient graves).

Great stone in front of the entrance to the Newgrange passage tomb in Ireland engraved with spirals. The opening above the door, called a roofbox, allows light to penetrate the long shaft precisely on winter solstice, although some light enters a few days before and after solstice.

Like its companion passage tombs, Knowth and Dowth, Newgrange was built around 3300 B.C. by Ireland's early argicultural people and consists of a large stone-and-turf mound containing a long passage that leads to central burial chambers. At Newgrange, three niches radiate from the end of the long passage to create a cruciform; each niche contains a huge stone basin that had once held cremated human remains and mortuary offerings such as beads, marbles, and pendants. The exterior base of the mound is ringed by nearly a hundred large, horizontally placed stones, many of which are carved with spirals, lozenges, zigzags, and other cultic symbols. The most striking of these is the massive stone that guards the entrance to the passage, and which bears three great spirals arranged in a triangular motif on one end and a series of three stacked pairs of coils on the other. Similar to those carved at cultic sites in Brittany, these markings are thought by some scholars to symbolize the Great Mother Goddess. Some of the stones lining the passageway and the ceiling of one niche also contain elaborate spiral carvings. In addition, a dozen out of an estimated thirty-five original standing stones à la Stonehenge ring the mound, although these were believed to have been added approximately a millennium later than the original structure, demonstrating its longevity as a sacred site.

One of Newgrange's most dramatic features is provided by its roofbox, a rectangular stone containing a three-foot-long and sixteen-inch-high opening in the center that is set above the entryway lintel. M. J. O'Kelly discovered this strange architectural element while excavating Newgrange in the 1960s, but at that time its function was unknown. Local tradition or myth held, however, that it allowed the sun's rays to penetrate the passage tomb, lighting it at some unspecified time during the year. Kelly investigated and discovered that this did indeed occur. On December 21, the winter solstice and shortest day of the year, the roofbox allows a slender beam of sunlight to pierce the long passageway precisely between 8:58 and 9:15 A.M. The decorative carvings in the three small chambers, usually obscured in complete blackness, are splendidly illuminated for those few precious moments. In ancient times, worshippers may have considered this event the symbolic mating of the sun god, Daghdha, who throws the shaft of light, and Danu, great mother goddess— a ritual act that would propagate humans, animals, and crops.

Despite its massive modern reconstruction, Newgrange retains a remarkable air of ancient mystery, one that reverberates with the fervent beliefs of a long-vanished people. Anyone wishing to experience the full impact of this singular phenomenon must hurry, however. When we visited Brú na Bóinne in 1999, I noticed that some of the designs had been lost as the stone surface flaked away, and asked the docent about the cause of the damage. "It's the moisture from so many people's breath," she replied. "In fact, the authorities have decided that within a short time, they will no longer allow the public to enter the shaft of the tomb." An understandable precaution, but a loss to future visitors wishing to experience a taste of ancient Celtic spirituality.

blood on the white snow and the black of a raven perched nearby, and determined to marry a man with such coloring. Her nurse told Deirdre that she knew of just such a fair man with rosy cheeks and dark hair, a nobleman named Naoise.

Deirdre contrived to meet Naoise, who, knowing that she was betrothed to King Conchobar, at first resisted her advances, because he was bound by a code of honor. But he eventually yielded to her abundant charms, and, accompanied by his two brothers, the couple fled to Scotland, where the men entered the service of that king. But it wasn't long before the Scottish king began to lust after Deirdre, and the foursome planned to flee again when word came that Conchobar had granted them a pardon. Deirdre divined that this was a trap and warned against returning to their homeland, but the men trusted the king. Once they returned to Ireland, Deirdre's fears proved well founded: Conchobar dispatched a nobleman named Eoghan to slay the three brothers and he imprisoned Deirdre for a year.

Upon her release, the king asked Deirdre to name the man she most despised, and she uttered with the utmost contempt, "Eoghan." Vengeful Conchobar then announced that he was giving her to her enemy and ordered a chariot to take her to Eoghan. Rather than submit to this fate, Deirdre leaped from the speeding chariot and dashed out her brains on the rocks below. The king's treacherous behavior, especially the killing of the three noble brothers, caused revolt and bloodshed in Ulster, fulfilling the Druid's prophecy (Kinsella 1970).

The Christian monks who wrote down the oral histories and legends in illustrated manuscripts were not kind to the women who appeared in them; over the centuries as new renditions of the old tales were written, the status of women deteriorated. The account of Macha's vengeance stands in strong contrast to Deirdre's plight. In Macha's story, which was recorded at least two centuries before Deirdre's, we are presented with a skilled, courageous woman who possesses both the will and the power to visit a long-lasting and painful revenge upon her tormentors. In some versions of the legend, she is elevated to the status of a warrior goddess and feared as a great slayer of men. By the time Deirdre's story is added to the Ulster Cycle, a passive heroine has come to the fore. Instead of unparalleled courage and phenomenal athleticism, Deirdre's outstanding characteristics are her ability to prey upon the mortal and moral weaknesses of men and her beauty, which in turn inspires lust in their hearts and (in line with monastical doctrine) leads them to dishonorable deeds. When confronted by her mortal enemies, Deirdre cannot defend herself or strike back. She has become the evil one who must not survive, but in this near-chivalrous society, the masculine must not defile the feminine. To fulfill destiny in the manner demanded by the monks of the time, Deirdre must destroy herself.

Irish mythology abounds with examples of strong women whose personalities were sublimated, but the stories evolved further to vilify the heroines and serve as cautionary examples of what women should not be, like the Greeks' Amazonian tales. The most prominent woman in Celtic folklore is Medb, the warrior queen of Connacht, who plays a pivotal role in *The Cattle Raid of Cooley* and challenges the mighty Cú Chulainn himself. One night during a playful session of pillowtalk, the story goes, Medb and her husband, Ailill, began comparing their individual wealth. When Medb bragged that she had entered the marriage with assets equal to or surpassing Ailill's, he was quick to point out that he owned a white bull far superior to any bull in her herd (a trump card in this cattle-loving land). Determined to get the upper hand, Medb set her sights on the only bull in the land that surpassed Ailill's, the fabulous Brown Bull of Cooley. At first, she was only interested in securing the animal's stud services for a year and sent emissaries with generous offers to its Ulsterman owner (including access to her "own friendly thighs" if the gentleman was so inclined—Medb and Ailill seemed to have had a spectacularly open marriage). But, negotiations went awry, the deal was canceled, and the queen plotted to steal the bull.

Before launching her raid, Medb sought the counsel of a beautiful young maiden named Fedelm, who was said to have the gift of prophecy. But even though Fedelm warned "I see it bloody, I see it red," and described the destruction that the young hero Cú Chilainn would visit upon Connacht, Medb decided to proceed. She did, however, try to stack the deck in her favor by seducing Fergus, a great Ulster warrior, and convincing him to lead her army into battle. As Fedelm predicted, the raid initiated a protracted war between Connacht and Ulster, in which Medb repeatedly confronted her opponents with clever military strategy, seductive wiles, and ruthlessness. And even though the men of Ulster were subject to Macha's curse and were thus rendered helpless from time to time, Cú Chulainn was magnificent, winning battle after battle single-handedly until Ulster ultimately emerged victorious.

There are many versions of Medb's exploits in Irish folklore, the earliest of which seems to date to the seventh century. The older tales tend to be leaner, more direct, and the queen doesn't display as prodigious a sexual appetite and thirst for wealth and power as in later versions. Some stories anoint her a warrior goddess, and as such she is associated with birds, carrying such a pet on her shoulder.[7] Her role as sovereignty goddess (meaning that only by sleeping with her could a king become worthy of the throne) meant she had to protect her virtue and, at the same time, be extremely sensual and sexual to ensure the fertility of the land. In later versions, though, the tone of the tales becomes censorious, and these sexual and other supposed vices are condemned, as some authors label her "a determined, domineering, and wanton woman" (Mallory 1992, 69).

Although some firmly maintain that Medb never existed, there's a great mound at Knocknarea that's said to be her tomb. If legend maintains she is buried there, then it seems a possibility that this queen—or at least a very high-ranking woman—at one time in the dim past really did exist. I was curious to see the Knocknarea mound, wondering whether it were really as large as I had heard, because size is so important in determining

---

7. The bird motif is also found on the Issyk headdress. See Chapter 6.

status. Whoever had depleted so many precious resources—vast quantities of time and effort by many people—to build a huge burial mound would have to have constructed it for someone of exalted rank. And in Connacht, who else except Medb?

Passage tomb at Sligo, near Medb's tomb.

In 1999, Matt and I left Northern Ireland, heading southwest, and soon were in Ireland, where the wide four-laned highways of the northern region immediately disintegrated into narrow, winding two-lanes that seemed uncommonly dangerous, especially since I was driving on what to me was the wrong side of the road. Within an hour or so we were in County Sligo, and I turned at an intersection west toward the Atlantic, soon encountering a nice bunch of small passage tombs in the pasture. I parked adjacent to the narrow lane to take photographs, and as I stepped out of the car into a blustering gale, I spotted Medb's tomb silhouetted against the gray sky. Thirty-five-feet high and two hundred feet in diameter, it stood at the very top of a great hill, and I was struck by its resemblance to the famous passage tombs in the Boyne Valley.

Winter seemed to have set in and my luck was diminishing; after hiking to the Interpretive Center that explained the tombs in the pasture, we found it locked tight for the winter. Back in the car, I began searching for the road or path that led to Medb's tomb, and within minutes found that I had bypassed it. The weather had worsened during the short drive. As I stepped from the car, I faced a full Atlantic gale and, glancing toward the open water, I notice a fog bank bearing down on the land. Bending near-double against the wind, I made my way into the only open business establishment.

"Could you tell me where the road to Medb's tomb is? And is it possible to drive there?" I asked.

The postmistress surveyed me for a half a minute. "It's an hour's walk up that hill." She nodded over her shoulder, turning back to stamping a package.

I glanced out the window toward the small mountain and shuddered, doubting that I could walk uphill for an hour in that wind, even if it were at my back.

"Not a good idee to go up there 'cause the fog be rolling in. They'll just be sending the search planes lookin' for ye."

I thanked her and left, but as I fought my way back to the car I wondered if they really sent search planes out in such weather. Probably not. They just waited until the storm ended and then searched. Disappointed, I conceded it would be absolutely foolish to try to walk to Medb's tomb today.

As happens so frequently in archaeology, the answer was just beyond my fingertips. I consoled myself: Maybe another opportunity would come when I could judge for myself whether Queen Medb really had been buried there, or whether she was only another chapter in the great book of Irish mythology.

✻

Like the Greeks and the Amazons, the Irish monks seemed to find the sexual voracity of Medb and other mythic heroines completely unsettling, and this fear of lascivious females is probably reflected in some of the most controversial artifacts ever recovered in Ireland: the Sheela-na-gigs. These carved stones depict naked haggish-looking women gleefully displaying their swollen genitalia. The stones were a source of contention and outrage from the moment they were first discussed by antiquarians in the 1840s, probably because the peculiar erotica was found incorporated into the walls of twelfth- and thirteenth-century churches. Although a number of Sheela-na-gigs have been collected, rarely are they featured in museum exhibitions, and scholars have usually explained them as pagan idols or a Christian warning against lust, the worst female vice in medieval times (men's principal vice was avarice). But other beliefs also have been associated with the Sheela-na-gigs, including one from the nineteenth century, when country folk thought the Sheelas weren't malevolent but were actually amuletic and could avert the dreaded evil eye. (See "The Curse of the Living Sheela-na-gigs," page 202.)

I had seen illustrations of Sheela-na-gigs, but Eileen Murphy arranged for me to view the only example uncovered to date in Northern Ireland. At the Ulster Museum, as curator Cormac Bourke hurried us to the storeroom, he commented on the probability of a museum exhibition featuring the lewd figures. "We'd like to display the Sheela-na-gig now, and I think we could . . . we probably will." His words seemed less directed toward Eileen and me than an attempt to muster his own resolve to face the criticism such a move was likely to engender. "People weren't always so receptive to these pieces," he noted. Even Patrick Wallace, the director of the Dublin Museum, had condemned any interest in the sculptures in 1990, railing in the *Irish Times,* "Why can't people focus on a Cistercian abbey instead? Sheela-na-gigs are ugly and unflattering to women."

Sheela-na-gig from the parish of Errigal Keerogue, County Tyrone.

I asked Bourke about the provenance of the stones. He explained that since they typically were found in Romanesque churches, they were presumed to date to that era (A.D. 1000–1200), and that instead of being upright, they were usually placed in the walls lying on their sides or angled to match the pitch of the roof's gable. That struck me as odd—if the

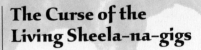

The Curse of the Living Sheela-na-gigs

Not only do superstitious people believe in the powers of stone Sheela-na-gigs, they also think that a person bewitched by the evil eye can be cured by a *living* Sheela. The afflicted party has to search for one of these creatures and persuade her to lift her skirt to display her genitals.

These living Sheelas don't always use their powers for good—they sometimes cast a malevolent spell. In a letter to the *Irish Times* dated January 23, 1977, an elderly man, Walter Mahon-Smith, recalls an incident of his youth: "In a townland near where I lived [in County Galway], a deadly feud had continued for generations between the families of two small farmers. One day, before the First World War, when the men of one of the families, armed with pitchforks and heavy blackthorn sticks, attacked the home of the enemy, the woman of the house . . . came to the door of her cottage, and in full sight of all (including my father and myself, who happened to be passing by) lifted her skirt high above her head, displaying her naked genitals. The enemies of her family fled in terror" (cited in Goode and Dexter 2000).

Sheela-na-gigs had been carved for the churches, why hadn't they been fit in the proper, upright orientation?

In the storeroom, Bourke gently pulled a small weathered gray stone from a shelf and positioned the carving so it stood illuminated in a shaft of light. Measuring about a foot wide and two feet high, the homely, leering figure grasped her labia with both hands, pulling them upward and outward so that they completely dominated the picture.

A few Sheelas have been found in France and England, and one of the English ones holds a circular object that could have been a mirror. The inclusion of this often cultic item made me wonder whether sculptors might actually have had fertility or divination, not wanton sexuality, in mind. I also imagined that the figures might have been carved much earlier and merely reused as building stones when the churches were constructed, a frequent occurrence when one culture replaces another. If this were true, they could have been intended not as a warning to good Christians of the evils of feminine sensuality, but for a completely different purpose. It is known, for example, that the ancient Irish believed that the nakedness of a woman held great power. Once Cú Chulainn's uncle sent Scandlach, his (female) teacher of warfare, and a company of women in their nakedness to calm Cú's warrior rage. Upon seeing them, "the hero gazed away and then laid his face against his chariot so that he might not see their nakedness" (translated by Miriam Robbins Dexter). Could it not be possible that the Sheela-na-gigs were fashioned for a similar purpose?

Eileen, intrigued by my theory, wanted to show me a possible precursor of the Sheelas. She and her husband, Colm, took Matt and me to the Chadragh cemetery on Boa Island in Northern Ireland. The island sits on the northern end of Lough Erne, and as we made our way down a narrow, overgrown path, the blustery wind carried the chill from the lake. The soft ground was covered with a dense carpet of grass, and flat gravestones were upthrust helter-skelter. Although it was midday, a canopy of swaying tree branches obscured the sunlight that dared struggle through the thick fog cover, and they filled the copse with an ominous rustling. I remembered that Druids conducted their mysterious ceremonies in groves such as this, and it took little imagination to visualize a procession of ghostly hooded images moving in single file toward the gravestones.

Two stone sculptures, elevated on modern cement bases, stood at right angles to each other. Eileen told us they had been transferred here in relatively recent times from a secret site on the island. The larger was the Chaldragh Idol, a four-foot-high Janus figure, its double profile pointing in opposite directions. Like the Roscommon Sheela-na-gig, the Janus bore crosshatching along both sides of the heads, probably a representation of heavy braids. Standing on tiptoe, Eileen pointed to a rectangular depression at the top of the figure between the Janus heads, now filled with rainwater.

"This is still used as a fertility font by the local women who want to get pregnant and can't." As Colm reached forward as if to swat her hand into the water, she quickly pulled away; we all laughed at her superstitiousness.[8] Her grinning husband explained that the closest parallels to this sculpture were from Gaul, dating to the first centuries B.C.[9] We turned to the other sculpture, known locally as the Lustymore Idol, after the island it is said to have been transplanted from, and I examined what appeared to be the representation of a female. The face was more diminutive than the Janus's, but stylistically similar, with the same pointed chin and broad forehead. Some scholars maintain that the pointed chin is suggestive of a beard, but it has no striations indicating hair. Rendered in stone identical to the Janus, its likely contemporary. Eileen noted, "Some Irish scholars think this image might be the precursor to the Sheelas—see how the arms lie across the torso and point toward the inverted V that represents the top of the vulva?"

I later found other similarities between the Janus sculpture and a Sheela-na-gig from County Tipperary as well as two Sheela stelae now in the Dublin National Museum: all four share chevron tattoos on their faces. Another interesting parallel is that the Sheelas are associated with women warriors in the same manner as Medb: the Sheela-na-gig from County Galway includes in her Celtic interlaced ornamentation a bird perched on a small rosette (Goode and Dexter 2000).

With the evidence I had gathered, I felt it preposterous to consider Sheela-na-gigs a symbol of feminine depravity. Certainly they had been carved much earlier than the Romanesque period and were fitted in the churches in an attempt to harness any mythical powers the figures might have. Their real function must have been to represent female omnipotence; they could have been amulets for fertility and fecundity; perhaps

---

8. In late spring 2000, I received this e-mail from Eileen: "I obviously didn't pull my hand away from the Janus figure and its fertility powers quickly enough . . . since I am three months pregnant!"

9. Gaul was an ancient Celtic stronghold in western Europe, consisting of what is now primarily France and Belgium.

they even calmed the furor of the masculine warriors. And in some capacity they were warrior women or they transmitted their power to warrior women.

As happened so frequently, the patriarchs again fabricated a contradictory belief system; they convinced the medieval illiterates that feminine endowments were not only negative, they were awful evil powers that must be assiduously avoided.

The Janus-head sculpture (right) and the female image (left). The latter is thought to be the precursor to the Sheela-na-gig figures. In recent times the lips of both sculptures have been marked with red pigment.

Evidence of the uneasy relationship between the early Christian church in Ireland and Irish women also exists in a curious little cemetery outside the village of Carrickmore, which lies roughly in the center of Northern Ireland. This region is rife with cultic monuments, including the Neolithic stone circles of Beaghmore on the southern edge of the Sperrin Mountains. Although much smaller than the standing rocks of Stonehenge, the circles were placed with a deliberate astrological orientation and in the black heather-covered boglands impart a similar air of mystery. Colm was an excellent guide, noting that Beaghmore has the greatest concentration of Neolithic stone circles ever excavated in Ireland—including one that was filled with more than eight hundred small stones planted upright like dragons' teeth.

He pointed north over the bogs. "There could still be hundreds of circles yet that haven't been excavated, and if they aren't excavated, they remain preserved." Although I was curious to know what else might be under the bogs, I knew that archaeological monuments, even stone, will disintegrate in the atmosphere from acid rain and pollutants in the air.

We left the Beaghmore circles and didn't have to travel far to reach our next destination: Relignaman, which Eileen translated as the "women's cemetery." "The locals have a saying about this place," she said after we picked our way through a boggy pasture, carefully stepping on tufts of grass—to slide off meant sinking knee-deep into gooey black muck." 'No living woman can come out, and no dead man can go in.'" In contrast to the soft bog, the climb up the rocky, bramble-covered ridge overlooking the Camowen River valley was a pleasure.

Finally, we arrived at a small, fence-enclosed graveyard, perhaps measuring sixty feet by sixty feet, overgrown with weeds and tall grasses that partially obscured the flat gray stones marking a little huddle of graves. As I stopped to study a large stone bearing a series of crudely carved crosses, Eileen recited the two main legends about the site, both of which revolve around Columba, the Irish saint who lived in the area in the sixth century. "The first is that there was a 'bad woman' who had a child out of wedlock, and when Columba confronted the woman and demanded that she disclose the identity of her lover, she named *him* as the child's

A stone circle in Beaghmore, Northern Ireland.

father. Furious, the saint decreed that when she died, she be buried away from hallowed ground and beyond the range of the church's bells.

"In the other version," Eileen continued, "the woman merely did a lot of things to annoy Saint Columba during her lifetime, so that when she passed away, the saint wanted her buried as far away from him as possible. In either case, the woman was put in a remote graveyard and not buried near the church." Nothing seems to be known about the other poor women buried in Relignaman, but they certainly had fallen from grace and so were interred in this desolate little cemetery far from consecrated ground.[10]

The gloomy Relignaman with its doomed women put both Eileen and me in mind of another type of Ireland's supernatural females, the *bean sí*, or banshee, as the word was later anglicized. I had long been acquainted with the term—my aunt used to admonish me "not to scream like a banshee" when I was a child—but I hadn't known that what we think of today as a banshee is actually an amalgam of two distinct characters from Irish folklore: the *sí*-woman and the *badb*-woman. Some of the tales concerning these wailing harbingers of death were first recorded in the eighth century, some in the twelfth, but all undoubtedly stem from prehistoric oral traditions.

Sí-women appear in the *Táin Bó Froech* (*The Cattle Raid of Froech*), one of the earliest epics from the Ulster Cycle. Froech, the son of a goddess of the underworld, came to Connacht to win the hand of Finnbair, the daughter of Medb and Ailill. Apparently his prospective in-laws did not think highly of the young swain, and through their treachery, Froech was wounded by a water monster and brought to Cruachan, the capital of Connacht, to recuperate. As he lay in the castle, 150 beautiful and elegantly dressed maidens appeared throughout the land, weeping in the most pitiful manner. Medb dispatched messengers to discover the cause

---

10. Separate, remote graveyards for children are more common throughout Ireland, because babies who died before they were baptized could not be buried in consecrated ground. In fact, a *Relig na paisde,* or children's graveyard, lies quite near Relignaman.

of their sorrow, and found they were crying for Froech because it was foretold that he would die. Froech learned of the prophecy and exclaimed, "This is the crying of my mother and the women of Boand (the otherworld)." Froech's injuries did prove fatal, and the lovely young *sí*-women who had forecast his death carried his corpse into the otherworld mound of Cruachan.[11] But not to be stopped even by the grim reaper, the hero later returned, accompanied by fifty ladies attired in otherworldly apparel; they fought valiantly by his side when he launched a cattle raid, and together they brought it to a successful conclusion.

Sí-women also appeared in several later epics, including *Táin Bó Cuáilnge* and *The War of the Gaedhil with the Gaill*. In all these tales, the *sí*-women are beautiful young women who comb their long hair as they loudly lament the imminent passing of a hero. These were socially elite supernatural prophetesses, for they followed only certain old noble families, such as the Fitzgeralds and the O'Briens. As Patricia Lysaght notes in her poem *The Banshee*: "In Dingle the crying did not grow faint,/And the hoarding merchants grew afraid,/But they need not fear for themselves,/Banshees do not bewail their sort." In fact, the men about to die would never hear or see the *bean sí,* and despite the women's being forecasters of doom, they were often considered protective patron spirits of the noble family they watched over.[12]

In *The Death of Cú Chulainn*, we meet another type of death messenger, the shape-shifting warrior goddess Badb, who appeared as a crow and then as a hag roasting dog-meat.[13] Later, Cú Chulainn and his warriors encountered a lovely maiden by a river on the plains of Emain engaged in the grisly business of washing a pile of bloody human body parts: "While moaning and complaining she squeezed and washed purple,

---

11. The mound seems to be a passage tomb allowing entry into the otherworld—the Celts believed that they could move freely between the realms of the living and the dead.
12. Banshees have been noted in recent times. Eileen Murphy's father told his family he had heard a banshee wailing when his neighbor, the last member of her family, died.
13. Again we find the dog as a symbol of the underworld.

hacked, wounded spoils on the bank of the ford" (Lysaght 1986). The Druid accompanying the troops told Cú Chulainn that the woman was Badb's daughter, and she was forecasting his death.

Although Cú Chulainn's prophetess was described as beautiful and young, most of the mythic Badb-women were ugly old crones who directly confronted the doomed men. In *The Triumphs of Turlough,* the army of Donnchadh O'Brien came across a loathsome creature washing a heap of severed heads and limbs on the shore of Lough Riasc in County Clare. When asked to whom the mangled remains belonged, the Badb-woman told O'Brien that they were his army's, and that his own head was included in the bunch. In another tale, hero Cormac Conloingeas was proudly riding to Ulster to assume the throne when he stumbled upon a Badb on the banks of the River Shannon. "Swarthy she was of hue and a dusky mantle covered her," the story relates, "her mouth was big and gray hair fell over her shoulders" (Lysaght 1986). Upon seeing the heir apparent, the Badb assumed the stance of a sorceress uttering a prophecy while standing on one foot and closing one eye—this is also said to be the pose of a Druid while prognosticating—and chanted that it was Cormac's blood-soaked harness she was washing (Lysaght 1986).

In modern times, the *bean sí* and the Badb have merged to become the banshee, whose hair-raising screeches and shrieks alert mortal listeners to an impending death. She is still associated with water, appearing at dusk, dawn, or midnight near ponds, lakes, or rivers.[14] Sometimes she appears in the mournful guise of a young *bean sí,* other times her long tresses have turned gray and matted and her shrill screams announce her grief. And sometimes she can still be found washing a load of ghastly laundry at the ford.

On the plane home from Dublin, I read passages from *The Banshee* and other mythic texts and wondered what insights into ancient Ireland could be gleaned from these colorful tales. After traveling through Ireland and

---

14. One wonders if this is a cultural memory of the water goddess so prominently displayed in ancient Near Eastern and Hittite iconography and at their religious sites. Many ancient stelae and sculptures depict women holding vases with flowing water.

seeing the stories' pervasive cultural influence and links with the archaeology, I was certain they shouldn't be dismissed as mere flights of fancy—
like all myths, they reflected the beliefs and social structure of the people
who created them. If one examines its distinguishing qualities, Irish
mythology is replete with images of strong females who are equal, or
superior, to their male counterparts. The genealogy of Irish mythic heroes
is always traced through the female line. Although we have no written
evidence, this nonetheless implies that the pre-Christian tribes, who created and embellished the myths, had to have been matrilineal.

An unusually large proportion of the feminine mythic figures are associated with the bellicose arts: the many war goddesses, Queen Medb,
vengeful Macha—even the great Cú Chulainn and other male heroes
were trained in the arts of war by women. We must assume that these
woman were also warriors in their own right.

It's reasonable to suppose that when the mainland Celts entered Ireland,
they also brought their cultic traditions. As horrific as they are, the banshees with their gift of prophecy, along with the mysterious Sheela-na-
gigs, are highly suggestive of the existence of a priestess class, which we
know existed in other Bronze and Iron Age societies. The Sheela-na-gigs
also display certain similarities—nudity and sexuality—to the images of
the Kangjiashimenzi dance ritual; these also relegate the explicit figures
to fertility and procreation. Queen Medb could well have originated as
a powerful fecundity cult leader if we consider her main focus throughout the long epic: *Táin Bó Cuáilnge*. She must obtain not just any bull, but
the very best bull in the entire land. Even more compelling: Without the
bull, her kingdom does not survive.

All these circumstances convince me that women of the Emerald Isle,
throughout the pre-Celtic and Celtic "dark ages," must have enjoyed significant power and dignified prestige. They were matriarchs and priestesses, fertility cult and religious leaders, and they excelled as warriors and
rulers.

CHAPTER TWELVE

FROM CELTS TO MONGOLS: WOMEN OF BUSINESS AND KINGMAKERS

My visit to Ireland fed my long-standing interest in the Celts, and I found my attention drawn to other Celtic strongholds in Great Britain and continental Europe, wondering whether these lands might also yield glimpses of women with substantial power and influence. I was rewarded with more stirring tales of mythological heroines, and firm archaeological evidence of actual warrior queens and other high-status women. As the exploration of one culture led naturally to another, I also discovered that my path eventually returned to its starting point, the steppes of Eurasia.

Like the Irish, the Celts who settled in parts of what is now Wales, England, and Scotland cloaked many of their goddesses in the garb of warriors. Andraste, "the invincible one," was invoked by Celtic Britons before they engaged in battle; Cymidei Cymeinfoll, whose name means "bloated with war," was considered both a war goddess and a derivation of resurrection; and tales of the mythic ancestresses of Wales—Branwen, Rhiannon, and Arianrhod—are rife with conflict and bloodshed. But unlike Ireland, where warrior queens remain the stuff of legend, England has yielded reliable evidence of real-life female rulers and military leaders, evidence that comes courtesy of the cruel but literate foreign invaders who overran the island in ancient times.

Tacitus, the first-century Roman historian, wrote that the Britons "are used to women commanders in war" and offered detailed reports on the exploits of two warrior queens, Cartimandua and Boudicca (also known as Boadicea). The former, whose name means "sleek pony," was queen of the Brigantes, a vast tribal confederation in north-central Britain. Although she ruled with her husband, Venutius, Cartimandua held the real power in the kingdom and had played an active role in choosing her mate and co-regent. When the Romans invaded, both Cartimandua and Venutius saw the political advantages in siding with these powerful aggressors, and Brigantia, around A.D. 50, became a thriving Roman client state. The queen lost popularity among her subjects, however, when she turned over the leader of the Celtic rebels to the Romans after he sought asylum at her court. Her power base further eroded when she divorced her husband and married his armor-bearer, thus making the former underling the new king. Her actions prompted a civil war, with the Romans entering the fray on Cartimandua's side and eventually defeating Venutius in A.D. 71.

While the Brigantine rebels were stirring up trouble, the Romans faced a fierce vengeance in the northeastern part of the island. Upon the death of her husband, Queen Boudicca, whom the Roman Dio Cassius, more than a century later, described as "very tall in stature, in appearance most terrifying, in the glance of her eye most fierce, harsh in voice . . . and with a great mass of bright red hair falling to her hips" (Werner 1994, and Fraser 1988), had become leader of the Iceni, in what is now Norfolk and Suffolk. Like the Brigantes, the Iceni had formed an alliance with the Romans that allowed them prosperity and a good measure of independence. Before his death in A.D. 60, Boudicca's husband, King Prasutagus, willed half his personal estate to Rome, hoping the gesture would prove his fealty and appease Nero. The emperor, however, would

Boudicca, queen of the Iceni, drives her chariot, victorious over the Romans, in this bronze
sculpture on the bank of the Thames in London.

never settle for half a fortune when he could have it all—especially if such
riches belonged to a mere woman—so Nero ordered his minions to seize
Prasutagus's estate and annex the Iceni territory. When Boudicca protest-
ed, the Roman soldiers flogged the queen and raped her two daughters.

Furious beyond words, Boudicca took command of her Iceni troops
and joined forces with Trinovante Celts from the south; together they
formed an immense army of both male and female soldiers, as Tacitus
noted. He also quoted the queen as saying, "I am not fighting for my
kingdom and wealth. I am fighting as an ordinary person for my lost freedom, my bruised body, and my outraged daughters." The queen offered
a hare to the war goddess Andraste before each battle, while the rebellious
Britons destroyed the Roman city of Camulodunum (Colchester) and
annihilated the Ninth Legion. Suetonius Paulinus, the Roman provincial
governor, counted on Boudicca to proceed immediately to Londinium

(London) but instead, the queen moved northward. Suetonius drafted all the men of fighting age into his army and, leaving the city undefended, marched north, knowing full well he might have been sacrificing Londinium. Meanwhile, after sacking Verulamium (St. Albans) twenty miles to the north, Boudicca moved on to the defenseless Londinium, determined to exact her revenge on the Romanized citizens. "Those who were unfit for war because of their sex (the Romans didn't draft the women into war as did the Iceni and other tribes), or too aged to go, or too fond of the place to abandon it, were butchered," Tacitus wrote. "They [Boudicca and her warriors] wasted no time in getting down to the bloody business of hanging, burning, and crucifying."

The warrior queen then turned her attention to Suetonius, tracking him down in north London. This time, however, Andraste abandoned her followers, and Suetonius, who had managed to join forces with another Roman legion, soundly defeated the Britons. Shortly afterward, Boudicca committed suicide, reportedly by taking poison.

The advent of Christianity dealt the fatal blow to the old Druidic ways in Britain, Ireland, and mainland Europe. Charismatic missionaries such as St. Columba and St. Patrick, with their inspirational rhetoric and promises of eternal salvation, gradually seized the imagination of the Celts, and new religious traditions began to infiltrate pagan rites and legends. Some of the most striking examples of this spiritual mélange can be found in *The Barzaz Breiz*, a collection of fifth- and sixth-century Celtic tales from Brittany filled with mystery and magic. One of the best-known tales concerns a powerful count named Conomor, who married five successive brides for their wealth and property. He then murdered each one when she became pregnant, due to a Druidic prophecy that had foretold Conomor would be killed by his own son.

For his sixth wife, Conomor sought the hand of the fair Triphine, the daughter of King Waroc of Broërec. Both the king and Triphine were reluctant to agree to such an unpromising union, but Waroc entrusted the bridal negotiations to his adviser, St. Gildas. Well aware of the count's military might and nasty temper, St. Gildas feared what might befall the kingdom if the wedding didn't proceed. In the end, the saint decided to give his blessing to the union, but he vowed to protect Triphine and gave her a magic silver ring that would warn her of imminent danger.

At first, the newlyweds got along well, but then Triphine became pregnant. Noticing that her ring had turned black, the frightened countess sought refuge in the last place she thought Conomor would look: the royal crypt in which the cold-hearted king had buried his five previous wives. As she pondered her fate, the wives' ghosts rose up before her and each one offered a bit of information or a device to help her escape from the castle. Triphine fled into the forest, where a raven from her father's court appeared at her side. She held up her magic ring and the bird carried it off to alert the king of his daughter's peril. While she waited, Conomor caught up with his runaway bride and beheaded her with a single blow. However, St. Gildas appeared on the scene and prayed for Triphine, who promptly came back to life, and refitted her severed head neatly upon her neck.

She returned to her father's court, where she gave birth to a son. Several years later, the boy was playing with some friends in the same forest where his mother had hidden. Conomor happened upon the group and recognized the boy as his own. Gratified by another chance to cheat the prophecy, the merciless count drew his sword and lopped off his son's head, but to no avail. Still under the protection of St. Gildas, the little boy calmly picked up his head and followed Conomor back to his castle. When the lad reached the fortress's walls, they crumbled, crushing Conomor to death.

The fact that Conomor married women for their fortune suggests that Celtic women could amass great personal wealth and own land, an assumption that has been supported by archaeological finds dating as far back as the sixth and fifth century B.C. Eastern France, southwestern Germany, and other areas of Celtic Europe are dotted with Iron Age tombs in which both male and female rulers were buried with rich troves of mortuary offerings.

In Holmichele, Germany, for example, a man and woman were found laid side by side in a lateral burial chamber while a single woman occupied the more important central burial—an arrangement that is reminiscent of Sauro-Sarmatian burials. One of the most elaborate tombs on the French Côte-d'Or belonged to the celebrated Lady of Vix, who was buried in the late sixth century B.C. in a Celtic hill fort. The lady, who was about thirty-five years old when she died, was laid on a wooden wagon, which was placed in a large, square grave chamber. She wore a gold torque and diadem; accompanying her were bronze bowls, an Attic Black Figure cup from Greece, an immense bronze krater (mixing bowl) of Greco-Etruscan workmanship, and many other treasures. That krater, in particular, has given historians and archaeologists pause. Some assert that its shape and great size are suggestive of the cauldrons that Herodotus and Strabo reported were used to catch the blood of human sacrificial victims, leading them to believe that the Lady of Vix might have been a priestess. Whether she was a priestess, a princess, or a noble woman of great wealth, the amassed mortuary offerings belonging to the Lady indicate the elevated status that a woman could obtain in the ancient Celtic world.

In the late eighth century A.D., the British Celts encountered a new threat to their peace and prosperity: seafaring raiders from Scandinavia, who became known as the Vikings. The first recorded attack befell the island of Lindisfarne, off the east coast of England, when the Vikings looted and slaughtered its inhabitants before razing its monastery. Soon attacks on the European coastal settlements were commonplace, and villagers trembled at the sight of long wooden ships with beast-shaped prows approaching their shores. Some Vikings were farmers in pursuit of less crowded lands in more hospitable climes; others were mercenaries lured by the prospect of gold, silver, slaves, and other booty. Some were traders eager to establish mercantile footholds in distant lands, while others sought the silver coinage minted in Persia (Iran). All in all, they enjoyed a three-hundred-year-long golden age. During this time, they discovered Greenland, Iceland, and North

America; founded colonies in Ireland, France, England, and the Netherlands; and both raided and traded with Spain, Italy, North Africa, Russia, the Middle East, and the Byzantine Empire.

I had seen evidence of the Vikings' passion for plunder and the sea during several visits to Scandinavia. Birgitta Gustafson, editor of the Swedish periodical *Popular Arkeologi,* invited me to Stockholm in 1997. One of the highlights was a visit to the Museum of National Antiquities, where I marveled at the tremendous hoard of gold torques and silver coins from Central Asia ensconced in a handsome display. The next year, when Matt and I returned to Sweden for an archaeological conference, our itinerary included a tour of the petroglyphs at Tanum, located north of the city of Göteborg and overlooking the North Sea. Dating to the time of the Vikings, hundreds of images of longships and men at oars had been carved onto these stone boulders, while scores of other petroglpyhs depicted warriors wielding spears, long swords, or axes. I noticed only a single petroglpyh that revealed the Vikings' agricultural provenance, a scene of ritual plowing, no doubt intended to ensure fertile fields. Clearly, the lure of the sea and its lucrative ports of call was foremost in the hearts of these bold marauders.

In the history books and the movies, the Vikings are muscle-bound, hairy, blond, bearded warriors who swing swords, leaping from their longboats to rape and pillage.[1] And Viking women, if considered at all, are pictured toiling at home, herding the animals, maintaining the hearth, all the while in anticipation for their menfolk to return with the spoils. In actuality, the women's roles were much more dynamic. With such a large part of the male population away at sea for long periods of time, Viking women enjoyed an amount of responsibility and freedom unusual for females of their era. They could divorce their husbands whenever

---

1. There were two groups of Vikings: the Western Vikings from Denmark and Norway, who terrorized Northern and Western Europe and explored the Atlantic, and the Eastern Vikings, who were predominantly Swedes and established trading centers in Eastern Europe, Russia, Ukraine, and Byzantium.

they chose, they owned property and goods, and they liberally shared in the booty their men returned with. In his *Risala,* the tenth-century Islamic historian Ibn Fadlan reported that the Viking women he encountered in his travels on the Volga "wore neck rings [status-symbol torques] of gold and silver" and that "each woman wears on either breast a box of iron, silver, copper, or gold; the value of the box indicates the wealth of her husband." The richest, he noted, were festooned with much-prized colored beads or large oval brooches from which dangled knives, keys, and combs.[2]

Ibn Fadlan's chronicles are not only backed by archaeological findings; the variety and value of Viking women's mortuary offerings usually exceeded the men's. Many wives also controlled the family's commercial businesses—about 25 percent of female burials, a higher percentage than the men's, held scales and weights used to measure Persian silver coins, the principle trading commodity from the Middle East sought by the Vikings. And women often were buried with keys, locks, and caskets, suggesting they were the ones in charge of the family fortunes.

Strength and physical fitness were prized equally in women, and even Ibn Fadlan, who deplored many of the customs of these people he termed "coarse infidels," had to admit that he had "never seen such perfect physical specimens, tall as date palms, blonde and ruddy." For recreation, women competed as equals with men in the sport of *glima,* a type of wrestling that is still popular today in Iceland. An ancient saga commemorated one such match between a male and a female that lasted for days before ending in a draw. Some women were probably also warriors, as they were entombed with an array of weapons to help them fight on in the otherworld.

With such a tradition of strong women, it isn't surprising that, like the ancient Celts, the Vikings counted many powerful females among their deities and often associated them with the art of war. Freya and Frigg are

---

2. Ibn Fadlan referred to the Eastern Vikings whom he encountered along the Volga as the *Rus,'* from which Western scholars believe the Russian nobility derived.

the chief goddesses in the Norse pantheon, which is divided into two contentious families of gods, the Vanir and the Aesir.[3] Freya, the ravishing Vanir goddess of love and fertility, possesses a zest for battle; her sacred boar is a symbol of war, and after a Viking skirmish, she divides the fallen warriors with Odin, the chief god of the Aesir. Frigg, Odin's wife, is the ultimate hearth woman—the goddess of marriage, fertility, and childbirth, she uses her prodigious common sense and domestic skills to keep everything running smoothly in Asgard, the Norse Olympus. She is commonly portrayed with a magical spinning wheel, which she uses to spin out the fates of humans, and usually outsmarts her impetuous husband when they have a disagreement.

There are many other goddesses—such as Eir, the great physician; soft-hearted Lofn, who intercedes for star-crossed lovers; and Gefiun, who attends all who die virgins—but the best-known females in Norse mythology are the Valkyries. These beautiful, heavily armed maidens on their winged horses are charged with deciding which of the Vikings who die in battle are heroic enough to dine with Odin. They escort the most valiant to Valhalla to serve Odin, and also function as his messengers. It is said that the sunlight reflecting off their armor as they ride on the god's errands causes the shimmering colors of the Northern Lights. The celebrated Brunhilde, of the breastplate and horned helmet, who figures prominently in Old Norse sagas as well as the German *Nibelungenlied*,[4] is sometimes referred to as a Valkyrie. In both traditions, she is a mighty warrior who vows to marry only a man who can surpass her in strength.

The heyday of the Western Vikings drew to a close in the twelfth century, just as a powerful new force from the East began to turn its atten-

---

3. In Chapters 8 and 9 I've described the unexpected red- or blond-haired, blue- or green-eyed Caucasoids who turned up throughout much of Eurasia. In contrast, the creation myths of the Vikings (blond and blue-eyed people) trace their ancestry to Odin and Frigg, who were said to come from Asia Minor, land of dark-skinned peoples.

4. A thirteenth-century German epic poem based on Scandinavian legends and featuring the exploits of the hero Siegfried.

tion to the West and the lucrative trade along the Silk Road. The wealth of the Rus' principalities in Ukraine also caught the eye of Genghis Khan, one of the greatest conquerors the world has ever known. On his march westward, he gained control of the ports along the Volga and Don rivers, once commanded by the Vikings, as well as land routes connecting East and West. Finally, his forces took Hungary, but soon afterward they mysteriously disappeared in the thunder of thousands of ponies' hooves, never to be seen again on the Western plains. It was 1241, Genghis Khan was dead, and the *quriltai*—the great council meeting in which all the lesser khans and their forces gathered to elect a great khan—had begun.

Shortly after, *The Secret History of the Mongols* was written—commissioned by the descendants of Genghis Khan, but penned by his Uygur scribes—and its generosity in crediting the women, who variously poured oil on troubled waters or stirred up court intrigue, is quite unexpected in the warrior-dominated culture. The *Secret History* begins with the story of Alan-Qo'a, a mythical ancestress of the Mongol people. Alan-Qo'a had given birth to two sons by the time she was widowed, then had three more children, whom she claimed were conceived in a rather unconventional manner: "Every night, a bright yellow man entered by the light of the hole at the top of the door and rubbed my belly," she is quoted as saying. "His light was wont to sink into my belly. When he went out, like a yellow dog he was wont to crawl out by the beams of the sun or moon." The youngest of these "pure sons" was Boduçhar, whose progeny, eight generations later, included Temüjin. Temüjin, born into the noble Borjigin tribe around A.D. 116, was the man destined to become Genghis Khan (Universal Ruler).

When Temüjin was about ten, a feuding nomadic tribe killed his father, Yesügei. Anxious to seize power, the Yesügei clan drove the family into the Kentei Mountains, where the strong and determined widow, Hö'elü Üjin, managed to survive with her children. Born "with the seat of courage," the resourceful Hö'elü Üjin not only adapted to a threatening environment, she protected and nurtured her children, digging for edible roots, collecting shallots and other plants, and gathering wild pears until the children were old enough to help her hunt and fish. In his early man-hood, her son Temüjin overcame this unpromising situation by using his intense charisma, immense strength, and shrewd intelligence, systemati-cally building tribal alliances until he had amassed a mighty army. Then he began his march to the West and into Europe.[5] By 1206, Genghis Khan had become the ruler of all Mongols.

His endeavors were always assisted by his wife Börte, the daughter of an influential tribal chieftain who held her in high esteem. *The Secret History* describes his love and admiration for her: "When he saw his daughter, he saw a maiden with light in her face, with fire in her eyes." Shortly after their wedding, misfortune fell when Börte and Temüjin encountered a band of Mäkrits—the same tribe that had killed Temüjin's father—who took the young bride captive. With the help of a sympathetic khan, whom Temüjin rendered even more sympathetic by giving him Börte's magnif-icent sable coat, a treasure of her dowry, the young warrior recovered his wife. Nine months after her capture she gave birth to her first son, Jochi, but the paternity of the child was never mentioned.[6] Throughout the years of Temüjin's reign, both his wife and his resilient mother, Hö'elü Üjin, were counted among his most trusted advisers, for theirs were the voices of reason calming his volatile nature in the most treacherous of situations.

After Genghis Khan's death in 1227 and intermittently for spans of years, Mongol *qatuns* (queens) were appointed regents and during their sovereign-

---

5. One of the principal ethnographic divisions of Asian peoples, the Mongols of the Genghis Khanite were composed of many Mongol and Turkic ethnic and linguistic tribes and are believed to have originated in the forest steppes of northeastern Mongolia. Today, they still speak Altaic languages related to the Turkic languages. Mongols ranged over what is now Mongolia and China's Inner Mongolia Autonomous Region, with their original home-land, that is, the homeland of Genghis Khan, south of present-day Ulan Bator. As the hordes of Genghis Khan spread westward, they intermarried with indigenous tribes, cre-ating the Caucasoid and Mongol admixture that is found today as far west as Turkey.
6. Less is known of Jochi than the other sons of Börte, probably because a cloud hung over his paternity.

The Mongols in the Thirteenth Century

By 1206, Genghis Khan had united the Mongol and Turkic tribes, pastoral nomads who hitherto had been divided into often fractious *ulus*, a Mongol word meaning both "tribes" and "small nations." A man of keen intelligence, ambition, and political flexibility, the Great Khan then used the military might of the unified tribes to amass the largest contiguous land empire ever assembled, one that eventually stretched roughly from Hungary to Korea, and from southern Siberia to Tibet.

Within the century, Koreans and Chinese in the East, Hungarians and Poles in the West, and the Rus' north of the Black Sea had felt the Mongol impact, and being literate societies they documented—and not necessarily in the most unbiased manner—the bloodcurdling attacks, the tenacious sieges upon the cities, the rapes, pillages, and the ultimate wholesale decimation of entire populaces.

The Mongol technique was simple, and the terms were always the same. Supported by as many as ten thousand highly trained archers on horseback, Genghis Khan

Mongol Khan and Qatun hunting with cheetahs.

approached a fortified settlement and issued an ultimatum: "Surrender and give me everything, or I'll annihilate you." Some were pragmatic enough to wave the white flag quickly, but many would not and the Mongols inevitably breached their defenses. The khan's troops would massacre the men except for the artisans, seize all the property, and turn the women and children into slaves and concubines. Like the Vikings', the Mongols' ruthlessness in battle and seemingly unslakable appetite for conquest caused them to be widely feared and reviled. Matthew Paris, a thirteenth- century English monk and historian, labeled them "a detestable nation of Satan that poured out like devils from Tartarus" (from the Greek *Tartaros*, a section of Hades reserved for the punishment of the wicked), thus giving rise to the popular term "Tartar" that hailed the Mongol for centuries. These "demons" at first were the Tartari, then Tartares, and finally Tartars. The word Tartar subsequently became confused with Tatar (Persian *Tātār*). The *Tatars*, however, are a distinctive ethnic group of Caucasoid-Mongol Turkic-speaking Muslims who live in the Autonomous Region of Tatarstan west of the Ural Mountains. Although the devil's scourge for the Rus' and the Europeans, once Genghis Khan had crushed his principal rivals and amassed his vast empire he proved to be a shrewd and imaginative ruler who learned much from the peoples he conquered.

ty were afforded the rights and privileges of ruling the entire Mongol Empire. Theirs was a stabilizing force, holding the nation together during the political turmoil that preceded the election of each subsequent khan. These queens were warrior women, brilliant politicians, astute businesswomen, holders of immense properties, who had become steeped in wisdom, and upon the death of a khan were powerful agents for choosing the next one.

The first of these remarkable women was Sorqaghtani Beki, a Keryait princess raised in Christianity, who excelled at political astuteness and as kingmaker.[7] Widow of Genghis Khan's youngest son, Tolui, who had died two years after inheriting the Mongol homeland from his father, Sorqaghtani Beki was a strong and forceful women.[8] She had been the

---

7. *Beki* is an official title usually reserved for men. See page 224 for the generations of Genghis Khanite rulers.
8. As was the tradition, the youngest son remained with his parents until they died and then inherited the remaining property, the older children who had left to establish their homes had already received their share of the inheritance. This tradition is still in force today among the Kazaks and Mongols.

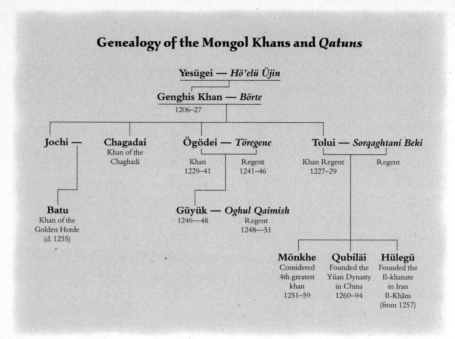

Genealogy of the Mongol Khans and *Qatuns*

Yesügei — *Hö'elü Üjin*

Genghis Khan — *Börte*
1206–27

Jochi —	Chagadai	Ögödei — *Töregene*	Tolui — *Sorqaghtani Beki*
	Khan of the Chaghadi	Khan / 1229–41 Regent / 1241–46	Khan Regent / 1227–29 Regent

Batu
Khan of the
Golden Horde
(d. 1255)

Güyük — *Oghul Qaimish*
1246–48   Regent
       1248–51

Mönkhe	Qubiläi	Hülegü
Considered 4th greatest khan 1251–59	Founded the Yüan Dynasty in China 1260–94	Founded the Il-khanate in Iran Il-Khāns (from 1257)

directing spirit of the house of Tolui even before her husband's death. When she was widowed, Tolui's older brother Ögödei attempted to force her to marry his son; it was the custom for widows to be assimilated into elder brothers-in-law's families. Asserting her independence, she refused, informing the khan that she had her own children to raise. In addition to the vast appanages inherited from her husband, she also had two feudal estates in different Chinese provinces that Ögödei decreed to her after he was elected khan. The rents from these estates—in reality, large villages—provided her with more than adequate wealth. She also maintained an *orda* (an encampment) at the summer pasture in the Altai Mountains where great herds of horses, sheep, camels, and yaks were managed by an entourage of more than a thousand families; she also had 12,900 soldiers who maintained her rule. Sorqaghtani Beki and her three sons were frequently lauded by the khan as examples of honesty and loyalty worthy of emulation.

According to a modern Mongolian historian, Ögödei's wife, Törogene, had been de facto ruler for the twelve years of her husband's reign, as his love for alcohol had rendered him less than competent. Her history is particularly fascinating, as she had been the wife of a Mäkrit khan before being captured by Genghis Khan, who then married her to Ögödei as his sixth wife. To have ascended to power from this relatively inferior position—as an outsider and sixth wife—she must have possessed charm, considerable astuteness, and extraordinary competence. Her influence in Ögödei's life was enormous. She also earned the respect of the lesser khans, for they appointed her regent following her husband's death in 1241. As regent she continued to command the empire for another four years and did not permit a *quriltai* to convene until 1246, when she was able to manipulate the politi-

A priestess of the thirteenth-century Golden Horde has the same accoutrements designating her status as those worn by priestesses a thousand years earlier: an elaborate headdress, a string of valuable beads, and a cultic cup analogous to the *kubok* excavated from Late Sarmatian graves north of the Black Sea.

cal command so that her son, Güyük, was elected khan. As fate would have it, Güyük died two years later, possibly of severe alcoholism.

Once again, a woman picked up the reins of power—this time Oghul Qaimish, Güyük's widow. An intense power struggle broke out between the lesser khans to elect the next great khan, weakening the empire. As had happened in the past, the diplomat Sorqaghtani Beki again demonstrated her finesse, and in collaboration with Batu, the powerful ruler of the Golden Horde, saw to it that her son Möngke was elected khan "by one vote" amid great political intrigue.[9] Once in power, Möngke set about eliminating the opposition. Oghul Qaimish was summoned to court and immediately taken to Sorqaghtani Beki's *orda,* where she and another opposing *qatun* were tried and "allowed to commit suicide" on the grounds they had used black magic against Möngke.

Sorqaghtani Beki was instrumental in manipulating Mongol politics until her death in 1252. In addition to Möngke's placement as khan (he is considered to be the greatest of all Mongol khans), two of her other sons followed in the footsteps of their illustrious grandfather, also becoming khans: Hülegü founded the Il-khanate in Iran, and Kublai unified China under the Yüan Dynasty. (See "End of an Empire," page 227.)

The story of regent *qatuns* doesn't end with Sorqaghtani Beki. In 1467 the Grand Khan Mandaghol (a descendant of Genghis Khan) died and his only remaining heir to the throne was Dayan, a five-year-old who had been orphaned. Mandaghol's young wife, Manduhai, adopted the child and soon had him proclaimed khan. She then assumed control of the court and went to war against the Oirat tribe, inflicting a decisive defeat upon them. In the ensuing years, her exploits were likened to those of the heroic mother of Genghis Khan. When Dayan turned nineteen, Manduhai married him, but she did not loosen her control over the Mongols. Ever the warrior, within a short time she led her loyal soldiers into battle, definitively overthrowing the Oirat horde so that the Mongols finally regained supremacy in the eastern regions of the holdings (Grousset 1970, 509).

Manduhai's name and deeds have gone into legend; Aigul, my translator, recounted more of the popular history of this *qatun* that she had learned as a child:

Upon reaching manhood, Dayan fell in love with a young and beau-

---

9. The Golden Horde, a mixture of Turks and Mongols, ruled the western portion of the Mongol Empire from the mid-thirteenth through the fourteenth centuries. The "golden" in their title alludes to their immense wealth, while "horde" is a corruption of the Mongol word *orda,* which means "summer pasture." (See Fedorov-Davydov 2001.)

End of an Empire

Kublai Khan, who reigned from 1260 until his death in 1294, presided over the Mongol Empire's greatest era of power and prosperity. An educated and relatively compassionate emperor who tried to earn the loyalty of his subjects through enlightened rule rather than terror, Kublai was also no slouch in the military department. Under his leadership, the Mongols reached a long-held military objective: the conquest of the Sung Chinese and the reunification of China under the Mongol Yüan Dynasty.

The strain of managing the enormous Mongol Empire began to show itself even during Kublai Khan's day, and political alliances among the lesser khans began to erode. None of his successors had the imagination, charisma, or political clout to prevent the gradual disintegration of the empire. In 1367, the Chinese Mings led a successful rebellion against their Mongol overlords, and, less than two decades later, the Golden Horde in Eurasia, already devastated by an incursion of the bubonic plague—which may have begun when infested pelts were traded to Europeans—retreated to the east and lost its territory along the Don and Volga rivers under an alliance of Rus' princes. Finally, in the seventeenth century, the Manchus of northeastern China launched a series of invasions into the Mongolian homeland—which I verified in an excavation in the Altai Mountains in 1999—setting off a complex chain of civil warfare and foreign interventions, driving Mongols and Kazaks from their ancient grazing lands. Today, the traditional Mongol homeland is split into two political entities: the present Mongolian Republic (Outer Mongolia) and the Inner Mongolia Autonomous Region, which is ruled by the Chinese.

tiful woman. And, although khans were permitted multiple wives, he couldn't marry her—even though she was pregnant with his child—because she was of a common family. Soon, however, intrigue permeated the court and a palace coup was in the making, centered on Manduhai. A childhood sweetheart of the *qatun* heard of her impending doom, warned her, and in the subsequent battle Manduhai and her court prevailed. As was the custom, Manduhai ordered all involved in plotting the coup summoned to court, tried, and those found guilty to be thrown into a great pit.

From its depths, Dayan pleaded for the life of his unborn child. "Great Qatun Manduhai, don't you want to save this child? The only heir of the great Genghis Khan?"

Manduhai stoically returned Dayan's gaze for only a short moment before turning to her general. "Fill the pit!" she ordered. And as the soldiers began to bury the victims alive, she strode away without a backward glance.

The world of the Mongols descended into literary darkness after the horrific Black Plague abruptly closed the passages between East and West in 1337, and our knowledge of this society became fractured. Western historians have defined the Mongol society as extremely cruel and abnormally patriarchial (a concept further fostered by patriarchal historians), one in which women didn't exist. The stories in *The Secret History of the Mongols* imply that without the Athena-like astuteness, diplomatic abilities, and survival instincts of Temüjin's mother and his wife, there might never have been a Mongol Empire. As we search through the history books for clues, however, we encounter other *qatuns* who were brilliant politicians, *qatuns* who were adroit and diplomatic, *qatuns* who were astute businesswomen, managing feudal estates and vast *ordas*. These were the *quatuns* who held the empire intact between *quriltais*. Their hands not only rocked the cradle, they continually rearranged the Mongol political sphere throughout the Genghis Khanite.

Can we imagine what would have happened if Töregene had followed the lead of her husband, Ögödei, and had continued the rape of Europe? Instead, she fostered the campaigns of Kublai Khan in China, thus allowing Europe to recover—and within a short time the Renaissance emerged to transform the world's cultures.

In 1992, as part of the UNESCO "Silk Road Dialogue" trip, a multinational group of some thirty journalists, fifty international scientists, and eighty Mongol support personnel visited Karakorum, the former capital of the Mongol Empire. As we motored along in our caravan of Jeeps, short yellow school buses, an army mess trailer, and trucks loaded with suitcases and massive gasoline tanks (where we were going, no gas stations had ever been built), we served as a great source of wonderment for the locals. And, at least one time, we were the source of animosity among the officials at the government center that had to prepare for about a hundred guests at a stand-up banquet (where can you find that many chairs in the steppe lands?). For four weeks, we explored historical and archae-

The many Silk Roads between the East and the West.

On the vast steppes of Mongolia, the sculpture (balbal) of a priestess of a Turkic tribe was probably carved as a burial marker around the middle of the first millennium A.D. She also wears a veil and holds a cup.

ological sites, nomad encampments, and petroglyphs—even finding unrecorded images on a rock outcropping—and we fought manic media photographers for shooting-room in front of *balbals, oovos,* and other archaeological wonders.[10] During the day, the terrain afforded a view of a half-dozen mountain ranges, each providing a backdrop for the next, and at night we camped under black skies filled with enormous and incredibly bright stars.

Once, in the central Mongolian mountains, a tribe of nomads prepared savory mutton for our midday meal. They seasoned the meat with wild shallots and roasted it in its own juices, packed between hot rocks in ten-gallon milk cans swaddled in heavy felts. After the meal, two young women came and sat beside me. Within moments, they pressed their faces, which wore the most curious expressions, closer and closer to mine. Finally, through a translator, they told me that this was the first time either had seen a white woman. I found it paradoxical that a culture that had once exerted such

---

10. *Balbals* are stone sculptures carved in the likeness of the people whose burial they marked. They are attributed to Turkic peoples dating from the sixth to ninth centuries, and are found from Tova and western Mongolia to Xinjiang, China, to points west into Eastern Europe. *Oovos* are cultic monuments composed of piled stones where Mongols offer sacrifices and make wishes.

The Mighty Woman Wrestler

Like the Vikings, the Mongols were much taken with the sport of wrestling and sometimes allowed men and women to compete as equals. I had seen bronze plaques of wrestlers posing in the traditional stance—shoulders pressed to shoulders—that date to the second and first

Medieval period wrestling scene with horses placed heraldically within the scene. The costume at this time does not include the frontless jacket. The scene is on a rhyton (drinking cup) and was discovered in 1866 in the Ural region.

centuries B.C., so I knew this traditional sport had a long history. Nowadays in early July of each year, Mongol families pack light summer tents, good boots, and festive deels, and ride and trail horses (for racing) from their summer pastures to villages or to Ulan Bator. They have one concern only: Nadaam festivities. On opening day at Ulan Bator, the stadium is filled with noisy spectators who have come to watch the proceedings; a procession of young warriors dressed in the costumes of the Genghis Khanite era, the archery competitions between both the men and women, and most important, the wrestling matches—more than seven hundred of them. In the center of the arena wrestler after wrestler is eliminated until only the champion of all of Mongolia remains. But the first time I saw a Mongol wrestling match I was curious about the unusual costumes worn

Mongol wrestlers at a provincial center celebrate Nadaam wearing their traditional costumes: boots, tight shorts, and sleeved jackets without a front.

231

by the competitors: heavy leather boots with up-turned toes, the skimpiest of shorts, and long-sleeved, frontless jackets held in place by narrow ties that stretched across ample bellies.

Since then, I've seen literally hundreds of these male-only matches, and finally learned the legend behind the odd outfits. In 1996 at one of the Mongol Nadaam celebrations, my Kazak translator Aigul told me that the costume harked back to the late days of the empire, when one of the Khans had a strong, aggressive daughter who excelled at wrestling. She decreed that any man wishing to wed her had to first defeat her in a wrestling match; if the would-be bridegroom lost, he had to forfeit to her a thousand horses. Suitor after suitor tried his luck, but the princess always won, and she eventually amassed a fortune—a herd of more than ten thousand horses.

Mongolian woman competing in an archery contest at the Nadaam festival in Ulan Bator.

Although Mongol men had sanctioned coed matches in the past, a woman such as this khan's daughter was anathema to their masculinity. They mandated that a new costume would be worn by wrestlers—one in which no woman could disguise her femininity, so she could never enter a match masquerading as a man, and could never be victor over a man.

influence on vast portions of the world had become so isolated that Caucasoid features now commanded such rapt attention.

After three weeks of winding through endless mountain passes, meandering through long stretches of plains, and fording almost unpassable rivers, we arrived at the site in central Mongolia where Genghis Khan had established his capital of Karakorum. I had eagerly anticipated this moment, but little remained to remind me that this once had been the center of a great empire. Unlike the Sinophile Kublai Khan, who built an elaborate enclave in his chosen capital at Beijing, replete with magnificent buildings and gardens, his grandfather established a less pretentious city at Karakorum, although Ögödei arranged for very elaborate fountains in his palace. But many diplomats from Western courts had made the arduous and dangerous journey over endless steppes, bringing their religions, a written alphabet for the Mongol court, and subtle innovations that modified this sturdy culture.

Today, a large grassy mound, a sculptured stone phallus, and a circular stone foundation mark the earth where the khan's massive ger-palace once stood. These are the only markers—hardly a fitting tribute to an era that had such a profound impact on world history.

CHAPTER THIRTEEN

THE LEGACY OF WARRIOR WOMEN

The revelations I've attempted to share with you in this book haven't come quickly or easily. Long, hot summers of excavating first the Saka nomads at Issyk in southern Kazakstan, then the Sauromatians and Sarmatians at Pokrovka in the southern Ural steppes was heavy work; the living conditions were purely primitive, and monetary rewards nonexistent. It took months of digging into kurgan mounds for skeletons and other ancient treasures, jostling over horse-made trails through summer pastures, sharing the nomads' yurts and their meals of boiled mutton dunked in hot broth washed down by salt-milk tea to even begin to fathom the survival tactics of the ancient nomads. It took my intense archaeological focus—countless hours of sorting artifacts and determining gender and status, and thousands more hours poring over bones and dusty pots—to arrive at the ten minutes of glorious recognition that the Gold Man was actually the Gold Woman. But it also took my presence as a guest of these hospitable people, observing their daily duties or their enjoyment during singing contests and wrestling, for me to begin to understand that in this nomadic world, egalitarianism, rather than patri-archialism, has always been the dominant way of life.

The clues in the artifacts we unearthed, as well as the common ritual practices and legends that live on in the present, allowed me to slowly piece together a global picture of warrior women. Though it is nearly impossible to pinpoint the beginning of ritual acts or how they evolved, my research has led me to believe that there are two great branches of rituals. The first encompasses those meant to encourage fertility. These were the rituals of the greatest concern in this world. The second branch involves burial rites, of utmost importance to gain entrance to the oth-erworld. It could not have been more fortuitous for me that the Early Nomads believed their possessions had to be included in their graves. Their intent was to ensure that all that they enjoyed in life would con-tinue in the otherworld, but these burials also provided the means for studying their way of life centuries later. Of course, it is also extremely lucky that the heavy alkaline soils of Pokrovka preserved bones and bronzes so well, providing us with an immense variety of artifacts, and enabling me to differentiate the statuses of Sauromatian and Sarmatian men and women.

Many of the central motifs of the enigmatic Animal Style and petro-glyphic scenes associated with the Saka, Sauromatians, and Sarmatians were also central to Celtic art in Western Europe. Thus I was drawn beyond the Central Asian steppes and into the literary genius of Celtic myths and legends of hidden heroines, where I found a cadre of power-ful women—anonymous, unnamed, sometimes maligned, always strong, frequently rich in gold and always wealthy in knowledge. Whether they dominated on the battlefield, acted as soothsayers, or ruled over the hearth, all had roles crucial to the survival of the tribe.

Among the steppe people, most of our ancient heroines belonged to the hearth—where oaths were sworn by the king, rites of passage were performed, and joyous births occurred, to be followed by somber and sorrowful deaths. The keepers of the hearth were also keepers of traditions, and of the culture, for in prehistoric societies without written languages, the traditions, tribal histories, and precious genealogies had to be memorized by each new generation. In times of illness, hearth women nursed the sick. And most crucial to survival, they prepared and distributed life-sustaining nourishment so that each received his or her share—no small task when all the tribe's food was restricted to portable portions which, during times of stress, could be mighty small. Through hundreds of generations, the strength and wisdom of unnamed hearth women guarded intrinsic power through which the family, clan, and tribe not only persisted but expanded exponentially, until nomads became mighty forces reckoned with throughout all of Eurasia.

Our excavations at Pokrovka revealed the earliest Sauromatian priestesses, who left us their unadorned divination mirrors, along with the single seashell they used while ministering to their extended families. During the course of the next 150 years, the increased value of priestesses' work was expressed by an elaborate medley of relics and heirlooms, embellished with gold to symbolize the sun's potency. In fact, by this point in history the images depicted on a priestess's tools did not only symbolize her own beliefs but the most significant beliefs of the entire tribe. Their icons of potency also centered on wild animals—deer, wolves, and great felines, and combinations that became mythical griffins. We encountered these magical animals in petroglyphs, cast in small gold plaques, carved from wood, and painted and tattooed on bodies. Priestesses had become seeresses of cultic rituals, manipulators of rites of passage, and healers of the body, mind, and spirit. Without a doubt, they held one of the single most important and revered roles in ancient communities. And, while providing divinations and prognostications, these women were also fundamental to the political and economic future of their tribes.

In fact, if we are to believe the linguists, women were also the first shamans. The roots of shamanism are to be found in Paleolithic Siberia, where a single term, most commonly *utygan*, always referred to the female shaman. Male shamans, in contrast, were called by various unrelated names.

In states of ecstasy, shamans communed with gods and spirits to cure human ills and to attain superhuman knowledge; they employed animal helpers to visit the otherworld. Long before a written language appeared, icons were recorded using the tools at hand. They included magical images of shamans, pecked into black slate at Tamgaly, dancing or ritually inseminating the magical horned horse. For nomads whose lifestyle is intimately connected with the forces of nature, sun and water are the givers of life, and nature symbols became imbued with the intensity of fertility, fecundity, and the ultimate result, reproduction. In the Kangjiashimenzi grotto, dancers choreographed the moment, while ancient artists preserved it in stone for as long as the storm gods are willing. Yet the dancers' postures reveal that the grotto was not the origin of this ritual, for it had traveled thousands of miles from its source in Neolithic Eastern Europe.

As the hierarchy of priestesses expanded, they performed greater services. If we interpret the accoutrements of the Tillya Tepe burial ritual with accuracy, we learn that warrior women served as priestesses and divined for the chieftains of great confederacies. Ritual swords and daggers were magnificently emblazoned with a golden profusion of parading winged horses and snow leopards, Trees of Life and birds, and Mistresses of Animals—all symbols of fecundity. Adding an international component, the image of Athena in the guise of a warrior from the Greek world complements representations of eunuchs driving chariots from China. Given their incredible wealth of gold and icons emblazoned with supernatural power, it takes little imagination to realize that these warrior-priestesses had attained authority on par with that of chieftains. Remarkable cross-cultural exchanges are revealed in the burial customs and mortuary offerings at Tillya Tepe, in the tombs of the Sauro-Sarmatian priestesses in the Ural steppes, those of the Saka women of the Tien Shan and Altai mountains, and the mummified women buried in the Taklamakan desert.

We do not know for sure where the line was drawn between the warrior-priestess and the woman warrior. But this much we know for certain: Warrior women there were! Many of the women discussed in these pages appear to have been warriors only, and did not act as priestesses. For example, Tomyris appears in ancient literature as the slayer of a great Persian king. Greek fables that centered on Amazons probably originated not only from tales of the Eurasian Sauromatians, but from North Africa, where matriarchy was central and the kings' elite troops were women. Fueled by anger, frustration, humiliation, and unimaginable courage, Queen Boudicca led her Iceni tribes against the most formidable Romans, and nearly defeated an army of superbly trained men. Medieval texts relate how the Mongol women were trained to fight, to shoot straight and deadly with bow and arrow, and not infrequently were called upon to serve as auxiliary troops in time of war.

As my crew and I wound our way through the Eurasian steppes and mountains, encountering the essence of undeniably high-status women, we discovered themes and icons that connected women of far-flung cultures. Many different ways of life had preceded the Early Nomads, and the Saka, Sauromatians, and Sarmatians were heirs to thousands of years of cross-cultural influences. Hunting-and-gathering groups foraged in southern Siberia, and later settled as agricultural villagers who spread into Eurasia along food-abundant rivers. These migrants carried concepts and assimilated others until beliefs became entwined, and icons representing the tenets evolved to hold multiple symbologies. Thus we find that shamans flew to the otherworld on a bird, while, in another context, birds held the souls of the yet-to-be-born. And, simultaneously, discrete icons might also represent a single belief: as a bird could hold the essence of life, so did the Tree of Life.

The reinterpretation of two icons in particular that represent women's fate over the centuries comes to mind: women's headdresses and the stone Sheela-na-gigs of Ireland.

Massive, elaborately decorated headdresses are special markers that we have followed throughout our search for women of status; they are one of the oldest cultural elements ever found. Elaborate headdresses, the only clothing the Kangjiashimenzi grotto women wear, define headgear as being paramount to ritual and status. Headdresses, then, are the hallmark of all women of status, from the stone-carved sculptures on the Mongolia steppes to those of the Pazyryk highlands in southern Siberia, to the Issyk warrior-priestess in southern Kazakstan, to the mummies of Xinjiang, China, to yet other sculptures north of the Black Sea. Then, in Europe around 1400, the conical headdresses dramatically metamorphosed into black hats that patriarchs deemed the identifier of women they fantasized to be witches, women they punished for imagined transgressions by burning them at the stake.

The second extraordinary example of this transformation is the Sheela-na-gigs, created in prehistoric antiquity as potent fertility images. However, several centuries before the nineteenth century (when they were first mentioned in the literature), the sculptures had been absurdly incorporated into church walls to warn against lust—a vice caused, of course, by women. From that point on, they were deemed embarrassing erotica. In the same milieu, Irish monks edited folktales so that strong warrior women became wanton women, or weak heroines whose only recourse to save their (always threatened) virtue was by preposterous self-destruction.

These two icons reveal the transition that occurred when egalitarian power shifted to patriarchal kingship-priesthoods. Women were purged from the positions of influence and eminence they had enjoyed for millennia and relegated to the lowest rungs of the status ladder, frequently maligned, or represented as satanic forces—the fate of the goddess Lilith is an excellent example. In ancient Greece, the myth of the Amazons—the hyperbolic caricature of the independent woman—was conjured up by Greek men, drawing from legends of warrior women in Eurasia, Anatolia, and Africa. These mythic women left their homes to fight the Greeks, they cut off their breasts to better shoot arrows, and, most damagingly, they murdered their male children. But despite their mask of invincibility, their challenge to male supremacy was a challenge punishable by rape or death—a task that fell, not so surprisingly, to the male Greek gods to perform.

We've only just begun to understand warrior women's dynamic and important roles in society during their lifetimes. By analyzing portable art forms and the permanent petroglyphs, we see their themes of creativity, their abilities for self-expression, and their obvious self-assurance. Weaving in mythology and literature, we see that intense feminine beings, with status, power, and position, persevered. These warrior women were the underlying foundation that held ancient societies together. They are our heritage, our role models. They deserve to come out of the shadows of history and be celebrated!

It has not been an easy road, but my work has been immensely rewarding on a personal and professional level. After so many years of raising children and living the life of a modern-day woman of the hearth, I am proud to have made an impact, however small, on our perceptions of women's roles throughout the ages. At lectures on my findings, numerous women—and even some men—have told me that hearing about my excavations and ethnographic research in "exotic lands" has inspired them to pursue their own dreams in this field. I am pleased at the prospect of finding more female colleagues joining excavations than ever before.

It is my sincere hope that the worlds I have unearthed will help create a sense of the powerful legacy of warrior women in today's society. May women everywhere find their place in this mysterious and grand history so that they may know themselves to be, as in the ancient past, the providers and protectors of the covenant of life.

GLOSSARY

ACHAEMENID PERSIANS Founded by Cyrus the Great (599–522 B.C.) after he united two nomadic tribes, the Medes and the Persians, who had originated in the Eurasian steppes, he consolidated his power from the Iranian plateau to Lydia in western Anatolia, creating the Achaemenid Empire. Marching into Central Asia, Cyrus was killed in battle with Tomyris although he is best known for liberating the Jews in Babylon. After his death, the throne was usurped by Darius the Great (522–486 B.C.), who became the greatest Achaemenid Persian ruler, noted for his administrative genius and building projects, including the great halls at Persepolis in southern Iran where they established their capital. Under Darius the empire extended from Egypt to India, including Central Asia, whose administrative centers *(satrapies)* had direct contact with nomadic confederacies as far east as Pazyryk. Darius's eldest son Xerxes (486–464 B.C.) inherited the throne, but from that time forward the Empire began to disintegrate. The last king, Darius III, was defeated by Alexander the Great and the invaders destroyed Persepolis in 330 B.C.

ALANS Nomad tribe along the north Black Sea in the first century A.D. had united, and by the third century had formed a single people known as the Alans, some of whom migrated to the Iberian Peninsula in the fifth century B.C. The Alans are considered descendants of the Late Sarmatians; the Ossetians living in the Caucasus Mountains are the descendants of the Alans.

AMAZONS Female warriors in Greek mythology who are said to have originated in northern Turkey.

ANIMAL STYLE The specific stylization of animals on nomadic portable art, weaponry, horse harness accoutrements, textiles, etc. Animal Style along with trilobed arrowheads, and horse accoutrements form the so-called Scythian triad, and are a hallmark of all Early Nomads.

ASSYRIAN EMPIRE In northern Iraq, the Assyrians were notable from the early second millennium B.C. for their caravans of black donkeys transporting textiles to eastern Anatolia in exchange for iron ore; far to the east they controlled precious stone imports from northern Afghanistan. The Neo-Assyrian Empire (858–627), with capitals at Assur and Nineveh, was under the inexorable control of dynamic kings, expanded to the eastern Mediterranean and Egypt, controlling all of Mesopotamia and much of Iran. The empire began to decline in the seventh century B.C.; in 626 B.C. the Scythians plundered Syria and Palestine, and in 612 B.C. the Medes and Babylonians allied destroying Nineveh, not only ending Assyria's rule but laying scourge to the lands.

AUL A village of yurt.

BACTRIA One of the Achaemenid Satraps (political divisions) encompassing present-day northern Afghanistan.

BRITONS Indigenous tribe in Britain before the invasion of the Anglo-Saxons in the fifth century A.D.

BRONZE AGE The period when people began manufacturing bronze items. Arsenic was found naturally mixed with copper and the first bronzes, known as arsenical bronze, were cast. True bronze is copper mixed with tin. The Bronze Age (4000–3000 B.C.) did not arrive in Eurasia until around 2000 B.C.

CELTS Early Indo-European people, archaeologically known as the Hallstatt Culture. Dating to about 1100 B.C., they were first excavated at Hallstatt near Salzburg, Austria, in an Early Iron Age context. In the early centuries of the first millennium B.C., they are known as the La Tène culture. These tribes spread over much of Europe, east to the Black Sea coast, and into Anatolia. Linguistically they have survived in the modern Celtic speakers of Ireland, Highland Scotland, Wales, and the Isle of Man.

CHALCOLITHIC AGE (also known as Eneolithis age) The time in cultural development, probably in the late seventh millennium B.C., when the Stone Age ended and people began incorporating hammered copper artifacts into their daily life.

CHOWHOUGOU An archaeological site in Xinjiang province adjacent to an oasis where Bronze Age and Early Iron Age peoples settled and nomadic populations buried their dead in three cemeteries. A fourth cemetery was used by the later-dated Hsiung nu. The cemeteries are located north of the Taklamakan desert and south of the Tien Shan Mountains with the closest city being Heijing.

COSSACK An extremely independent Caucasoid ethnic group living in the northern hinterlands of the Black and Caspian seas. In exchange for military service, they gained considerable privileges in czarist Russia. As the men were frequently away on military duty, the women were responsible for the livelihood of the families and, consequently, became quite independent.

CUCUTENI-TRIPOLYE Sedentary agricultural peoples during the fourth and third millennium B.C. who were excavated in Romania as the Cucuteni culture, and in Moldova and the western half of the Ukraine as the Tripolye culture. Subsequently, archaeologists recognized that the peoples living in the two regions belonged to the same culture, hence the hyphenated name. In the third millennium B.C., the eastern factions began migrations into the Don and Volga regions and probably farther east. They are known for their beautiful handmade painted pottery.

CZAR KURGAN An extremely large burial kurgan in which a high ranking chieftain was buried with many artifacts and sometimes retainers and horses; rich lateral burials at the edge of the kurgan have also been excavated, such as Issyk. The central burial of all these mounds have been robbed, either in antiquity (possibly to reclaim the burial artifacts for reuse) or, beginning in the sixteenth century by the Russians as they expanded across Siberia. Most of the massive gold artifacts in Animal Style were melted for monetary value, although after Peter the Great (1682–1725) issued an edict, some were brought to him and now are in the Hermitage museum's Gold Room in St. Petersburg.

DERBETS (Also Dörböt) One of the ancient Mongol tribes whose descendants currently live in western Mongolia.

DJUNGARS (Also spelled Jungar and Dzungar; also known as the Oirat and Kalmyks) In the early 1600s, the Oirat Mongols were driven westward by the Khalka Mongols into Siberia and around the Ili River and the Djungar Basin in western China. Earlier, in the fifteenth century, the Djungars had controlled and plundered a huge territory stretching from the outskirts of Beijing to western Turkestan.

EARLY NOMADS The first Eurasian nomadic tribes, specifically the Scythians, Sauromatians, Sarmatians, and Saka, that practiced transhumance, following their animals from pasture to pasture as required for feed and shelter.

GOLDEN HORDE The Russian designation for the Ulus of Jochi, the eldest son of Genghis Khan. The Golden Horde attained its power and prestige under Jochi's son Batu and flourished in the western part of the Mongol Empire from the mid-thirteenth to the end of the fourteenth century. Batu founded his capital, Sarai Batu, on the lower stretch of the Volga River. Over time the Horde became Turkified, adopting Islam under Khan Öz Beg. Plague, the horrific Black Death, struck in 1346–47, marking the decline of the Golden Horde. The people of the Golden Horde were Turkic and Mongol tribes, with the latter constituting the aristocracy. (See also **UZBEKS**.)

HAN CHINESE The appellation used for ethnic Chinese people, to distinguish them from minority nationalities in China.

HAN DYNASTY (206 B.C.–A.D. 220) The second great Chinese imperial dynasty, considered the prototype for all later Chinese dynasties. The Chinese of the Han Dynasty frequently interacted with nomads, particularly the Hsiung-nu.

HSIUNG–NU A confederacy of pastoral nomads who were also aggressive mounted warriors. They began to dominate much of Central Asia beginning in the early third century B.C. and continued their mastery for about five hundred years. Their repeated invasions into China became a forceful threat that caused China to begin construction of the Great Wall. Later, the Hsiung-nu confederacy split into the Eastern tribe, which submitted to China, and the Western tribe, which ultimately was driven into Central Asia.

HUNS A confederacy of nomadic peoples that originated east of the Volga River and migrated westward. As pastoral nomads, they invaded southeastern Europe around A.D. 370, built an enormous empire, and sacked Rome (which apparently had violated a treaty). By 455 they had faded from the historical scene. A unique Hunnic cultural tradition was skull deformation: they tied a silk band around the small child's head, causing the skull to elongate, apparently a sign of beauty. Skeletons with such deformed skulls dating to the second century A.D. were excavated at Pokrovka in the southern Urals, thus indicating a line of migration.

ICENI A tribe in Britain that occupied modern Norfolk and Suffolk. Under their queen, Boudicca, they revolted against, attacked, and nearly defeated the Romans in the first century A.D.

IRON AGE The time when iron was smelted into weaponry. This varies from 1200 B.C. in Anatolia to ca. 500 B.C. in the Eurasian steppes.

KALMYKS Oriat Mongols that, in the seventeenth century, were driven into the steppe lands north and west of the Caspian Sea, but many returned to the pastures in the high Tien Shan Mountains in Xingiang. Under Sovietization, they were banished to the gulags of Siberia, but managed to reestablish themselves in Kalmykia following Stalin's death. (See also DJUNGARS and OIRAT.)

KAZAKS Known in historical sources as the Kirghiz-Kazakhs, the Kazaks were a huge group of tribes who had separated from the Uzbeks around 1465. The Kazaks divided into three hordes; their collective homeland ranged over the modern territory of Kazakstan and into the western Altai Mountains in Mongolia. Their way of life was pure nomadic—as proclaimed by Khan Qasim (1509–1518):"We are men of the steppe; all our wealth consists of horses; their flesh is our favorite food, mare's milk our best drink. Houses we have none. Our chief diversion is to inspect our flocks and our herds of horses" (Grousset 1970, 480). During the Russian expansion in the mid-eighteenth century, Kazak tribes fled to the Djungarian Basin in western China, only to be forced by the Djungars into the Tien Shan Mountains in western China, while others sought refuge in the western Mongolian province of Bayan Ulgii. Here they were officially given territory and continue to this day to maintain their pure nomadic way of life. In Kazakstan, those who survived the devastation of Sovietization now practice a sedentary lifestyle on collective farms. Ethnically, the Kazaks are a mixture of Caucasoids and Mongoloids. (See also UZBEKS.)

KUSHAN EMPIRE In the second century B.C., the Hsiung-nu drove the Yüeh Chih from present day Xinjiang and they migrated westward into ancient Bactria (northern Afghanistan) where they subjugated the remaining Seluccids (Alexander the Great's army who had settled there after his death). The Yüeh Chih chieftain of the Kushan confederacy gained political supremacy and a century later under King Kaniska, the Kushans reached their political height and were equal to the other Eastern powers, including China. Their power abated about A.D. 200. The Kushans were instrumental in spreading Buddhism in Central Asia, India, and China.

LA TÈNE A Late Iron Age culture in Europe that evolved in the mid-fifth century B.C. when the Celts came into contact with Greek and Etruscan influences south of the Alps. (See also CELTS.)

MASSAGETAE A Saka tribe living in the vicinity of the Aral Sea who under the leadership of their queen, Tomyris, defeated and killed Cyrus the Great, Achaemenid Persian king, when he tried to invade her lands, in 530 B.C.

MONGOLS An Asiatic group of closely related tribal peoples who originated in, and form the majority population of, Mongolia; they share a common language (an Altaic tongue) and nomadic traditions. Today in Mongolia, the principle tribes are the Khalka, Derbet, Ölöt, Oirat, and Torgut. Mongol tribes also live in enclaves in Xinjiang, Tibet, Manchuria, the Kalmyk Republic, and Russian Siberia. In Siberia the Buryat live near Lake Baykal.

NEOLITHIC PERIOD (New Stone Age) The stage of human development when stone tools shaped by polishing and grinding were used. Animals and plants were domesticated, the people lived in permanent villages and developed pottery and weaving. The time periods vary in different parts of the world. The Neolithic period is followed by the Bronze Age.

245

OIRAT A Mongol tribe, particularly powerful during the medieval period, whose descendants now live in western Mongolia. (See also DJUNGARS.)

PALEOLITHIC PERIOD (Early Stone Age) The stage of human development when the people made and used rudimentary, chipped stone tools. The Stone Age period is divided into three periods: Paleolithic, Mesolithic, and Neolithic.

PARTHIANS A nomadic dynasty (c. 141 B.C.–A.D. 224) in Iran famous for its combat cavalry and fine archers, and for breeding horses that were highly sought after by the Han Dynasty emperors. The Parthians amassed significant wealth by controlling the western Silk Route between Rome and China. Although employed by other nomads, the technique of firing arrows at high speed on horseback while shooting over the shoulder is known as the "Parthian shot."

PAZYRYK The name given to tribes belonging to the Saka confederacy that inhabited the region of the same name (Pazyryk) in southern Siberia from about 450 to 300 B.C. Their frozen tombs in large kurgans, excavated in the 1950s, revealed an elaborate assortment of usually lost organic materials including textiles, carpets, carved wooden artifacts, human remains, and sacrificed horses.

PHRYGIANS People living in west-central Anatolia who probably migrated from Thrace. From their capital at Gordium, the Phrygians dominated Asia Minor between the twelfth and seventh centuries B.C., when they were destroyed by the Cimmerians. Around 750 B.C. the legendary King Midas of the golden touch became their ruler.

POKROVKA An archaeological site of many kurgan cemeteries, located in the southern Ural steppes adjacent to the Kazakstan border about 90 miles south of Orenburg, used over an eight-hundred-year period. Bronze Age people were the first to construct modest kurgans to bury their deceased. In turn, Early Iron Age Sauromatians and Sarmatians buried their dead in the same kurgans or, more frequently, constructed new mounds.

PROTOME Representation of the head and neck of an animal. Used on the end of an object as a decorative element in nomadic art.

SAKA A confederacy of Early Nomads who practiced pastoral transhumance in the Tien Shan and Altai mountains, the Ferghana Valley, and the Syr Darya delta region in Kazakstan from the eighth through third centuries B.C. The Saka were Caucasoids and spoke an Indo-Iranian language. (See also EARLY NOMADS.)

SARMATIANS Between the fourth century B.C. and the second century A.D., tribes of nomadic pastoralists who succeeded the Sauromatians in Russia's southern Ural steppes and along the Volga and the Don rivers, where they had their summer pastures. These Caucasoid peoples, who varied significantly in physical type, are further subdivided by time periods into the Early, Middle, and Late Sarmatians. The Sarmatians spoke an Indo-Iranian language. (See also EARLY NOMADS.)

SASSANIANS An Iranian dynasty (A.D. 224–651) that evolved in Persia as their first king, Ardashir I, continued his conquests against the Parthians. The Sasanians controlled parts of Afghanistan in the east, and in the west their dynasty included Mesopotamia. The Sasanian period marks the end of the antique period and the beginning of the early medieval period. The Arabs destroyed the Sasanians between 637 and 651.

SAUROMATIANS Tribes that practiced pastoral nomadism and interred their deceased in Russia's southern Ural steppes beginning in the sixth century B.C. and along the Volga and the Don rivers in the seventh century B.C. Herodotus reports their genesis as being from the Amazons and Scythians. The Sauromatians, who preceed the Sarmatians, were Caucasoids and spoke an Indo- Iranian language. (See also EARLY NOMADS.)

SAURO-SARMATIANS An abbreviated form to indicate both Sauromatians and Sarmatians.

SCYTHIANS Between the seventh and third centuries B.C., the Scythians, one of the four Early Nomad tribes, were pastoralists north of the Black Sea, where they developed a symbiotic relationship with Greek colonists who established cities in the same region. Over time some Scythians became agriculturists, producing grain for export to mainland Greece, while others maintained their pastoral status. (See also EARLY NOMADS.)

THRACIANS One of the three tribal groups in the Balkans who settled in present-day southern Bulgaria. In the first millennium B.C., they interacted with both the Greeks and the Scythians.

TOCHARIANS Very little is known of these people except that they spoke a now-extinct early Indo-European language during the first millennium A.D. Discovered in the Tarim Basin in western China, their earliest written documents are dated between 500 and 700 A.D., and attest to a Tocharian A and a Tocharian B language. These are most closely related to Celtic.

TUVANS A Turkic tribe living in the Tuva Autonomous Region in southern Siberia; a few Tuvans also live in the Altai Mountains of western Mongolia.

ULUTI A Celtic-speaking tribe, ancestors of the Ulstermen, the people during the heroic era in Northern Ireland. It is likely the first Celts came from England to Ireland around 500 B.C., with the introduction of the more sophisticated La Tène people around 200 B.C. The Uluti may have descended from these people, but there are no written records until around A.D. 800.

UYGURS Today a sedentary population in western China, they migrated into the Tarim Basin in the twelfth century. Known in southern Mongolia from before the eighth century, they adapted their vertically written alphabet to the Mongol language and became the traditional scribes for the court of Genghis Khan and that of the subsequent Mongol khans. The Uygurs are a Caucasian and Mongol admixture and speak a Turkic language.

UZBEKS A tribe descended from the Golden Horde, who took their name from the admired Khan Öz Beg (1312–1341). In 1428 Khan Abu'l-Khayr led the Uzbeks from southern Siberia to the north bank of the Syr Darya, where many of the tribes, taking the name of Kazak, broke away. In 1468 Abu'l-Khayr was killed and the Uzbek confederacy shattered while in battle with the Djungars. By 1495, the Uzbeks had recovered, conquering and moving into the territory known today as Uzbekistan, where they occupied Samarkand, Bukhara, and other important cities. During the next century, Uzbek hegemony extended eastward as far as the Badakhshan region of Afghanistan and east Turkestan and westward to the Khorasan region of Iran. The sedentary Uzbeks are a Caucasoid and Mongol admixture, and speak a Turkic language. (See also **GOLDEN HORDE, KAZAKS, DJUNGARS.**)

VIKINGS The word *Viking* means "man from Vik," Vik being the very large bay that lies between Cape Landesnes in Norway and the mouth of the Göta River in Sweden. During the Viking Age (A.D. 800–1500), the western Scandinavians plundered in Ireland, Scotland, England, and France, while those of the eastern regions of Scandinavia explored and became merchants, traveling down the Volga River to the Caspian Sea. They traded for the much sought after silver coinage from Iran.

YÜEH CHIH One of three nomadic confederacies west of the China heartland. In the second century B.C., they forced the Saka west and south from their homeland and in the first century B.C. were in turn forced out of Xinjiang by the Hsiungnu. They migrated into ancient Bactria where the strongest of the five chieftains unified the tribes and founded the Kushan Empire. (See **KUSHAN EMPIRE.**)

ZOROASTRIANISM The religion founded by Zoroaster in Persia either in the early first millennium B.C. or in the middle of the first millennium B.C. Its teachings include the worship of Ahura Mazda (also known as Ormazd) in the context of a universal struggle between the forces of good and evil, and light and darkness.

BIBLIOGRAPHY

Akishev, Kemal. 1978. *Issyk mound: The art of Saka in Kazakhstan.* Moscow: Iskusstvo Publishers.

Allsen, Thomas T. 1987. *Mongol imperialism: The policies of the Grand Qan Möngke in China, Russia, and the Islamic lands, 1251–1259.* Berkeley: University of California Press.

Allworth, Edward A. 1990. *The Modern Uzbeks: From the Fourteenth Century to the Present.* Stanford: Hoover Institution Press.

Andersen, Jørgen. 1977. *The witch on the wall: Medieval erotic sculpture in the British Isles.* Copenhagen: Rosenkilde and Bagger.

Balzer, Marjorie Mandelstam. 1997. Soviet superpowers. *Natural History.*

Barber, Elizabeth Wayland. 1997. On the origins of the Vily/rusalki. In Miriam Robbins Dexter and Edgar C. Polomé, eds., *Varia on the Indo-European past: Papers in memory of Marija Gimbutas. Journal of Indo-European Studies.* Washington, D.C.: Institute for the Study of Man (Monograph No. 19).

——— 1999. *The mummies of Ürümchi.* New York: Norton.

Bunker, Emma C., C. Bruce Chatwin, and Ann R. Farkas. 1970. *Animal Style art from East to West.* New York: Asia Society.

Carpini, Giovanni DiPlano. 1996. *The Story of the Mongols Whom We Call the Tartars,* trans. Erik Hildinger. Boston: Branden Publishing Company, Inc.

Catallus, 1893. *Catallus.* "Poem 63." E. T. Merrill. Cambridge: Harvard University Press.

Chavannes, E. 1903. *Documents sur les Tou-Kiue (Turcs) occidentaux (Documents on the Western Tou Kiue* [Turks]. St. Petersburg, Russia: Academia Nauk (Academy of Science).

Christian, David. 1998. *A history of Russia, Central Asia, and Mongolia.* Vol. 1. *Inner Eurasia from prehistory to the Mongol Empire.* Malden, Mass.: Blackwell.

Davis-Kimball, Jeannine. 1989. Proportions in Achaemenid art. Ph.D. diss., University of California, Berkeley. Ann Arbor, Mich.: University Microfilms International.

——— 1997a. Chieftain or warrior-priestess? *Archaeology,* September/October, 44–48.

——— 1997b. Sauro-Sarmatian nomadic women: New gender identities. *Journal of Indo-European Studies 25.*

———— 1997/98. Amazons, priestesses, and other women of status: Females in Eurasian nomadic societies. *Silk Road Art and Archaeology* 5. Kamakura, Japan: Journal of the Institute of Silk Road Studies.

———— 1998. Tribal interaction between the Early Iron Age nomads of the southern Ural steppes, Semirechiye, and Xinjiang. In Victor H. Mair, ed., *The Bronze Age and Early Iron Age peoples of eastern Central Asia.* Washington, D.C.: Institute for the Study of Man and the University of Pennsylvania Museum Publications.

———— 2000a. The Beiram Mound: A Nomadic Cultic Site in the Altai Mountains (Western Mongolia). In Jeannine Davis-Kimball, Eileen Murphy, Ludmila Koryakova, and Leonid T. Yablonsky, eds. *Kurgans, Ritual Sites, and Settlements: Eurasian Bronze and Iron Age.* British Archaeological Reports, International Series 890. Oxford: Archaeopress.

———— 2000b. Enarees and Women of High Status: Evidence of Ritual at Tillya Tepe (Northern Afghanistan). In Jeannine Davis-Kimball, Eileen Murphy, Ludmila Koryakova, and Leonid T. Yablonsky, eds. *Kurgans, Ritual Sites, and Settlements: Eurasian Bronze and Iron Age.* British Archaeological Reports, International Series 890. Oxford: Archaeopress.

———— 2001a. Village Life to Nomadism: An Indo-Iranian Model in the Tien Shan Mountains (Xinjiang, China). In Karlene Jones-Bley, Angela Della Volpe, Miriam Robbins Dexter, Martin E. Huld, eds. Proceedings of the Twelfth Annual UCLA Indo-European Conference Los Angeles May 26–28, 2000. *Journal of Indo-European Studies Monograph Series.* Washington, DC: Institute for the Study of Man, 243–268.

———— 2001b. Fertility Rituals: The Kangjiashimenzi Petroglyphs and the Cucuteni Dancers. Dragos Gheorghiu, ed. In *Material, Virtual, and Temporal Compositions: On the Relationship between Objects.* British Archaeological Reports, International Series 953. Oxford: Archaeopress.

————2001c. Book Review: *Late Prehistoric Exploitation of the Eurasian Steppe.* Marsha Levine, Yuri Rassamakin, Aleksandr Kislenko, and Nataliya Tatarintseva with an introduction by Colin Renfrew. *American Journal of Archaeology,* 105.2: 25–26.

———— 2002. Katuns: The Mongolian queens of the Genghis Khanite. In Sarah Nelson ed., *The quest for queens in archaeology.* Walnut Hills, Calif.: AltaMira Press.

Davis-Kimball, Jeannine, and Leonid T. Yablonsky. 1995. *Kurgans on the left bank of the Ilek: Excavations at Pokrovka, 1990–1992.* Berkeley, Calif.: Zinat Press.

Davis-Kimball, Jeannine, Vladimir A. Bashilov, and Leonid T. Yablonsky, eds. 1995. *Nomads of the Eurasian steppes in the Early Iron Age.* Berkeley, Calif.: Zinat Press.

Davis-Kimball, Jeannine, Eileen Murphy, Ludmila Koryakova, and Leonid T. Yablonsky, eds. 2000. *Kurgans, Ritual Sites, and Settlements: Eurasian Bronze and Iron Age.* British Archaeological Reports, International Series 890. Oxford: Archaeopress.

Debaine-Francfort, C. 1999. *The Search for Ancient China.* New York: Harry N. Abrams.

Donnelly, Colm J. 1997. *Living places: Archaeology, continuity, and change at historic monuments in Northern Ireland.* Belfast: Institute of Irish Studies, Queen's University of Belfast.

Eliade, Mircea. [1964] *Shamanism: Archaic techniques of ecstasy.* Trans. Willard R. Trask. Princeton, N.J.: Princeton University Press.

Fedorov-Davydov, German. 2001. *The Silk Road and the cities of the Golden Horde.* With a contribution by V. V. Dvornichenko. Ed. Jeannine Davis-Kimball. Trans. Alexander Nymark. Berkeley, Calif.: Zinat Press.

Francfort, H. P., F. Soleilhavoup, J. P. Bozelle, P. Vidal, F. D'Errico, D. Sacchi, Z. Samashev, and A. Rogozhinskij. 1997. Les petroglyphes de Tamgaly (The petroglyphs of Tamgaly). *Bulletin of the Asia Institute* 9.

Fraser, Antonia. 1988. *The Warrior Queens: The Legends and the Lives of the Women Who Have Led Their Nations in War.* New York: Vintage Books.

From the land of the Scythians. 1973–1974. Metropolitan Museum of Art Bulletin No. 5 (Exhibition Catalogue). New York: Metropolitan Museum of Art.

Frye, Richard. 1996. *The Heritage of Central Asia: From Antiquity to the Turkish Expansion.* Princeton.: Markus Wiener Publishers.

Gimbutas, Marija. 1991. *The Language of the Goddess.* San Francisco: HarperSanFrancisco.

Goode, Starr, and Miriam Robbins Dexter (2000). Sexuality, the Sheela na gigs, and the goddess in ancient Ireland. *ReVision* 23, no. 1 (Summer): 38–48.

Grousset, René. 1970. *The empire of the steppes: A history of Central Asia.* Trans. Naomi Walford. New Brunswick, N.J.: Rutgers University Press.

Hadingham, E. 1994. The mummies of Xinjiang. *Discovery,* April, 68–77.

Herodotus. 1975. Trans. A. D. Godley. Cambridge, Mass.: Harvard University Press, Loeb Classical Library.

Jacobson, Esther. 1993. *The deer goddess of ancient Siberia: A study in the ecology of belief.* Leiden, The Netherlands: E. J. Brill.

Jettmar, Karl. 1967. *Art of the steppes.* Trans. Ann E. Keep. New York: Crown.

Jones, David E. 1997. *Women warriors: A history.* Washington: Brassey's.

Kamberi, Dolkun. 1994. The three thousand year old Chärchaän man preserved at Zaghanluq. *Sino-Platonic Papers* No. 44 (January).

Khazanov, Anatoly M. [1984] 1994. *Nomads and the outside world.* Trans. Julia Crookenden. Madison; University of Wisconsin Press.

Kinsella, Thomas, trans. 1970. *The Tain: Translated from the Irish epic Táin Bo Cúailnge.* Oxford: Oxford University Press.

Kuzmina, Elena. 1994. *Where had the Indo-Iranians come from? The material culture of the Andronovo tribes and the origins of the Indo-Iranians (Ot Kyda Indo-Iranians).* Moscow.

Levine, Marsha, Yuri Rassamakin, Aleksandr Kislenko, and Nataliya Tatarintseva. 1999. *Late prehistoric exploitation of the Eurasian steppe.* Introduction by Colin Renfrew. Cambridge, England: McDonald Institute for Archaeological Research.

Ligabue, Giancarlo, and Sandro Salvatori. 1988. *Bactria: An ancient oasis civilization from the sands of Afghanistan.* Italy: Erizzo.

Lysaght, Patricia. 1986. *The banshee: The Irish supernatural death-messenger.* Dublin: Glendale Press.

Lysias. 1930. W. R. M. Lamb, trans. Cambridge: Harvard University Press.

Mair, V. H. 1995. Mummies of the Tarim Basin. *Archaeology,* March/April, 28–35.

Mallory, J. P., ed. 1992. *Aspects of the Táin.* Belfast: December Publications.

Mallory, James P., and Victor H. Mair. 2000. *The Tarim Mummies: Ancient China and the Mystery of the Earliest Peoples From the West.* London: Thames and Hudson.

Mallory, James P., and D. Q. Adams. 1997. *Encyclopedia of Indo-European Cultures:* London and Chicago: Fitzroy Dearborn Publishers.

Mayor, Adrienne. 2000. *The first fossil hunters: Paleontology in Greek and Roman times.* Princeton, N.J.: Princeton University Press.

Melyukova, Anna I. 1995. Scythians of southeastern Europe. In Jeannine Davis–Kimball, Vladimir A. Bashilov, and Leonid T. Yablonsky, eds. *Nomads of the Eurasian steppes in the Early Iron Age.*

Minns, Ellis H. 1913. *Scythians and Greeks.* Cambridge: Cambridge University Press.

Moorey, P. R. S. 1971. *Catalogue of the ancient Persian bronzes in the Ashmolean Museum.* Oxford: Clarendon Press.

Moorey, P. R. S., Emma C. Bunker, Edith Porada, and Glenn Markoe, 1981. *Ancient bronzes, ceramics, and seals.* Los Angeles: Los Angeles County Museum of Art.

Morgan, David. 1986. *The Mongols.* New York: Basil Blackwell.

Murphy, Eileen. 1998. An osteological and palaeopathological study of the Scythian and Hunno–Sarmatian period populations from the cemetery complex of Aymyrlyg, Tuva, south Siberia. Ph.D. diss. Queen's University, Belfast.

Olcott, Martha Brill. 1987. *The Kazakhs.* Stanford: Hoover University Press.

Pletneva, S. A., ed. 1981. *Stepi Evrazii v Epokhu Srednevekovia.* Moscow: Nauka (The Steppes of Eurasia in the Middle Ages).

Polosmak, Natalya. 1994. A mummy unearthed from the pastures of heaven. *National Geographic,* October, 89–103.

Polosmak, N. B. 1996. La prêtresse altaâque (The Altai priestess). In B. Bioul, A. Jeannelle, H. Durand, and V. Maily, eds. *Tombes gelées de Sibérie.* Dossiers Archeologie 212. Dijon: Editions Faton SA., 28–35.

Rolle, Renate. 1989. *The world of the Scythians.* Trans. F. G. Walls. Berkeley: University of California Press. Originally published in German in 1980.

Roller, Lynn E. 1999. *In search of God the Mother: The cult of Anatolian Cybele.* Berkeley: University of California Press.

Rosenfield, John M. 1967. *The dynastic arts of the Kushans.* Berkeley: University of California Press.

Rudenko, Sergei I. 1970. *Frozen tombs of Siberia: The Pazyryk burials of Iron Age horsemen.* Trans. M. W. Thompson. Berkeley: University of California Press.

Sarianidi, Viktor. 1985. *The golden hoard of Bactria: From the Tillya-tepe excavations in northern Afghanistan.* Trans. Arthur Shkarovsky-Raffé. New York: Abrams.

Scott, George Riley. 1996 *The History of Prostitution.* London: Senate.

The secret history of the Mongols. 1982. Trans. and ed. Francis Woodman Cleaves. Cambridge, Mass.: Harvard-Yenching Institute, Harvard University Press.

Tacitus. 1996. *Tacitus: The Annals of Imperial Rome.* London: Penguin Books.

Treasures of the warrior tombs. Ed. E. Bespali et al. C. E. Batey. Glasgow, Scotland: Glasgow Museums.

Ustinova, Yulia. 1999. *The supreme gods of the Bosporan kingdom: Celestial Aphrodite and the Most High God.* Boston: Brill.

Wang Bing-Hua, ed. 1992. *Tienshan petroglyphs: A testimony of fertility worship.* Ürümqi: Cultural Relics Publishing House.

Werner, Alex. 1999. "Bodies at the Museum of London." *History Today,* November.

Wilde, Lyn Webster. 2000. *On the trail of the women warriors: The Amazons in myth and history.* New York: Thomas Dunne Books, St. Martin's.

INDEX

Achilles, 116

Actaeon, 119

Adam, 94

Aeschylus, 116

Afghanistan, 64, 148
    see also Bactria

afterlife, 24, 70–71, 75, 218
    Pokrovka burial mounds and, 45, 48
    warrior women and, 56, 60

Agamemnon, 116, 119

Ahura Mazda, 181

Ailill, 197, 207

Aisha, 41–42

aites (singing contest), 39–41

Akhinjanov, Serjhan, 80–81

akinakes (sword shield), 169–71

Akishev, Kemal, 100–101, 103–4, 106

aksakal (white-haired one), 31

Alan-Qo'a, 220

Alans, 63, 66, 108

Alexander III (the Great), King of Macedonia,
    117, 181

Almaty, 6–7, 80–81, 98
    Academy of Science in, 88
    Archaeological Museum in, 104

Alphabet of Ben Sira, The, 94

Altai Mountains, xiii–xiv, 60–61, 111, 134, 148,
    182, 237
    burial mounds and, 11, 73–76, 79–80, 82
    Kazaks and, 33, 35–36, 40, 43
    Mongols and, 224, 227
    Saka of, 9
    spirituality and, 85, 89–90

altars, 24, 70–71, 93, 181
    China's mummies and, 144–45
    Pokrovka burial mounds and, 29, 47

Alykhardaakh, 84–85

Amazons:
    Greeks and, 113–21, 129–31, 197, 200, 238–39
    Herodotus and, xiv, 11, 52, 114, 117–18, 121
    origins of, 120–21

    savagery and failings of, 118–19
    warrior women and, 53–54, 65, 114–21,
        129–31, 238–39

amulets, 5
    Pokrovka burial mounds and, 28, 45
    Sheela-na-gigs and, 201, 204
    spirituality and, 70, 74, 91–92, 94
    warrior women and, 57–58

ana (mother of the tribe), 41

Anacharsis, 176–77

Anatolia, *see* Turkey

ancestor worship, 25, 92, 162

Andraste, 211, 213–14

Andrews, Roy Chapman, 110

animals:
    bones of, 14, 24–25, 28, 35, 56, 72, 97, 109–11
    sacrifices of, 72, 79–80, 90, 95, 126, 128, 176
    see also livestock; *specific types of animals*

Animal Style, animal depictions, xiii, xvi,
    165, 173, 185, 235
    China's mummies and, 136–37
    Gold Man and, 101–5
    Kangjiashimenzi petroglyphs and, 157, 159–60
    Pokrovka burial mounds and, 45, 96
    Saka and, 100
    Scythian burial mounds and, 10–11
    spirituality and, 70–71, 75, 77–79, 81–83
    and women of Irish legends, 187

Antiope, 115–16

Anu, 192–93

Aphrodite Urania, 69, 178

Apollo, 69, 119

Aral Sea, 9–12, 32

archaeological excavations, 77–79, 164, 240
    Barkol stone house and, 167–68
    Beaghmore and, 205–6
    south of Aral Sea, 9–12
    in Taklamakan desert, 135, 138
    in Tell Dor, xiv–xv
    warrior women and, 55–61
    see also burial mounds

Archaeology, 106
archery, 232, 238
Arctinus of Miletus, 116
Ares, 115, 117–18
Arianghais, 85*n*, 87
Arimaspians, 8–9, 109
Aristophanes, 125
armor, 28, 32, 47, 54
arrowheads, 14, 24
    Pokrovka burial mounds and, xii, 28, 46
    Saka and, 100
    warrior women and, 56–58, 60–61, 65
Arses, King of Persia, 179
Artaxerxes III, King of Persia, 179
Artemis, 118–20, 131, 126–27
artifacts, xiii, xvi, 6, 24–29, 31–33, 162–65, 234–35
    Barkol stone house and, 168
    China's mummies and, 140–41, 144–45,
        147–48, 151, 153
    of Cucuteni-Tripolye, 162–64
    Gold Man and, 98–107, 234
    Pokrovka burial mounds and, xi–xii, 13, 17,
        25–29, 35, 45–48, 96–98, 235–36
    Scythian burial mounds and, 10–11
    spirituality and, 68–71, 73–77
    in Tarim Basin, 150
    Tillya Tepe and, 182–85, 237
    warrior women and, 54–60, 65
    and women of Irish legends, 193
    see also specific types of artifacts
Atlantis, 131
Attila, King of the Huns, xiv, 9, 63
Attis, 175–78
Augustus, Emperor of Rome, 179
auletridi (dancing girls), 123
Austen, Jane, 1
axes, 148

Baatar, Tsayangiin, 89–90
babies, 5
    China's mummies and, 143–46
    Pokrovka burial mounds and, 161*n*
    spirituality and, 92–95
Bactria, 169–71, 180–83
    Cucuteni-Tripolye and, 164–65
    eunuchs and, 180
    mother goddesses and, 173, 175, 185
    Tillya Tepe and, 181–83, 185
Badb, 208–9
Bagoas, 179
Baipakov, Karl, 98

balbals, 230
Balkans, 63, 68*n*
balks, 21
Balzer, Marjorie Mandelstam, 84–85
banshees, 207–10
Barber, Elizabeth Wayland, 92, 136*n*, 137, 148–49
Barkol, stone house at, 167–68
Barzaz Breiz, The, 214–15
Bashilov, Vladimir A., 54
Batir, Kurumbai, 37, 40
Batu Khan, 225–26
BBC, 147
beads, 24, 135
    Gold Man and, 105
    Mongols and, 225
    Newgrange and, 194
    Pokrovka burial mounds and, 28, 45, 47–48
    spirituality and, 73–74
    Vikings and, 218
    warrior women and, 60
Beaghmore, stone circles of, 205–6
Beauty of Loulan, 145, 148
Bible, xv, 51, 93–94, 178
birds, 215, 237
    Gold Man and, 103–5
    shamans and, 83–84, 87, 238
    spirituality and, 75, 79, 92–95
    Tillya Tepe and, 183
    and women of Irish legends, 198, 204
Black Sea, 10–11, 51–53, 63, 77*n*, 135, 164, 225, 239
    Amazons and, 114–15, 117, 120
    Mongols and, 222
    Sauromatians and, 52–53
    Scythians and, 51
Black Storms, 67–68
blankets, 22, 24, 36–37, 75
Boa Island, 203
boars' tusks, 58
Boduçhar, 220
Bolsheviks, 64, 84
bones, *see* skeletal remains
Börte, 221
Bosporus Kingdom, 77
Boudicca, Queen of the Iceni, 212–14, 238
Bourke, Cormac, 201–2
bracelets, 61, 76–77
Brauron (Vravrona), 120, 127
bronze, bronzes, bronze artifacts, xii–xiii,
        xv–xvi, 24, 111, 134, 148, 170, 173*n*, 216
    Barkol stone house and, 168
    Gold Man and, 105

bronze, bronzes, bronze artifacts, *(continued)*
Luristan, 165
Pokrovka burial mounds and, xii, 13, 27–28, 35, 46–48, 235
Scythian burial mounds and, 10
spirituality and, 70, 73, 81
in Tarim Basin, 150
warrior women and, 54–57, 59–61, 65
wrestling and, 231
Bronze Age, xv, 22, 67, 154, 166–68, 182, 210
Barkol stone house and, 167–68
China's mummies and, 133, 140
Kangjiashimenzi petroglyphs and, 159
Tamgaly and, 81–82
and women of Irish legends, 189
Brunhilde, 219
bubonic plague, 63, 227–28
Buddhism, 82, 84, 89, 182*n*
Bukhara, 1–3, 109
burial mounds (kurgans), 32–33
in Altai Mountains, 73–76, 79–80, 82
Amazons and, 114–15
China's mummies and, 138, 140–41, 143, 145, 152
construction of, 22–25
Elizavetovskoye and, 115
Gold Man and, 98–107
in Issyk, 97–98, 234
in Kobyakova, 76–77
mother goddesses and, 171–73, 184–85
in Pazyryk, 11, 22, 73–76, 79–80, 82, 109
in Pokrovka, xi–xii, 12–13, 15–29, 32, 35, 45–49, 55–61, 68, 70–72, 96–98, 114, 121, 138, 161*n*, 169, 190*n*, 234–36
of Saka, 44
schematic of components of, 23
Scythians and, 9–11, 114
spirituality and, 68–80
Tillya Tepe and, 181–85
warrior women and, xii, 12–13, 51–52, 54, 121
and women of Irish legends, 198–200
see also archaeological excavations
burials, burial rites, 22–25, 41*n*
Saka and, 100
spirituality and, 74–75, 81
Tillya Tepe and, 237
warrior women and, 235

Callisto, 119
camels, 5, 28, 72, 82, 90, 135, 154, 224

caravans, xiv, 66, 108, 154
caravansaries, 2
Carrickmore, 205
Cartimandua, Queen of the Brigantes, 212
carvings, 24, 230*n*
mother goddesses and, 173–74
Newgrange and, 194–95
Pokrovka burial mounds and, 27, 29, 47, 96
Sheela-na-gigs and, 200–205
spirituality and, 70–71, 81, 95
see also petroglyphs
Caspian Sea, 52, 64
catacombs, 18, 23–24, 55–59
Çatal Hüyük, 171–73
cat's eye, 20–21, 23
Cattle Raid of Cooley, The (Táin Bó Cuáilnge), 191–92, 197–98, 208, 210
Cattle Raid of Froech, The (Táin Bó Froech), 207–8
Catullus, 177–78
Caucasoids, 31–32, 99, 146, 148–51, 219*n*, 221*n*, 223
China's mummies and, 135–39, 141, 148–49, 151
Kangjiashimenzi petroglyphs and, 160, 162
Mongols and, 230–32
Pokrovka burial mounds and, 13
Sarmatians and, 32
Sauromatians and, 52
in Tarim Basin, 150
Caucasus Mountains, 10, 63, 164
celebrations, 35, 37–41, 120
Greece and, 126–29
Kazaks and, 38–41
Mongols and, 231–32
spirituality and, 91–92
and women of Irish legends, 191–92
wrestling and, 231–32
Celts, 13, 32, 208*n*, 211–16, 218, 235
China's mummies and, 149
Chritianity and, 214
Great Britain and, 211–13, 216
Newgrange and, 195
and women of Irish legends, 187–93, 204, 210
Central Asia, 48, 64, 135, 149, 235
Amazons and, 117
Kangjiashimenzi petroglyphs and, 154
mother goddesses and, 171
spirituality and, 82, 84
Central Europe, 148–49
Chalcolithic Age, 166
Chaldragh Idol, 203–4

Chärchär, 136, 143, 145, 148

Charleton, Ian, 143

cheese, cheese making, 5, 33–34, 89

"Chieftain or Warrior-Priestess?" (Davis–Kimball), 106

chieftains, 10, 12, 22, 237
    Gold Man and, 101, 105–6
    Issyk burial mounds and, 98
    Kazaks and, 41–42, 44
    Silk Road and, 109
    spirituality and, 69–72, 74, 76
    warrior women and, 51, 66

children, 5
    Amazons and, 118
    Greece and, 122–27, 129
    Kazaks and, 33–36, 39, 43
    Mongols and, 220–22
    mother goddesses and, 174
    Pokrovka burial mounds and, 28, 46–47
    Relignaman and, 206–7
    spirituality and, 90, 92–95
    warrior women and, 53, 55, 61

China, 41–42, 48, 50, 63–68, 108–11, 133–69, 221n, 230n
    Barkol stone house and, 167–68
    dinosaurs and, 109–10
    eunuchs and, 179
    and fall of nomads, 63–64
    Kangjiashimenzi petroglyphs and, 153–65, 167
    Kazaks and, 34, 41
    Mongols and, 144, 222, 224, 226–27, 229, 232–33
    mummies of, 133–53, 158, 160, 162, 187, 237, 239
    riding skills of women in, 60–61
    Silk Road and, xiv, 108
    spirituality and, 76–79
    warrior women and, 65–66

Chowhougou, 150–51

Christians, Christianity, 82, 84, 178
    Great Britain and, 214
    Relignaman and, 207
    seashells in architecture of, xvi
    Sheela-na-gigs and, 200–204
    and women of Irish legends, 187

Chulainn, Cú, 189, 192, 197–98, 203, 208–10

Cimmerians, 50–51, 165n

clans, see kinship groups; tribes

Claudius I, Emperor of Rome, 177

Clavijo, Ruy Gonz lez de, 131

clay, clay artifacts, 14, 173n
    Pokrovka burial mounds and, 45, 47
    spirituality and, 70–71
    warrior women and, 60

cloth, clothing:
    Amazons and, 114–15
    China's mummies and, 136, 143, 149
    Gold Man and, 101, 104–5
    Kazaks and, 36–40, 42
    Mongols and, 231–32
    Pokrovka burial mounds and, 27–29, 48, 96
    spirituality and, 70, 76, 84–87, 92
    Tillya Tepe and, 183–84

Columba, Saint, 206–7, 214

Conchobar, King of Connaught, 193–96

Conloingeas, Cormac, 209

Conomor, 214–15

copper artifacts, 27

corpses, 22–25
    China's mummies and, 136, 138, 141
    Pokrovka burial mounds and, 27–29
    spirituality and, 74–75, 79–80

Corybants, 176

Crunniuc, 191

Ctesias, 44, 110

Cucuteni-Tripolye, 162–66

Cybele, 175–79, 184–85

Cymidei Cymeinfoll, 211

Cyrus II (the Great), King of Persia, 44, 51, 100

Daghdha, 195

Danu, 189, 192–93, 195

Daphne, 119

Darius I, King of Persia, 99

Darius III, King of Persia, 179

Dayan (Kazak camp), 35

Dayan (Mongol khan), 226–28

death, deaths:
    Badb and, 209
    Kangjiashimenzi petroglyphs and, 162
    spirituality and, 92–93
    and women of Irish legends, 207–8

Death of Cú Chulainn, The, 208–9

Debaine-Francfort, Corinne, 135

deel, 85–87

Deidre, 186, 193–97

Demeter, 126–28

Derbets, 85n, 89

Dexter, Miriam Robbins, 202–4

dicteriadi (prostitutes), 123–24

dinosaur nests, eggs, and bones, 97, 109–11

Dio Cassius, 212
Diodorus of Sicily, 130–31
Dionysus, 126, 128, 176
Discover, 137, 139, 172*n*
disks, 84, 96
divorces, 43
Djungars, 40
Donnelly, Alton, 8
Donnelly, Colm, 190, 203–6
Don River, xiv, 164
    burial mounds near, 76–77
    Mongols and, 220, 227
    Sauromatians and, 9, 11, 52
    warrior women and, 55, 61
dragons, 108, 110–11
Druids, 190, 193, 203, 209, 214
Dublin Museum, 201, 204
Dubs, Homer, 65–66
dyes, dye vats, xv, 5

Early Iron Age, 10, 73, 83, 97–99, 133–34, 161*n*
earrings, 28, 47, 60, 105
Eastern Europe, 66, 92, 163–65, 230*n*, 237
egalitarianism, 125, 235, 239
    Kazaks and, 36–39, 43, 49
Eliade, Mircea, 84, 180
Elizavetovskoye, Five Brother kurgans of, 115
Emain Macha, 186, 189, 192, 198
emasculation, 175–80, 185
Enarees, 178–79, 183–84
Eoghan, 196
Ephesus, 120, 131
epinetrons, 112–13, 130
eunuchs, 177*n*, 178–80, 183, 185
Eurasia, xvi–xvii, 3–4, 63, 219*n*
    gold–producing regions in, 97
    headdresses and, 103
    important archaeological sites in, xvii, 78
    Mongols and, 227
    nomads of, xiii–xiv, xvi, 3, 31–33, 45, 54,
        105, 165*n*, 187, 236
    Silk Road and, 108
    spirituality and, 92
    steppes of, xiii–xiv, xvi, 4, 8–12, 33, 45,
        50, 137, 187, 211, 238
    transvestitism in, 180
    and women of Irish legends, 187
Europe, 9, 48, 50, 66, 148–49, 162, 235, 239
    Chritianity and, 214
    Mongols and, 223, 227, 229
    mother goddesses and, 184

    Silk Road and, 108–9
    spirituality and, 92
Europoids, *see* Caucasoids
"Exile of the Sons of Uisliu, The," 193–96

families, *see* kinship groups
Fedelm, 198
felines, xiii, 83, 169–74, 183–85, 237
    Gold Man and, 102–4
    Kangjiashimenzi petroglyphs and, 157, 160
    mother goddesses and, 171–74, 176–77, 185
    Pokrovka burial mounds and, 45
    Saka and, 100
    Scythian burial mounds and, 10
    spirituality and, 70, 79
    Tillya Tepe and, 183–84
Female Riding a Feline, 173–74, 183–84
Feodorovo, Vitaly, 72
Fergus, 198
fertility, fertility cults, fertility rites, 202–4, 219,
        237
    of Cucuteni-Tripolye, 163–65
    Enarees and, 178
    Gold Man and, 104–5
    Greece and, 126–28
    Kangjiashimenzi petroglyphs and, 157, 159–
        65, 169
    mother goddesses and, 173–76
    Sheela-na-gigs and, 202, 204, 210, 239
    spirituality and, 75, 91–95
    Tamgaly and, 82–83
    warrior women and, 235
    and women of Irish legends, 192–93, 198
    see also sexuality
Flaming Hills, 110
food, 5, 25, 230*n*, 236
    China's mummies and, 148
    Greece and, 128–29
    Kazaks and, 31–33, 35–37, 42
    Pokrovka burial mounds and, 17–19, 28–29,
        35
    spirituality and, 72–73, 89–90
France, 32, 202, 215–17
Fraser, Antonia, 212
Freya, 218–19
Frigg, 218–19
Froech, 207–8
Funeral Oration (Lysias), 118–20

gems, 14, 28, 43, 48, 76–77, 105, 182
Genghis Khan, xiv, 9, 63, 220–28, 231–33

Georgraphical Journal, 44
Germany, 95, 215–16, 219
Gildas, Saint, 214–15
glass artifacts, 24, 60, 73
    Pokrovka burial mounds and, 45, 47–48
gold, golden artifacts, 9–11, 96–111, 174*n*,
       235–37
    Kazaks and, 43, 106
    Pokrovka burial mounds and, 28, 45, 47, 96–
       98, 236
    protection of, 97, 107–11
    of Saka, 44
    Scythian burial mounds and, 10–11
    Silk Road and, 108
    spirituality and, 71, 73, 76–77, 79, 91–92
    Tillya Tepe and, 181–85, 237
    Vikings and, 216, 218
    and women of Irish legends, 193
Golden Horde, 225–27
Gold Man, 98–107, 234
Goode, Starr, 202, 204
Gorbachev, Mikhail, 3, 17
Great Britain, 187*n*
    Lilith and, 95
    Sarmatians and, 32
    Sheela-na-gigs and, 202
    Vikings and, 216–17
    warrior queens of, 211–14
Greco-Persian wars, xiv, 52, 115
Greeks, Greece, xiv–xv, 8, 13, 44, 50–54,
       109, 112–31, 193, 216, 237–39
    Amazons and, 113–21, 129–31, 197, 200, 238–
      39
    mother goddesses and, 175–76, 185
    prostitution in, 122–24
    Scythian burial mounds and, 10
    spirituality and, 68–69, 76–77, 82, 115–23,
      126–29, 131
    status of women in, 121–26, 129–30
    Tillya Tepe and, 182–83
    warrior women and, 51, 53–54
griffins, 8–9, 236
    Gold Man and, 101–2
    gold protected by, 97, 108–11
    spirituality and, 73, 79
Grousset, René, 226
Gustafson, Birgitta, 217
Güyük, 225

Hades, 127–28, 223
Hadrian's Wall, 32

hallucinogenic plants, 25, 70
Hami, 139–41, 147–48
Han Dynasty, 65–66, 76–77
Haumavarga, 99
headdresses, 103–7, 176, 198*n*, 225, 238–39
    Gold Man and, 103–6
    Kangjiashimenzi petroglyphs and, 157, 160,
      162, 239
    spirituality and, 73–80, 84, 90–93
hearths, hearth women, 5, 46–50, 138, 235–36
    Pokrovka burial mounds and, 46–49
    spirituality and, 70–72, 91
    Vikings and, 217, 219
    warrior women and, 60, 62
Hecate, 120, 177*n*
He Dexiu, 142–43, 145, 151–52
Hedin, Sven Anders, 135, 138
Hellanicus, 8–9
Hercules, 115–16
Hermitage, 10, 107, 169–71
Herodotus, 8, 10–11, 22, 95, 216
    Amazons and, xiv, 11, 52, 114, 117–18, 121
    Enarees and, 178
    legacy of, 52
    mother goddesses and, 176
    on Saka, 44
    on Sauromatians, xiv, 52–54, 114, 121
    spirituality and, 69, 74
    on warrior women, 51–54
Hestia, 69, 119
hetairai (courtesans), 122–23
hewana (Mother Eve), 41
Hippolyte, 115–16
Histories (Herodotus), 51–52
History of Prostitution, The (Scott), 123
Hittites, 120, 209*n*
Hodder, Ian, 172
Hö'elü Üjin, 220–21
Homer, 109, 116
homoeroticism, 124–25
horses, xiii, 90–91, 134, 224
    Amazons and, 114, 116–17
    bones of, 25, 28, 35
    Kazaks and, 34–35, 39–42, 60–61
    Mongols and, 60–61, 231–32
    sacrifices of, 72, 79–80, 95
    Saka and, 100
    Silk Road and, 108
    spirituality and, 74–76, 79–83, 91, 95
    in Tarim Basin, 150–51
    Tillya Tepe and, 183, 237

horses, *(continued)*
    warrior women and, 51, 54
    and women of Irish legends, 191–92
    see also riding equipment, riding skills
Hsiung–nu, 63, 65–66, 147, 168, 182
Hülegü, 226
Hungary, xiii, 63, 220, 222
Huns, xiv, 9, 63, 66, 108
Huntington, Ellsworth, 44
Hutubei, 67, 154

Iambe, 128
ibex images, 165
Ibn Fadlan, 218
I Ching, 109
Idanthyrsos, King of the Scythians, 69
Iliad (Homer), 116
India, 68, 108–9, 180
inheritance laws, 37–38, 44–45, 49
Iphigenia, 119
Iran, 48, 76, 99, 104, 148–49, 160, 165,
    173*n*, 178*n*, 226
Iraq, 76–77
Ireland, 186–212, 214, 217
    Beaghmore and, 205–6
    legends of, 186–93, 197–200, 203–4, 207–10
    Relignaman and, 206–7
    Sheela-na-gigs and, 200–205, 210, 238–39
    warrior queens of, 186–200, 204, 208–10, 212
iron, iron artifacts, 24, 218
    Gold Man and, 102
    Pokrovka burial mounds and, xii, 28, 46
    warrior women and, 56–58, 60
Iron Age, 31, 121, 159, 182, 210, 215
    China's mummies and, 133, 140, 151
    Pokrovka burial mounds and, 13
    Tamgaly and, 81, 83
    and women of Irish legends, 187, 190
Isaiah, 93
Islam, 42–43, 84, 149*n*, 172, 179, 184, 223
    art and architecture of, xvi, 2
    Kazaks and, 36, 43
    shamanism and, 88, 92
    Tamgaly and, 81–82
Ismagulov, Orazak, 106–7
Ismagulova, Ainagul, 107
Israel, xiv–xv
Issodonians, 109–10
Issyk, 81, 97–107, 109, 169, 198*n*, 239
    burial mounds in, 97–98, 234
    Gold Man and, 98–107

ivory, 169–71
jailou (summer pasture), 30–44, 49
Janus, 203–4
Jeremiah, 51
Jochi, 221
Judaism, 82, 84, 94–95

Kangjiashimenzi petroglyphs, 153–65, 167,
    210, 237, 239
    China's mummies and, 158, 160
    dating of, 158–60
    Eastern Europeans and, 163–65
    fertility rites and, 157, 159–65, 169
    schematic of, 156
    transvestism and, 180
Karakorum, 229, 232–33
Kazak Academy of Sciences, 6–8
Kazakh/American Research Project, Inc., 8
Kazak Institute of History, Ethnography, and
    Archaeology, 80, 98–100, 106
Kazaks, Kazakstan, 3–8, 22, 98–99, 134, 139*n*,
    146–47, 150, 155, 223*n*, 227, 232, 234,
    239
    arts and ethnography of, 3–6
    Davis-Kimball's observation of, 30–44, 49,
    85–87
    Davis-Kimball's trip to Moscow from, 6–8
    and fall of nomads, 64–65
    Gold Man and, 106
    history of, 40–41
    horses and, 34–35, 39–42, 60–61
    Pokrovka burial mounds and, xi–xii, 12–13
    spirituality and, 42–43, 71, 76–77, 81, 85–
    86, 88, 90–93, 95
    warrior women and, 66
kelen (one who comes from outside), 41
Kelia, 135
Kelly, Eamon, 193
Khagan, 88
Khan Bukha-noion, 89–90
Khazanov, Anatoly M., 44–45
Khoito teebi (Northern Granny), 90
Khokhlatch kurgan, 77
Khrushchev, Nikita, 64
King's Stables, 189–90
Kinsella, Thomas, 192, 196
kinship groups, 4–5, 25
    Barkol stone house and, 167–68
    Kazaks and, 35, 36*n*, 37–39, 41–44
    Pokrovka burial mounds and, 28, 35, 236
    spirituality and, 70–72, 88, 91–92

Kishinev, 121, 162
knives, 24, 46, 148, 218
Knocknarea mound, 198–99
Kobyakova kurgan, 76–77
Konya, 114, 172
Korla, 142–46, 149
kraters, 114
Kublai Khan, Emperor of China, xiv, 169, 226, 229, 232–33
Kul Oba kurgan, 10
Kunenbaeva, Alma, 33, 36*n*, 41*n*, 90
Kunstkammer, 10
kurgans, *see* burial mounds

Lady of the Lake, The, 73
lariats, 5, 35
La Tène, 187
leather:
    Kazaks and, 35
    Pokrovka burial mounds and, 27–28
    spirituality and, 73–74
    warrior women and, 56–58
lekythos, 114
Levine, Marsha, 164
Lilith, 93–95, 174, 239
livestock, 4
    Barkol stone house and, 167
    Kazaks and, 30–39
    Mongols and, 224
    Pokrovka burial mounds and, 47
    in Tarim Basin, 150
    warrior women and, 65
Lop Nur, 78, 109, 135
Louvre, 112–13
Lui EnGou, 150
Luristan bronzes, 165
Lustymore Idol, 204
Lysaght, Patricia, 208–9
Lysias, 117–20
Lysistrata (Aristophanes), 125

Ma, 120
mac Cumaill, Finn, 189
Macha, 186, 191–92, 196–97, 210
Mahon-Smith, Walter, 202
Mair, Victor H., 136*n*, 140, 142–43
Mäkrits, 221
Mallory, James P., 136*n*, 198
Manchu Dynasty, 227
Manchuria, xiii, 63–64
Mandaghol, Grand Khan, 226

Manduhai, 226–28
Marathon, Battle of, 115
Marjan, 85–88, 111
marriages:
    Gold Man and, 106
    Greece and, 122*n*, 123–25, 127, 129
    Kazaks and, 38, 41*n*, 43
    polygamous, 43
    spirituality and, 74, 91–92
    warrior women and, 53
Massagetae Saka, 44, 51, 99–100
Matar, 173–75
matriarchies, 69–70, 238
matrilineality, 44–45, 49
mats, 5, 27
Matthew, Saint, 178
Matthew, Warren (Matt), 1–3, 7, 16, 31, 67, 80, 100, 134, 203, 217
    Kangjiashimenzi petroglyphs and, 154, 157–58
    Pokrovka burial mounds and, 18, 20
    and women of Irish legends, 186–89, 193,199
Mayor, Adrienne, 109
Medb, Queen of Connacht, 186, 197–200, 204, 207–8, 210
Mellaart, James, 171–72
Melyukova, Anna, 54
men, males, 5, 11–13
    Amazons and, 115–18, 121, 129–31, 239
    China's mummies and, 137, 140, 143–44
    Greece and, 122–26, 128–29
    Kangjiashimenzi petroglyphs and, 157, 161, 163
    Kazaks and, 34–41
    Mongols and, 222
    mother goddesses and, 175–77
    Pazyryk kurgans and, 11
    Pokrovka burial mounds and, 12–13, 28, 46–48, 96
    Relignaman and, 206
    spirituality and, 69–76, 84–87, 89–92, 94
    Tillya Tepe and, 183
    warrior women and, 53–55, 65
    and women of Irish legends, 210
Mesopotamia, 93, 149*n*, 160, 173, 175
Midas, King of Phrygia, 50, 174*n*
Middle East, *see* Near East
Ming Dynasty, 179, 227
Minns, Ellis H., 44
Minusinsk Valley, 148
mirrors:
    Gold Man and, 105

mirrors *(continued)*
    Pokrovka burial mounds and, 13, 27, 47, 236
    Sheela-na-gigs and, 202
    spirituality and, 70–71, 73–74, 76–77, 84,
        87, 90
    Tillya Tepe and, 183
    warrior women and, 59, 61
miscarriages, 90
Mistress of Animals, 173, 185
Moldova, 121, 162, 164
Möngke, 225–26
Mongols, Mongolia, 4–5, 108, 118, 139*n*, 144,
     146, 151, 169, 220–33, 238–39
    end of empire of, 227
    and fall of nomads, 64–65
    horses and, 60–61, 231–32
    Kazaks and, 30–44, 49
    spirituality and, 73, 85–90, 92
    geneology of khans and qatuns of,
       224
    Silk Roads and, 229–33
    of thirteenth century, 220–27
    warrior women and, 66, 223, 226
    wrestling and, 13, 231–32
Moscow:
    Davis–Kimball's train trip to, 6–8
    Institute of Ethnography in, 3–8, 26
    overland route to Pokrovka from, 19–20
    Pokrovka burial mounds and, 15–16, 18–20,
      26
    train trip to Sol Iletsk from, 15
Moshkova, Marina, 11
mother goddesses, 121–22, 126, 169–81, 182*n*
    eunuchs and, 179
    Newgrange and, 195
    Tillya Tepe and, 184–85
    and women of Irish legends, 192–93
mothers:
    Amazons and, 118
    Greece and, 125–26
    Kazaks and, 35–36
    Mongols and, 220–21
mummies:
    of China, 133–53, 158, 160, 162, 187, 237,
      239
    Kangjiashimenzi petroglyphs and, 158, 160,
      162
    spirituality and, 74–76, 95
"Mummies of Xinjiang, The," 137, 139
Munich Frauenmuseum, 172
Murphy, Eileen, 59, 189–90, 201, 203–4, 206–7,

    208*n*
Museum of National Antiquities, 217
music:
    Kazaks and, 38–41
    mother goddesses and, 175–76
Mysterious Mummies of China, 153

Nadaam festivities, 231–32
Naoise, 196
National Museum of Ireland, 193
nature gods, 68, 88, 95
Near East, 50, 66, 115, 173*n*, 182, 209*n*
    Enarees and, 178
    mother goddesses and, 171, 176
    Vikings and, 217–18
Neolithic period, 159, 237
    Beaghmore and, 205
    mother goddesses and, 171–72
    Newgrange and, 194
    Silk Road and, 108
    and women of Irish legends, 189
Nero, Emperor of Rome, 212–13
Newgrange, 193–95
New Testament, 178
Nibelungenlied, 219
nomads, xi–xiv, 3–5, 8–13, 87–88, 146–47,
     154–55, 163, 170, 185, 234–38
    Amazons and, 115, 120
    Barkol stone house and, 168
    burial rites of, 22–25
    China's mummies and, 133, 136–37, 151
    definition of, 4
    of Eurasia, xiii–xiv, xvi, 3, 31–33, 45,
     54, 105, 165*n*, 187, 236
    fall of, 63–65
    Gold Man and, 104–5
    hearth women and, 50
    Kangjiashimenzi petroglyphs and, 154, 159,
     161*n*
    Kazaks and, 33, 40–44
    marauding tribes of, 50–51
    Mongols and, 220, 230*n*
    Pokrovka burial mounds and, xi–xii, 12–13,
     15–18, 21, 28, 45–48
    protecting gold of, 107–9
    Saka and, 98–99
    Scythian burial mounds and, 9
    spirituality and, 21, 68–69, 73, 75–83, 88, 95
    of steppes, 4–5, 8–12, 33, 36*n*, 107, 181–82
    in Tarim Basin, 150–51
    warrior women and, 54, 61–62, 66

Nomads of the Eurasian Steppes in the Early Iron Age (Davis-Kimball, Bashilov, and Yablonsky), 54

Northanger Abbey (Austen), 1

Nova, 133, 139–43, 145–47, 149, 153, 162

Nurapiesov, Beken, 81, 98–101, 106

O'Brien, Donnchadh, 209

Odin, 219

Oghul Qaimish, 225–26

Ögödei, 224–25, 229, 233

Oiropata, 53–54

O'Kelly, M. J., 195

Old Testament, 51, 93–94

On the Trail of the Women Warriors (Wilde), 121, 127, 131

oral tradition, 33, 40–41

Orenburg, 11, 15, 26

Oxus River, 170–71

Paleolithic period, 4, 236

Paris, Matthew, 223

Parthians, 108, 149*n*

passage tombs, 194–95, 199

pastoral nomadism (transhumance), 4

pasturelands:
  and fall of nomads, 64–65
  Kazaks and, 31–44, 49
  Saka and, 32
  spirituality and, 75
  warrior women and, 61–65

patriarchies, 235, 239
  Kazaks and, 36–37
  Mongols and, 228
  mother goddesses and, 175
  spirituality and, 93

Patrick, Saint, 214

Pazyryk, 182, 239
  burial mounds in, 11, 22, 73–76, 79–80, 82, 109
  Gold Man and, 101–3, 105
  headdresses and, 103

pendants, 96, 194

Penthesilea, Queen of the Amazons, 116

perfume bottles, 76–77

Persephone, 127–28

Persia, Persians, xiv, 44, 68, 115, 165*n*, 218
  Achaemenid Dynasty of, 51–52, 76–77, 99, 104, 170, 179
  Herodotus on, 51–52
  Lilith and, 94–95

Silk Road and, 108

Scythians and, 51

spirituality and, 76–77

Peter I (the Great), Tsar of Russia, 6*n*, 10

Peterson, Nancy, 134

petroglyphs, 95, 235–37, 239–40
  Kangjiashimenzi, 153–65, 167, 169, 180, 210, 237, 239
  at Tamgaly, 80–84, 98, 103, 159, 237
  at Tanum, 217

Phoebe, 120

Phoenicians, Phoenicia, xv, 178

Phrygia, Phrygian, 50, 173–74, 174*n*, 175*n*, 177*n*

plaques, xiii, xvi, 236
  Gold Man and, 100–102, 104
  Pokrovka burial mounds and, 27–28, 45, 96
  Scythian burial mounds and, 10
  Tillya Tepe and, 183
  wrestling and, 231

Plato, 116

Pliny the Younger, 131

Plutarch, 122*n*, 125–26

podbois, 23–24

Pokrovka:
  burial mounds in, xi–xii, 12–13, 15–29, 32, 35, 45–49, 55–61, 68, 70–72, 96–98, 114, 121, 138, 161*n*, 169, 190*n*, 234–36
  drivers in, 16–18
  living conditions in, 15–17, 20, 26
  overland route from Moscow to, 19–20
  plundering tombs in, 29, 45, 96–98
  preservation in burials at, 27–29
  spirituality and, 21, 28, 45, 48, 68, 70–72
  types of soil at, 20–21
  volunteer crews in, 17–27
  warrior women and, xii, 12–13, 55–61, 121

Polo, Marco, xiv, 135, 169

pottery, 14
  Amazons and, 114–15
  China's mummies and, 140, 148, 151
  of Cucuteni-Tripolye, 162–64
  Kangjiashimenzi petroglyphs and, 163
  Pokrovka burial mounds and, 26, 28–29, 45, 47
  Tell Dor and, xv
  warrior women and, 56

Prasutagus, King of the Iceni, 212–13

pregnancy, 90–91, 119, 204
  Greece and, 125, 127
  mother goddesses and, 171–72
  spirituality and, 91, 93
  and women of Irish legends, 191–92

priests, priestesses, 119, 210, 216, 239
 China's mummies and, 135, 137, 144–46
 duties of, 72
 eunuchs and, 179
 in Greece, 121–22
 headdresses and, 103
 Kangjiashimenzi petroglyphs and, 161–62, 165
 Kazaks and, 41*n*
 Mongols and, 225, 230
 mother goddesses and, 174, 176–77, 185
 Pokrovka burial mounds and, xii, 12, 28–29, 46–47, 49, 96, 236
 spirituality and, 66, 68, 70–79, 82, 89, 92, 95
 Tillya Tepe and, 183–85, 237
 warrior women and, 56–62
 and women of Irish legends, 193
 see also warrior-priestess, warrior-priestesses
Procne, 130
prostitution, 122–24

quivers, xii, 24, 56, 65, 73

Rassamakin, Yuri, 164
Reid, Howard, 133, 139, 141–43, 162
religion, *see* spirituality
Relignaman, 206–7
riding equipment, riding skills, 5, 71
 Kazaks and, 34–35, 60–61
 Saka and, 100
 in Tarim Basin, 150–51
 warrior women and, 54, 60–66
rings, 102, 105
Risala (Ibn Fadlan), 218
Roberts, Charlotte, 140–41, 143–45
Rolle, Renate, 54–55, 65, 74
Roller, Lynn E., 174
Romans, Roman Empire, xiv–xv, 32, 44, 63, 68, 82, 169, 193, 238
 Amazons and, 120–21, 130–31
 eunuchs and, 179
 Great Britain and, 212–14
 mother goddesses and, 175, 177, 185
 Silk Road and, xiv, 108
 Tell Dor dig and, xv
 Tillya Tepe and, 182–83
 warrior women and, 54
Rosenfield, John M., 182
Rudenko, Sergei, 11, 73–74, 76
rugs, 5, 36–37, 40, 43
Russia, 9–12, 44–45, 107, 137–38

Amazons and, 114–15, 120
and fall of nomads, 63–64
Issyk burial mounds and, 98
Kazaks and, 31*n,* 36
Mongols and, 220, 222–23, 227
Pokrovka kurgans and, xi, 12, 15–19, 26, 28
spirituality and, 73, 76–79, 84–88
Vikings and, 217, 219*n*
warrior women and, 53–54, 59
 see also Soviet Union
Russian Academy of Science, xi

sacrifices:
 Amazons and, 118
 China's mummies and, 145
 Greece and, 126, 128
 of humans, 119–20, 126, 145, 190, 216
 Mongols and, 230*n*
 mother goddesses and, 175–77
 Pokrovka burial mounds and, 28–29
 spirituality and, 70–73, 79–81, 89–90, 95
 and women of Irish legends, 190
St. Petersburg, 6*n,* 107, 169
Saka, 9, 21, 31–33, 38, 51–52, 98–110, 134, 150, 234–35, 238
 confederacy of, 99–100
 Gold Man and, 98–107
 Herodotus on, 44
 Sauromatians and, 52
 Silk Road and, 108
 spirituality and, 68–69, 71, 76–79, 100
 status of women among, 44
 warrior women and, 51, 54–55
Samarkand, 1–3, 109
sarcophagi, 24, 27, 79, 100–101, 114
Sargon II, King of Assyria, 50
Sarianidi, Viktor, 180–84
Sarmatians, 9–11, 21–24, 31–33, 107–8, 137, 151, 182–83, 216, 225, 234–38
 fall of, 63
 Pokrovka burial mounds and, xi–xii, 13, 19, 24, 27–28, 32, 45, 47*n,* 48–49, 96, 114, 234–35
 Silk Road and, 108
 spirituality and, 68–72, 76–77, 90–91
 status of women among, 44–45
 warrior women and, 56, 60, 62–66
Sassanians, 149
Sauromatians, 9–13, 21–22, 31–33, 52–56, 116, 137, 151, 182–83, 216, 234–38
 Amazons and, xiv, 121

female domination of, 12
  Herodotus on, xiv, 52–54, 114, 121
  Pokrovka burial mounds and, xi–xii, 13, 24,
      27–28, 45, 47*n,* 49, 96, 114, 121, 234–36
  Silk Road and, 108
  spirituality and, 68–72, 90–91
  status of women among, 44–45
  warrior women and, 53–56, 61–66
Scandlach, 203
Scott, George Ryley, 123
scroll motives, xiii, xvi, 73
sculptures, 135, 203–4, 230, 233, 239
Scythians, 9–11, 21–22, 31–33, 51–54, 107,
      110, 121, 131, 171, 182, 190*n*
  Amazons and, 117
  Enarees and, 178
  Herodotus on, 51–52, 114
  mother goddesses and, 176–77, 185
  Pazyryk kurgans and, 11
  Pokrovka kurgans and, 114
  Sauromatians and, 52–53
  spirituality and, 68–69, 74, 77, 91
  status of women among, 44
  warrior women and, 54, 65
seashells, xvi, 24, 163
  Pokrovka burial mounds and, 28, 47, 236
  spirituality and, 70–71, 74
  warrior women and, 57–60
Secret History of the Mongols, The, 220–21, 228
sexuality:
  Amazons and, 116–17
  Greece and, 122–27
  Sheela-na-gigs and, 200–202, 204, 210, 239
  and women of Irish legends, 198
  see also fertility, fertility cults, fertility rites
Shakhanova, Nurilya, 6–7
shamans, 66, 82–92, 111, 159–60, 236–38
  Gold Man and, 105
  Kangjiashimenzi petroglyphs and, 160
  and resurgence of religion, 89–92
  Tamgaly and, 82–84
  transvestism and, 180
  women as, 84–88, 90
shape-shifters, 92, 208
Sheba, Queen of, 95
Sheela-na-gigs, 200–205, 210, 238–39
sheep, 89–90, 224
  bones of, 24, 28, 72
  Kazaks and, 31, 33–35, 37
  sacrificing of, 90
Shemashko, Irina, 3–8

Siberia, xiii, 3, 10–11, 64, 107, 182, 238–39
  burial mounds in, 73–80, 82
  China's mummies and, 148
  headdresses and, 103
  Mongols and, 222
  Pazyryk kurgans and, 11, 22
  Pokrovka kurgans and, 20
  Scythian kurgans and, 10
  shamans and, 236
  spirituality and, 82, 84, 87
  status of drivers in, 16–17
  transvestism and, 180
  warrior women and, 59
Silk Road Dialogue program, 86, 229–33
Silk Roads, xiv, 1, 76, 108–10, 140, 149*n,*
      167, 169, 220
  China's mummies and, 147–48
  Kangjiashimenzi petroglyphs and, 154
  spirituality and, 82
  Taklamakan and, 135
silver, silver artifacts:
  Gold Man and, 105
  Kazaks and, 43
  Pokrovka burial mounds and, 28
  spirituality and, 77, 91–92
  Vikings and, 216, 218
skeletal remains, 32–33, 190, 234–35
  of animals, 14, 24–25, 28, 35, 56, 72, 97,
      109–11
  Barkol stone house and, 168
  China's mummies and, 140–41
  Gold Man and, 100–102, 105–7
  Pokrovka burial mounds and, xi–xii, 12, 17,
      25–29, 35, 46, 48–49, 235
  Sarmatians and, 32
  spirituality and, 70–71, 75
  in Tarim Basin, 150–51
  warrior women and, 55–58
Sligo, passage tomb at, 199
Smirnov, K. F., 11
Sol Iletsk, 15
Sophocles, 130
Sorqaghtani Beki, 223–25
Soviet Union, xiii, 11, 15–17, 33
  collapse of, 4, 8, 15, 88
  Davis–Kimball's visits to, 1–8
  glasnost in, 3
  Gold Man and, 101, 106–7
  politics and, 3–6, 132–33
  status of drivers in, 16–17
  see also Russia

Spain, 66, 131, 217
spindle whorls, 29, 47, 60, 164
spirals, 194
spirituality, 21–25, 66–95, 159–62, 176–85
    Amazons and, 115–20, 131
    eunuchs and, 179
    Great Britain and, 211, 213–14
    Greece and, 68–69, 76–77, 82, 115–23, 126–29, 131
    hierarchy of, 70–72, 91, 237
    Kangjiashimenzi petroglyphs and, 159–61, 165
    Kazaks and, 42–43, 71, 76–77, 81, 85–86, 88, 90–93, 95
    Lilith and, 93–95, 174, 239
    Newgrange and, 195
    Pokrovka burial mounds and, 21, 28, 45, 48, 68, 70–72
    resurgence of, 89–92
    Saka and, 68–69, 71, 76–79, 100
    secular customs and, 91–92
    Tamgaly petroglyphs and, 80–84
    Tillya Tepe and, 181–85
    transvestism and, 176–78, 180–81
    Vikings and, 218–19
    and women of Irish legends, 190, 193, 208–9
    see also afterlife; mother goddesses; priests, priestesses; sacrifices; shamans
spoons, 72–73, 105, 144–45
Stalin, Joseph, 6, 64
statues, statuettes, xiii, xvi, 10, 44, 165
Stein, Sir Aurel, 135, 138
steppes, 23, 107–9, 117, 221n, 233–35, 237–39
    Amazons and, 115, 120
    of Eurasia, xiii–xiv, xvi, 4, 8–12, 33, 45, 50, 137, 187, 211, 238
    and griffins' protection of gold, 109
    hearth women and, 50
    Kazaks and, 6, 31, 39, 42–43, 49
    life of archaeologists in, 14
    Mongols and, 230n, 233
    nomads of, 4–5, 8–12, 33, 36n, 107, 181–82
    Pokrovka burial mounds and, 12–13, 28
    Saka and, 9, 98–99
    Sarmatians and, 11, 32
    Silk Road and, 108–9
    spirituality and, 66, 74, 79–82, 90–91
    terrain of, 6
    vegetation of, xiii–xiv
    warrior women and, 53, 55, 62–66

    weather of, xiv, 68
stone, stones, 24, 173n
    Barkol and, 167–68
    Beaghmore and, 205–6
    Mongols and, 230n
    mother goddesses and, 173–74
    Newgrange and, 194–95
    Pokrovka burial mounds and, 27–29, 47
    Sheela-na-gigs and, 200–205
    see also petroglyphs
Stonehenge, 195, 205
Subashi, 77
Suetonius Paulinus, 213–14
sun gods, 81–82
Syria, 48, 173, 193n

Tabiti, 69
Tacitus, 213–14
Takht-i Sanguin, 170–71
Taklamakan desert, 109, 149–50
    archaeological excavations in, 135, 138
    China's mummies and, 134–38, 140–44, 149, 237
    Cucuteni–Tripolye and, 165–66
    oil fields in, 146
Talmud, 94
Tamerlane, 2, 6, 131
Tamgaly, petroglyphs at, 80–84, 98, 103, 159, 237
Tanum, petroglyphs at, 217
Tarim Basin, 135, 138, 148–51
    changing lifestyles in, 150–51
    Cucuteni–Tripolye and, 163, 165
    Kangjiashimenzi petroglyphs and, 160
Tatars, 223
tattoos, 236
    China's mummies and, 136, 144, 151
    Sheela-na-gigs and, 204
    spirituality and, 79, 95
    warrior women and, 59
Tell Dor, xiv–xv
Thalestris, Queen of the Amazons, 117
Thermodon, battle at, 53
Thesmophoria, 127–28
Thrace, Thracians, 68, 131, 175
Tien Shan Mountains, 6, 60, 67, 79, 134, 150–51, 167–69, 182, 237
    Barkol stone house and, 167–68
    China's mummies and, 140, 148
    dinosaurs and, 109–10

headdresses and, 103
Kangjiashimenzi petroglyphs and, 154–55
Pokrovka burial mounds and, 45
Saka and, 9, 32, 98–99
Tigraxhauda, 99–100
Tillya Tepe, 181–85, 237
Tocharians, 149–51
Tolui, 223–24
Tomyris, Queen of the Massagetae Saka, 44,
    51, 99–100, 238
tools, 45, 47–48, 81
Töregene, 224–25, 229
torques, 216
    Gold Man and, 101–2
    spirituality and, 76–79
    Vikings and, 218
    and women of Irish legends, 193
trade:
    Issyk burial mounds and, 98
    Pokrovka burial mounds and, 48
    spirituality and, 76, 82, 92
    warrior women and, 66
    see also Silk Roads
transvestites, transvestism:
    spirituality and, 176–78, 180–81
    Tillya Tepe and, 183, 185
Trees of Life, 75–77, 165, 237–38
    and Gold Man, 103–5
    and shamans, 87
    and Tillya Tepe, 183
tribes, 236
    of marauding nomads, 50–51
    spirituality and, 74–75, 77–79, 83–84, 91,
    95
    warrior women and, 58
    see also kinship groups
Tringham, Ruth, 172
Triphine, 214–15
Triumphs of Turlough, The, 209
Trojan War, 116, 119, 130–31
Tuatha Dé Danann, 189
Turkestan, 6, 110
Turkey, 50, 52–53, 221n
    Amazons and, 114, 117–18, 120, 131
    eunuchs and, 180
    mother goddesses and, 169, 171–77, 185
    spirituality and, 77, 92
Turkic languages and peoples, 31, 221n, 223,
    226n
Turkmenistan, 12, 109
turquoises, 48, 76–77, 105, 182

Tuvans, 85, 88, 111
Twelve Labors of Hercules, 115–16

Ufa, 72–73
Ukok, 77–79, 103
Ukraine, 10, 51, 64, 162, 220
Ulan Bator, 86, 221n, 231–32
Ulster Museum, 201–2
Uluti, 190–91
Ulyasta, 89–90
United Nations Educational, Scientific, and
    Cultural Organization (UNESCO), 86,
    229
Ural Mountains, 9, 11, 223, 231, 234, 237
    human sacrifices in, 72–73
Ürümqi, 134–37, 139, 141–42, 144–45, 147,
    151, 153–54
Ustinova, Yulia, 69
Uygurs, 139, 146–47, 220
Uzbekistan, 1–6, 99, 109–10, 164n, 182

Valkyries, 219
Venutius, King of the Brigantes, 212
Vikings, 13, 32, 216–20, 222–23
villages, 4
    Barkol stone house and, 168
    Kangjiashimenzi petroglyphs and, 161
    Kazaks and, 30–44, 49
    Pokrovka burial mounds and, 96–97
    spirituality and, 70–72, 91–92
Vix, Lady of, 216
Volga River, xiv, 9, 11, 63, 164, 218
    Mongols and, 220, 227
    warrior women and, 54–55

Wallace, Patrick, 201
wall hangings, 75–76
Wang Bing-Hua, 138, 153–55, 158–59, 161,
    167–68
Wang Guowang, 139, 142
Waroc, King of Broërec, 214–15
War of the Gaedhil with the Gaill, The, 208
warrior-priestess, warrior-priestesses, 169–
    70, 237–39
    Gold Man as, 105–6
    headdresses and, 103
    Pokrovka burial mounds and, 138
    Tillya Tepe and, 182–83
warrior queens, 13
    Great Britain and, 211–14
    of Ireland, 186–200, 204, 208–10, 212

warrior women, 9, 47, 51–66, 137
  Amazons and, 53–54, 65, 114–21, 129–31, 238–39
  and fall of nomads, 65
  Herodotus on, 51–54
  legacy of, 234–40
  Mongols and, 66, 223, 226
  Pokrovka burial mounds and, xii, 12–13, 55–61, 121
  Sheela-na-gigs and, 204–5
  spirituality and, 70, 72
  Vikings and, 218
weapons, xvi, 171
  Amazons and, 114, 117
  Gold Man and, 101–2, 105–6
  Pokrovka burial mounds and, xii, 28, 45–47
  Saka and, 32
  Tillya Tepe and, 183–84, 237
  Vikings and, 218
  warrior women and, 54–58, 60–66
  see also arrowheads
weather, xiv, 4–5, 22, 67–68, 155
  China's mummies and, 136
  Greece and, 127–28
  Kangjiashimenzi petroglyphs and, 161, 165
  Kazaks and, 31–34
  Newgrange and, 194
  Pokrovka burial mounds and, 17–19, 26–27, 47
  spirituality and, 68, 75, 82, 89
  in Tarim Basin, 150–51
Werner, Alex, 212
whetstones, 46, 60, 73
Wilde, Lyn Webster, 121, 122n, 127, 131
women:
  bear-nature of, 127
  hidden history of, 13
  as kingmakers, 223–28
  status of, xii, xvi, 13, 41–42, 44–49, 54–55, 60, 75–77, 121–26, 129–30, 138, 144n, 162, 193–97, 205, 211, 215–16, 218, 221–25, 235–36, 238–40
  wealth and land amassed by, 215–16, 223–24, 228
wood, wooden artifacts, 141, 144–45, 148–49, 236
  Gold Man and, 103
  Pokrovka burial mounds and, 27
  spirituality and, 70, 75, 79
  warrior women and, 56

wrestlers, wrestling, 13, 40, 231–32
Wupu, 140–41, 148

Xinjiang, 110, 150, 230n
  Barkol stone house and, 167
  China's mummies and, 133–35, 137–39, 141, 146–48, 153, 158, 187, 239
  and fall of nomads, 64–65
  Kangjiashimenzi petroglyphs and, 153, 155, 158, 163
  mother goddesses and, 184
Xinjiang Institute of Archaeology, 67, 138

Yablonsky, Leonid T., 9–12
  Pokrovka burial mounds and, xi, 12, 15, 18–27, 47, 96–98, 114
  warrior women and, 54, 57–58
yaks, 30–34, 37
Yesevi, Ahmed, 6
Yesügei, 220
Yüan Dynasty, 226–27
Yüeh Chih, 149, 168, 181–82, 185
yurts, 4–5, 87–88, 91
  Kazaks and, 30, 33–34, 36–38, 40–41, 43

Zaghanluq, 143–44
Zagros Mountains, 165, 173n
Zarina, Queen of the Saka, 44
Zeus, 69, 115, 119
Zheng He, 179
Zhu Jun, 139
Zoroastrianism, 68, 181